# TOURISM EDUCATION
## Principles, Theories and Practices

# TOURISM EDUCATION

## Principles, Theories and Practices

Shashi Prabha Sharma

KANISHKA PUBLISHERS, DISTRIBUTORS
NEW DELHI-110 002

**KANISHKA PUBLISHERS, DISTRIBUTORS**
4697/5-21A, Ansari Road, Daryaganj
New Delhi -110 002
Phones : 2327 0497, 2328 8285
Fax : 011-2328 8285
E-mail : kanishka_publishing@yahoo.co.in

*Tourism Education:*
*Principles, Theories and Practices*

First Published-2004
Edition-**2017**


PRINTED IN INDIA

Published by Madan Sachdeva for Kanishka Publishers, Distributors, 4697/5-21A, Ansari Road, Daryaganj, New Delhi-110 002, Typeset by Sunshine Graphics, Delhi, and Printed at Rajdhani Printers, Delhi.

# Preface

The habit of travelling is inherent and attached to the human being from the very beginning. With evolution, growth and development of human civilization it gradually developed into a pleasure but it was only after the advent of industrialization, people started moving in large numbers to places away from their home with a desire for leisure and pleasure, which continued till tourism became a socio-economic phenomenon and this phenomenon to-day has evolved into one of the largest and fastest growing industries of the world.

After Second World War the economic potential of tourism received careful consideration from each and every country in the world, therefore, more and more destinations of tourism emerged on the horizon all over the world.

Apart from economic benefits, tourism has multiplier effects in terms of employment generation, income generation and development of infrastructure in tourist destination areas along with conservation of our heritage and cultural deposits, hence the importance of tourism as an employer, as a contributor to the improvement of socio-economic, socio-political and politico-economic understanding as well as a means of promoting cultural exchanges and international understanding and cooperation; paved the way for its fastest growth.

It is true that now some of the negative aspects of tourism or over tourism have come to light, which demand careful consideration and regulations to stop the negative impact of tourism and ensure full benefit of tourism to the tourists as well as the places of tourist destinations and inhabitants residing at and around tourist destinations.

India alike a developing country is a developing tourist destination, hence, problems concerning tourism deserve careful academic consideration and understanding. Therefore, as per need of the hour many institutions have started teaching tourism at undergraduate and postgraduate level, but there is a dearth of textbooks, on the subject, written by Indian authors and students are forced to read books written by foreign authors in which the subject had been discussed without taking Indian realities into consideration.

Here it may also be mentioned that the Indian authors have written books which are as per need of particular institution or university. Therefore, there is a basic need of a book which may be useful to all the students in Indian tourism institutions.

This book on tourism is a small textbook on the subject for students at the college level and informal layman who have an interest in the subject to enable them to understand the basic concepts of the subject most interesting. The present work is the modest attempt to explain the subject in a simple and lucid language and covers all aspects of tourism and we hope that this book will be helpful for the students getting education in tourism anywhere in India.

The present work among several others, published in India claims to be the most comprehensive. This book lays down the basic concepts of tourism as required to be understood by every specialist of the subject. This book contains point analysis and description of the subject in Indian socio-educational, socio-political and socio-cultural context. It covers the syllabi of all the Indian Universities and tourism institutions on the subject drawing examples from Indian social realities.

Chapter 26 captioned "Status of Tourism and Tourist Education in India" and Chapter 27 captioned "Areas of Career Opportunities in Tourism Industry" are the special features of this book, which no other book written on the subject contains. Hence, this book will be most useful to the reader.

Planned as a textbook for the students and reference for the scholars and teachers, this book is critical constructive appraisal of the subject. While I have tried my best to make this book the best on the subject, the students, scholars, teachers and other readers are the best judge of its merits.

Suggestions for improvement, are, therefore, cordially invited.

**Shashi Prabha Sharma**

# Contents

# 1

# Understanding the Tourism Terminology

Tourism is not a subject of general or usual educational system. It is a discipline of specialist vocational nature, therefore, students undertaking study of tourism for any degree or diploma need to understand the terminology of tourism before they attend regular instructions imparted by the teacher in the class, as it would enable them to follow teacher's instructions naturally. With this view in mind, however, we will discuss the meaning of some of the usual tourism terms very briefly:

**Affinity Group:** A group bound together by a common interest or affinity. Where charters are concerned, this common bond makes the members eligible for charter flights. One must have been a member of the group for six months or longer. They must travel together, on the departure and return flight, but they can travel independently where ground arrangements are concerned.

**Adventure Tourism:** The nature-based tourism in an unusual, remote and exciting environment. A type of tourism which presents a challenge to the tourist as it requires testing of the tourist's skills and physical fitness.

**Airline:** Any air transport enterprise offering or operating a scheduled international air service.

**Alternative Tourism:** A form of tourism that advocates smaller scale and limited tourism in terms of numbers of tourists involved and the dimension of tourism development. It is also called green tourism or responsible tourism.

**Amenities:** Features which enable a visitor to enjoy various attractions and which draw him to a country and for the use of which he normally has to pay. These refer to recreational and entertainment programmes, cultural and art centres, hotels, restaurants, transport services, etc.

**Antiquities:** Art objects which are more than one hundred years old and which cannot be traded.

**Attractions:** Natural or man-made features which collectively or singly create the appeal of a country.

**Baggage:** Personal property of passengers or crew carried on an aircraft by agreement with the operator.

**Baggage Accompanied:** The baggage carried on the same aircraft as that on which the passenger is carried.

**Baggage Excess:** That part of the baggage which is in excess of the free baggage allowance and for which the passenger has to pay extra freight charges.

**Brochure:** A pamphlet bound in the form of a booklet.

**Campaign:** A connected, integrated and organized series of advertising and promotional efforts.

**Camping Site:** A place providing simple and inexpensive shelter to travellers. The site provides wayside amenities for tourists travelling by long-distance coach tours and self-driven cars.

**Cargo:** Equivalent to the term "goods", meaning anything carried or to be carried in an aircraft, other than mail or baggage, provided that unaccompanied baggage moving under an airway bill is also cargo.

**Cargo Transfer:** Cargo arriving at a point by one flight and continuing its journey by another flight of the same or a connecting carrier.

**Cargo Transit:** Cargo arriving at a point and departing therefrom by the same through flight.

**Carrier:** A public transportation company such as air or steamship line, railroad, bus, etc.

**Carriage:** Equivalent to the term transportation, meaning carriage of passengers and/or baggage by air.

**Carriage, Domestic:** Carriage in which, according to the contract of carriage, the place of departure, the place of destination or stopover and the entire transportation are within one nation or its territories.

**Carriage, International:** Carriage in which, according to the contract, the place of departure and any place of landing are situated in more than one nation. As used in this definition, the term 'national' includes all territory subject to the sovereignty, mandate, authority, or trusteeship thereof.

**Charter:** The bulk purchase of any carrier's equipment (or part thereof) for passenger or freight. Legally, charter transportation is arranged for time, voyage or mileage.

**Charter Flight:** A flight booked exclusively for the use of a specific group of people who generally belong to the same organization or who are being 'treated' to the flight by a single host. Charter flights are generally much cheaper than regularly scheduled line services but are not open for sale to the general public. These may be carried out by the regularly scheduled or supplemental carries.

**Conducted Tour:** A pre-paid, pre-arranged vacation in which a group of people travel together under the guidance of tour leader who stays with them from the start to the end of the trip. Also referred to as an "escorted tour".

**Coupons:** Documents issued by tour operators in exchange for which travellers receive pre-paid accommodation, meals, sightseeing trips, etc. Also referred to as vouchers.

**Courier:** A professional travel escort who accompanies carriers.

**Cultural Impact:** The effect of tourism activity or tourism development on the culture of the region or locality.

**Cultural Tourism:** A form of tourism in which the culture and traditions of the region is the main attraction.

**Destination:** The place at which a traveller terminates his journey. The ultimate stopping place according to contract of carriage.

**Destination Facilities:** All plant and infrastructure available in a country, an area or locality.

**Destinational Tourist:** A tourist who terminates his journey at a particular country for the purpose of making a tour travelling from place to place for pleasure in that country.

**Destinational Traffic:** Persons (tourists) carried by transportation lines and terminating their journey at one particular place.

**Disembarkation:** The leaving of an aircraft after a landing, except by crew or passengers continuing on the next stage of the same through flight.

**Domestic Independent Travel:** A tour constructed to meet the specific desire of a client within a single country.

**Domestic Tourism:** A form of tourism where people of a country travel within the boundaries of their country.

**Domestic Tourist:** A local person who makes a tour travelling from place to place for pleasure, business, family, mission, meeting, etc., within the country.

**Ecotourism:** Ecology-oriented green tourism in which tourists seek out environmentally sensitive travel or vacations which help improve the knowledge of an environment of the area.

**Embarkation:** The boarding of an aircraft for the purpose of commencing a flight.

**Escort:** A professional tour escort often called tour manager or courier.

**Exchange Voucher:** A document issued by a carrier or its agents requesting issue of an appropriate passenger ticket and baggage check or provision of services to the person named in such document.

**Excursionist:** A temporary visitor staying less than twenty-four hours in the country visited.

**Facilitation:** The act of assisting progress or helping to move forward. Promoting any measure which will facilitate international travel with prime emphasis on achieving minimum entry and exit formalities for temporary visitor.

**Facilities:** Services which enable tourists to enter and move around the country with the maximum of ease and the minimum of obstacles and to secure maximum enjoyment of their visit.

**Fly/Drive Tour:** An independent tour that allows travellers to visit multiple destinations during their trip and usually includes air transport, a car rental and lodging at several hotels.

**FN/Cruise Tour:** A tour where travellers fly to a port of embarkation and then board a cruise ship for most of the tour.

**Folder:** One piece of illustrated paper which can be folded. It is usually printed on a single sheet and then folded for easy handling.

**Ground Arrangements:** All services provided for the traveller by his tour operator after the traveller reaches his first foreign destination. Also referred to as Land Arrangements.

**Guaranteed Tour:** A tour which is guaranteed to operate unless cancelled 60 days prior to departure. In the event of cancellation within 60 days of the departure date, full commission is paid to agents of sold clients.

**Guide:** A person who is licensed to take paying guests on local sightseeing excursions.

**Guided Tour:** A tour conducted only by local city guides.

**Hosted Tours:** A tour where participants have an opportunity to travel independently, but also to receive guidance and assistance from a host at each of the destinations.

**Hotelier:** A person, firm or corporation which provides hotel accommodation and/or meals, refreshments, etc., to visitors.

**Inclusive Tour:** A tour which includes all elements of an itinerary, making it unnecessary for a passenger to spend money for anything except personal extras during the course of the tour.

**Independent Tour:** A tour where participants travel independently without a group or a guide.

**Infrastructure:** The basic public services needed for the successful operation of tourism enterprises and for optimising the comfort of the visitors. It includes such services as roads, electricity, water, security, sanitation and health services, telephone and postal communication, railways and airports.

**Land Arrangements:** All services provided for the traveller by his tour operator after the traveller reaches his first foreign destination. Also referred to as Ground Arrangements.

**Market:** The totality of actual and/or potential buyers of a given product or service in a specified geographical location at a given point in time or during a given period of time.

**Mass Tourism:** Large-scale movement of travellers and the development of a standardized product.

**Motel:** A place which provides wayside amenities for tourists travelling by road, by automobiles. It provides under one roof all usual facilities expected by the tourist including attached bath.

**Motivators:** The factors which motivate consumers to buy a particular type of holiday.

**National Park:** An area which is strictly reserved for wildlife and where activities such as forestry, grazing and cultivation are not permitted.

**National Tourist Organization:** The body responsible for the formulation and implementation of national tourist policy. It is the agency and the instrument for the execution of the national government's responsibilities for the control, direction and promotion of tourism.

**Optional:** In travel literature the word means that the traveller has a choice of taking or not taking the service mentioned. If he takes it, there is always an additional charge which is not included in the basic tour price.

**Package:** A travel plan which includes most elements of a vacation, such as transportation, accommodations and sightseeing.

**Passenger, Transfer:** A passenger arriving on one flight and continuing his journey on another.

**Packaging:** The practice of combining different elements of products and services (often from different firms) into a single package for one price. Travel package, for example, often include airfare, hotel, meals and sightseeing for a single price.

**Passenger, Transit:** A passenger continuing his journey on the same through-flight.

**Passport:** A document issued by national governments to their own citizens as verification of their citizenships. It is also a permit to leave one's own country and return.

**Pension:** A French word, widely used throughout Europe, meaning guest house or boarding house.

**Promotion:** All activities in producing and increasing sales, including advertising, publicity, personal selling. The activities that supplement and make more effective advertising and personal selling. Special events individually treated to bring public attention to specific products.

**Public Relations:** Continuous and consistent representation of an organization's policies to the public at large and to sections of the public who have a special interest in the organization's activities.

**Resort, Resort Complex:** A self-contained site which provides all or most of the products and services required by a tourist. They tend to combine attractions with support services such as accommodation and catering.

**Rest and Recreation:** Specified time usually included in most planned tours to allow the traveller time to relax and/or shop and visit places of interest not included in the tour.

**Rest House:** Semi-hotel establishment situated in out-of the - way places. The rest houses are popular establishments in India and most of these are owned by the State governments. These establishments at certain places are also called Circuit Houses and Dak Bungalows and are scattered all over India close to National Highways. Primarily meant for Government officials on tour, foreign tourists can also stay under certain conditions. These are convenient for tourists travelling by road.

**Sample Survey:** Study of a given population through only a part or a fraction thereof.

**Sales Letter:** A direct mail material through which an attempt is made to gain agreement of favourable action towards a product.

**Social Tourism:** All the relations and phenomena resulting from the accession to tourism of low-income groups made possible or facilitated by specific social measures. It is the type of tourism practised by those who, otherwise, would not be able to meet the cost without social intervention, *i.e.*, without the assistance of an association to which the individual belongs.

**Stopover:** A point, between origin and destination of an itinerary, at which passenger remains for a period of time.

**Statistics:** The branch of science which deals with the frequency of occurrence of different kinds of things or with the frequency of occurrence of different attributes.

**Suggested Itinerary:** A preliminary itinerary provided by tour operators for the traveller's consideration. This generally shows routings and approximate times as well as recommended hotels and suggested sight-seeing excursions, and spells out the conditions under which these services will be provided.

**Supplementary Accommodation:** Various types of accommodation other than the conventional hotel type. It includes accommodation for travellers in youth hostels, motels, camping sites, guesthouses, etc.

**Tour:** Journey to various places and coming back in the end to the place the journey started from. Tour can be of many types such as package tour, guided tour, holiday tour. Strictly speaking a tour is undertaken for a period of more than 24 hours.

**Tour Operator:** Persons or a company which organizes and sells tours, destination, travel, fixes itinerary.

**Tourist:** Persons who goes on holiday to visit places away from his home. There are two kinds of tourists *i.e.* foreign tourists and domestic tourists.

A *foreign tourist* is a person visiting India on a foreign passport staying at least 24 hours in India, purpose of whose journey can be classified as under:

(*a*) Leisure-recreation, holiday, health, study.
(*b*) Business, family, music, meeting

A *domestic tourist* is a person who travels within the country to a place other than his usual place of residence and stays at hotels or other rented place, uses the sight seeing facilities for a duration of not less than 24 hours. One night and not more than 6 months.

**Traveller:** Is the person who goes from one place to another for satisfying his needs and wants.

**Travel:** It is the movement of people from one place to another for satisfying ones needs and wants. These wants can be of primary or secondary type. Travel can be domestic or foreign.

**Travel Agency:** Offices which arrange travel and accommodation for customers.

**Tariffs:** The published fares, rates, charges, and/or related conditions of carriage of a carrier.

**Tour Conductor:** A professional employee of a tour operator who accompanies a group on tour. Not to be compared with guide.

**Tour Manager:** One who controls, directs, and manages an enterprise with judicious economy and care.

**Tour Organizer:** A person who organizes a group of passengers to participate in a specially prepared itinerary.

**Tour Package:** A travel plan which includes most elements of a vacation, such as transportation, accommodation and sightseeing.

**Tour Wholesaler:** The company that combines various components of travel industry such as hotels, airlines and local attractions into a "package" for sale by retailers.

**Tourism:** The practice of touring or travelling for pleasure or recreation and the guidance or management of tourists as a business.

**Tourism Facilities:** Facilities which include accommodation like hotels, boarding houses, guesthouses, youth hostels, etc. They also include recreational and sport facilities of great variety and also all the necessary infrastructure like transportation and utilities.

**Tourism Policy:** Guidelines and decisions designed to assist the tourism industry in meeting objectives and goals. Tourism policy usually result from the actions of the government's various agencies and organizations.

**Tourism Research:** Investigation relating with various aspects of tourism. The main objective of tourism research is to find out how people travel, where they travel and why they travel. The areas like travel, demand, domestic and international tourism, accommodation, transport, planning, etc., are covered in the research. The findings of the research become the base for planning and implementation of various programmes connected with tourism.

**Tourist Centre:** A village or town with a definite concentration of tourist resources, material base and infrastructure of tourism development.

**Tourist Charter:** A flight booked exclusively for the use of a specific group of tourists who generally belong to the same organization or who are being 'treated' to the flight by a single host.

**Tourist Complex:** A massive architectural installation specifically meant for the infrastructure of tourism.

**Tourist, Domestic:** A local person who makes a tour, travelling from place to place for pleasure, business, family mission, meeting, etc., within the country.

**Tourist Flow:** Undisturbed and even movement of tourists from one country to another for the purpose of travelling for pleasure.

**Tourist, International:** A person who makes a tour travelling from place to place for pleasure to areas foreign to his residence.

**Tourist Lodge:** A small house providing temporary accommodation to a tourist. The accommodation provided is inexpensive as compared to a conventional hotel. The lodge also offers meals.

**Tourist Object:** Any object from a natural, socio-economic or cultural-historical viewpoint which has some specific attractions for the tourists.

**Tourist Product:** A sum total of a country's tourist attraction, infrastructure and tourist services which hopefully result in consumer satisfaction.

**Tourist Region:** A branch of economic region with specific high dependence on natural and man-made tourist attractions.

**Tourist Visa:** A document issued under the authority of the Government to a person visiting a particular country as a tourist.

**Transit Traffic:** Persons (tourists) carried by transportation lines and passing through a country en route to some other destination.

**Transit Visitor:** A visitor who is passing over or through a country en route to some other destination. Unlike Destination Tourist, be spends limited time and visit few places of tourist interest.

**Travel Agent:** A person, firm or corporation qualified to provide tours, cruises, transportation, hotel accommodation, meals, transfers, sightseeing and all other elements of travel to the public as a service.

**Travel Kit:** A sort of container which contains accessories or tools. Travel kit contains various types of materials like folders, pamphlets, exhibits, presentation items, give-aways, etc., which helps travel manager in promotional activities. It is an aid which helps in promoting and projecting a product. The contents of a kit, however, vary depending on the area where it is to be used and also amount set aside for the purpose.

**Travel Magazine:** A magazine which contains articles and other reading material devoted to all types of travel and tourism. The main objective of a travel magazine is promotion of tourism.

**Vacationer:** A person staying away from home for at least four nights on any one trip and may in some instances include tourists travelling for a combination of business and pleasure.

**Visa:** An endorsement on the passport issued by the representative of a government. The endorsement enables a person to travel to a country for which it is issued.

**Visa, Entry:** An endorsement on passport issued to persons who wish to visit a country for purposes of business, employment, permanent residence, profession, etc. Initially issued for a period of three months, these are extendable to a further period of three months.

**Visa, Tourist:** An endorsement on passport issued to a person who wishes to visit a country as a tourist. The visa is effective for a period of three months. Tourists must arrive within six months of the date of the issue of visa. The tourist can extend his stay for a further period of three months if he applies to the concerned authorities.

**Visa, Transit:** An endorsement on passport which is issued to a tourist whose destination is somewhere else and is passing across. Such visitors passing through a country en route to some other destination are granted Transit Visa on production of through tickets for the onward journey.

**Visitor:** Any person visiting a country other than that in which he has his usual place of residence, for any reason other than following an occupation remunerated from within the country visited.

**Visitor Plant:** All accommodation, transport, etc., parks, points of interest in a destination area.

**Vouchers:** Documents issued by the tour operators in

exchange for which travellers receive pre-paid accommodation meals, sightseeing trips, etc. Also referred to as Coupons.

**Wholesaler:** A travel-oriented organization that creates and presents ready-made travel package or tailor-made travel programmes exclusively at the request of a travel retailer (travel agent). The travel agent communicates with the prospective traveller, and discusses with him whether he needs a ready-made or tailor-made itinerary.

**Youth Hostel:** A building which offers clean, simple and inexpensive shelter to young people exploring their own country or the world, travelling independently or in groups for holiday or educational purposes.

# 2

# Tourism: The Basic Concept

The concept of tourism as we see it today is considered as a new phenomenon but in real spirit of the word this concept is as old as early human civilization. Hereunder, we will discuss basic concept related with tourism briefly.

## INTRODUCTION

Sporadic travels by the nomads in ancient times has now become the world's most flourishing industry namely TOURISM. Early man travelled under compulsion primarily to satisfy his biological needs. In later ages, the emergence of various empires led to travel for political, business and religious purposes. Travelling in olden times was difficult due to lack of proper transport facilities, safety and comfort en route. Time and cost were the other major constraints. Travel became a little organised for religious purposes. The development of roadside *sarais*, inns and *dharamshalas* made way for business travels, political visits and journey made for the sake of knowledge.

As technology and science advanced in leaps and bounds, coupled with industrialization, it led to economic and social progress. The spread of education also fostered a desire to travel. There was great progress in the air transport industry and tourist facilities which led to the phenomenal growth of tourism. So Herman Kahn's forecast that "2 billion people will be travelling in the year 2000, ranking tourism as one of the largest, if not the largest industries of the world" has become a truth.

Tourism contributes in the development of understanding among people, provide employment, create foreign exchange and raise the standards of living. To many countries, it is the only form of sustaining their economy.

Tourism is concerned with pleasure, holidays travel and going and arriving somewhere. These are the motivations that make people leave their "normal" place of work and residence for short-term temporary visits to "other" places.

Modern tourism is one of the most striking phenomena of our times and offers us an opportunity to learn, enrich humanity and to identify what may be termed as goals for a better life and a better society.

As an industry, the impact of tourism is manifold. Tourism industry nourishes a country's economy, stimulates development process, restores cultural heritage, and helps in maintaining international peace and understanding. Tourism at present is India's third largest export industry.

The most significant feature of the tourism industry is the capacity to generate large scale employment opportunities even in backward areas, specially to women, both educated and uneducated. Another important feature of tourism is that it contributes to national integration of the people who live in different regions of the country with diverse cultures and languages.

## MEANING AND DEFINITION

It is difficult to describe tourism. Some think of tourism as an industry. If an industry is defined as a number of firms that produce similar goods and services, in competition with each other, then tourism cannot be conceived as an industry because tourism offers complementary services.

Tourism is not an industry, it is better to call it an activity. It is an activity that takes place when people move to some other place for leisure or for business and stay at least for 24 hours.

Tourism and travel are not synonyms. All tourism involves travel but all travel is not tourism. All tourism occurs during leisure time but all leisure is not given to tourist pursuits.

Tourism means the business of providing information, transportation, accommodation and other services to travellers. The travel and tourism industry is made up of companies that provide services to all types of travellers, whether travelling for business or pleasure.

Tourism moves people from one region of the world to another. It may be said to be a 'dream machine'. It helps to realise a dream or fantasy in the tourist's otherwise toilsome life.

Tourism is unique. It involves industry without smoke, education without classroom, integration without legislation and diplomacy without formality.

Francis Bacon aptly remarked, "Travel in the young sort is a part of education and in the elder, a part of experience," Tourism as a form of education is a part of civilized existence. Tourism allows people to escape from their normal humdrum lives. Mark Twain had aptly said, "Even heaven can be boring after a while." The human animal needs change if it is to operate at optimum levels; travel provides that change. However, the level of satisfaction achieved from tourism depends on the age, health, energy and background of the individual. The younger and better educated travel more than the elderly and less educated.

There are three reasons that necessitate the accurate definition of tourism.

1. In order to describe tourism phenomenon systematically for the purposes of study, it is necessary to define what it covers;
2. In order to measure any phenomenon statistically it must be defined clearly; and
3. Definition of tourism is also necessary for legislative and administrative purposes since legislation may apply to certain activities alone and not to others.

Although travelling is perhaps as old as the human civilization itself, one of the earliest available definition of tourism was, however, provided by Hermann V. Schullard, an Austrian economist, as late as in 1910. He defined tourism as, ".......the sum total of operators mainly of an economic nature, which directly relate to the entry, stay and movement of foreigners inside and outside a certain country, city or region."

A more technical definition was provided by a couple of Swiss Professors—Hunziker & Krapf—in 1942. They believed that 'tourism is the totality of the relationship and phenomena arising from the travel and stay of strangers, provided that the stay does not imply the establishment of a permanent residence and is not connected with a remunerated activity.

Burkart, A.J. and S. Medik provided yet another definition of tourism by saying that, 'Tourism denotes the temporary, short-term movement of people to destinations outside the place where they normally live and work including their activities during their stay at these destinations.

Man has been fascinated by travel and tourism from the earliest historical period. He always has had the urge to discover the unknown, to explore new and strange places, to seek changes of environment and to undergo new experiences. Travel to achieve these ends is not new, but tourism is of a relatively modern origin. Tourism is distinguishable by its mass character from the travel undertaken in the past. This is largely a post-Second World War phenomenon.

Until recently, only affluent people participated in tourism. Increased leisure, higher incomes and greatly enhanced mobility have combined to enable more people to participate in tourism. Revolution in transport, technological progress and the emergence of a middle class with time and money to spare for recreation, has led to the growth of tourism— 'the modern holiday industry'. Thus tourism is no longer the prerogative of a few but is an accepted part of life of a large number of people.

In the Sanskrit literature there are three terms for tourism with the suffix "ATANA' meaning going or leaving home for some other place. These are:

1. *Paryatana*: meaning going out for pleasure and knowledge.
2. *Desatana*: meaning going out of the country primarily for economic gains; and
3. *Tirthatana*: meaning going out to places of religions merits.

Tracing out the original sense in which tourism would have been used for the first time, Jose Ignacie De Arrillaga, believes that "Tourism in its first place is considered as a spot or rather as a synthesis of automobiles touring, cycling, alpinism, camping, excursions and yachting."

Making it a little more precise and crisp, Professor Hunziker and Krapf found tourism as the "sum total of the phenomenon and relationship arising from travel and stay of non-residents, is so fare as they do not lead to permanent residence and are not connected with any earning activity."

This definition also finds favour with the International Association of Scientific Experts in Tourism (AIEST) Prof. Hunziker has described tourism, at another place, as "an entirely of relations and facts constituted by the travel and sojourn of persons out of their normal place of domicile, as far as this sojourn and travel are not motivated by any lucrative activity whatever.

Carrying this economic aspect of tourism further, he again tries another definition which encompasses all major aspects and consequences of tourism. This definition describes tourism as the 'total relationship and pronounces as linked with stay of foreign persons to a locality, on condition that they do not settle there to exercise a major permanent or temporary activity of a lucrative nature.

According to the Oxford Dictionary, tourism is basically 'travelling for pleasure'. It involves a discretionary use of time and money.

On the other side, Dr. Ziauddin takes a completely social aspect of tourism by describing it as 'a social movement with a view to rest, diversion and satisfaction of cultural need". From this social aspect of definition, Primault attempted an all-encompassing most general definition of tourism. He considers tourism as "exploration of all that is unknown in all spheres of human activity and in all aspects of nature.

An amalgamation of these definitions brings out the following distinct elements of tourism.

1. involvement of travel by non-residents.
2. stay of temporary nature in the area visited; and
3. stay not strictly connected with any activity involving earnings.

The word tourism relates to tour derived from Latin Word 'Tomos' which means a tool for describing a circle or turnner's wheel. Tour is also a Hebrew derived from the term 'Torah' which means learning, studying or searching. Thus tour means an attempt by the traveller to discover something about the place.

Tourism is a word having very wide concept. Nassau Bahamas Development Board and S.L. Sand's describe tourism to include the following:

- In a world overflowing with the wonders of science and industry, I have become a giant among giants.
- I have demolished archaic concept of time and distance,

until no spot in the world is more than 25 hours from any other place in the world.

- I have developed new, faster, easier ways of transportation, bridging once impenetrable frontiers and creating invisible highways through the air above the broadcast oceans.
- I have given the nations of the world a new way to strengthen their economics, in the Free World my vitality has helped far-sighted statesmen to life from their people the heavy burden left by War.
- I am the livelihood of millions.....in a thousand different countries, my by-products are so numerous that when I prosper, all business benefits.
- The currency I distribute throughout the world penetrates deeply into the economy, raising the standard of living of even the most lowly.
- I introduce the people of the world to each other, teaching them each other's customs and generating mutual understanding and respect.
- I encourage people to satisfy their intellectual curiosity, making it possible for them to know man's noblest works, wherever they may be preserved.
- In a world fraught with tension, I bestow the`precious gift of physical and mental well-being upon those who make proper use of the opportunities I offer.
- I am big as earth, and there are those who say I shall one day outgrow in and reach into space.

## THE TOURIST

Keeping in mind the above descriptive definition of tourism the self portrait of tourist is as follows:

- "I am the raison d'etre, without there can be no tourism.
- I come for pleasure, education, understanding, goodwill and peace.
- I bring glimpses of my country (and culture), and act as its ambassador.
- I am not an invader nor an exploiter and come not to desecrate or debase culture, tradition and ways of life, but to appreciate them.

- I come to enjoy and admire natural resources and beautiful creations old and new.
- I come not to kill tourism—it is my very life and existence—but to have it prosper, so that multitudes may come, adore and return.
- I need accommodation, transportation and other infrastructure, and I prompt the growth of a variety of tourist industries and enterprises.
- I use local facilities and services and buy mementos and gladly pay in foreign currencies contributing to progress and prosperity.
- I come unknown and leave as a friend and well-wisher. A warm welcome and kindness overwhelms me.
- I look forward to beautiful memories of my visit to many more returns in the future.

Most of the definitions cited above, however, are of general nature and non-measurable. The need was, therefore, felt to provide a definition of 'tourist' that could be measured as well. The 'League of Nations' did some pioneering work in providing a statistically measurable definition of tourist. It defined the term 'foreign tourist' as "any person visiting a country, other than that in which he usually resides, for a period of atleast 24 hours."

The following persons were to be considered tourists within this definition:

(*i*) Persons travelling for pleasure, for domestic reasons, for health etc.

(*ii*) Persons travelling to meetings or in a representative capacity of any kind (scientific, administrative, diplomatic, religions, sports etc.)

(*iii*) Persons travelling for business purposes.

(*iv*) Persons arriving in the course of sea cruise, even when they stay for less than 24 hours.

The following categories were not to be recognised as tourists:

(*i*) Persons arriving, with or without a contract of work, to take up an occupation or engage in any business activity in the country.

(*ii*) Persons coming to establish a residence in the country.

(*iii*) Students and young persons in boarding establishment or schools.

(*iv*) Residents in a frontier zone and persons domiciled in one country and working in an adjoining country.
(*v*) Travellers passing through a country without stopping, even if the journey takes more than 24 hours.

The International Union of Official Travel Organisation (IUOTO) proposed in 1963 has described 'visitor' as any person visiting a country other than that in which he has his usual place of residence, for any reason other than following an occupation remunerated from within the country visited."

This definition covers:

(*i*) Tourists, that is, temporary visitors staying at least twenty four hours in the country visited and the purposes of whose journey can be classified under one of the following headings:
  (*a*) leisure (recreation, holiday, health, study, religions and sport;
  (*b*) business, family, mission, meeting.
(*ii*) Excursionists, that is, temporary visitors staying less than twenty four hours in the country visited (including travellers on cruises).

These definitions are gradually being accepted by most of the countries. India, however, recognised this definition a little later in 1971. From 1971, the definition of tourism adopted by the Government of India reads as:

> "A person visiting on a foreign passport for a period of not less than 24 hours for non-immigrant, non-employment tourist purposes."

In India, statistics do not include the following:

(*i*) Nationals of Pakistan and Bangladesh;
(*ii*) Nationals of Nepal entering India through land routes; and
(*iii*) All foreigners entering India from Bhutan by land.

## DECLARATION OF WORLD TOURISM CONFERENCE, 1980

The declaration reads as follows, which emphasised that tourism be considered as an integrated activity:

1. Tourism is considered as an activity essential to the life of nations because of its direct effects on the social, cultural educational and economic sectors of national societies and their international relations. Its development is linked to the social and economic development of nations and can only be possible if man has access to creative rest and holidays, and enjoys the freedom to travel. Its very existence and development depends entirely on the existence of a state of lasting peace, to which tourism itself required to contribute.
2. On the threshold of the 21st century and in view of the problems facing mankind, it seems timely and necessary to analyse the phenomenon of tourism, in relation fundamentally to the dimensions it has assumed since the granting to workers of the right to annual paid holidays moved tourism from a restricted elitist activity to a wider activity integrated into social and economic life.
3. As a result of people's aspirations to tourism, the initiatives taken by States regarding legislation and institutions, the permanent activities of voluntary bodies representing the various strata of the population and the technical contribution made by specialised professionals, modern tourism has come to play an important role within the range of human activities. States have recognised this fact and the great majority of them have entrusted the WTO with the task of ensuring the harmonious and sustained development of tourism, in cooperation, in appropriate cases, with the United Nations and the other international organisations concerned.
4. The right to use of leisure, and in particular the right to access to holidays and to freedom of travel and tourists a natural consequences of the right to work is recognized as an aspect of the fulfilment of the human needs by the Universal Declaration of Human Rights as well as by the legislation of many states.
5. There are many constraints on the development of tourism, nation and groups of nations should determine and study those constraints and adopt measures aimed at attenuating their negative influence.
6. The share tourism represents in national economies and

in international trade makes it a significant factor in world development. Its consistent major role in national economic activity in international transactions and in securing balance of payments equilibrium makes it one of the main activities of the world economy.

7. Within each country, domestic tourism contributes to an improved balance of the national economy through a redistribution of the national income. Domestic tourism also hightens the awareness of common interest and contributes to the development of activities favourable to the general economy of the country. Thus, the development of tourism from abroad should be accompanied by a similar efforts to expand domestic tourism.
8. The economic returns of tourism, however, real and significant they may be, do not and cannot constitute the only criterion for the decision by States to encourage this activity. The right to holidays, the opportunity for the citizen to get to know his own environment, a deeper awareness of his national identity and of the solidarity that links him to his compatriots and the sense of belonging to a culture and to a people are all major reasons for stimulating the individual's participation in domestic and international tourism through access to holidays and travel.
9. The importance that millions of our contemporaries attach to tourism in the use of their free time and in their concept of the quality of life makes it a need that government should take into account and support.
10. Social tourism is an objective which society must pursue in the interest of those citizens who are least privileged in the exercise of their rights to rest.
11. Through its effect on the physical and mental health of individuals practising it, tourism is a factor that favours social stability, improves the working capacity of communities and promotes individual as well as collective well-being.
12. Through the wide range of services needed to satisfy its requirement, tourism creates new activities of considerable importance which are a source of new

employment. In this development in all the countries where it is practiced irrespective of their level of development.

13. With respect to international relations and the search for peace, based on justice and respect of individual and national aspirations, tourism stands out as a positive and ever-present factor in promoting mutual knowledge and understanding and a basis of reaching a greater level of respect and confidence among all the people of the world.
14. Modern tourism results from the adoption of a social policy which led to the workers' gaining annual paid holidays and represents the recognition of a fundamental right of the human being to rest and leisure. It has become a factor contributing to social stability, mutual understanding among individuals and people and individual betterment. In addition to its well-known economic aspects, it has acquired a cultural and moral dimension which must be fostered and protected against the harmful distortions which can be brought about by economic factors. Public authorities and the travel trade should accordingly participate in development of tourism by formulating guidelines aimed at encouraging appropriate investment.
15. Youth tourism requires the most active attention since young people have less adequate income than others for travelling or taking holidays. A positive policy should provide youth with the utmost encouragement and facilities. The same attention should be paid for the elderly and handicapped.
16. In the universal efforts to establish a new international economic order, tourism can under appropriate conditions, play a positive role in furthering equilibrium, cooperation, mutual understanding and solidarity among all countries.
17. Nations should promote improved conditions of employment for workers engaged in tourism and confirm and protect their right to establish professional trade unions and collective bargaining.
18. Tourism resources available in various countries consist at the same time of space, facilities and values. These are

resources whose use cannot be left uncontrolled without running the risk of their deterioration or even destruction. The satisfaction of tourism requirements must not be prejudicial to the social and economic interest of the population in tourist areas, to the environment or, above all to natural resources, which are the fundamental attraction of tourism, and historical and cultural sites. All tourism resources are part of the heritage of mankind. National communities and the entire international community must take the necessary steps to ensure their preservation. The conservation of historical, cultural and religious sites represents at all times, and notably in time of conflict, one of the fundamental responsibilities of states.

19. International cooperation in the field of tourism is an endeavour in which the characteristics of people and basic interests of individual states must be respected. In this field, the central and decisive role of the WTO as a concept utilizing and harmonizing boys is obvious.
20. Bilateral and multilateral technical and financial cooperation can not be looked upon as an act of assistance since it constitutes the pooling of the means necessary for the utilization of resources for the benefits of all parties.
21. In the practice of tourism, spiritual elements must take precedence over technical and material elements. The spiritual elements are essentially as follows:

    (*a*) the total fulfilment of the human being;
    (*b*) a constantly increasing contribution to education;
    (*c*) equality of destiny of nations;
    (*d*) the liberation of man in a spirit of respect for his identity and dignity;
    (*e*) the affirmation of the originality of cultures and respect for the moral heritage of peoples.

22. Preparation for tourism should be integrated with the training of the citizen for his civic responsibilities. In this respect, governments should mobilise the means of education and information at their disposal and should facilitate the work of individuals and bodies involved in this endeavour. Preparation for tourism, for holidays and

for travel could usefully form part of the process of youth education and training. For these reasons, the integration of tourism into youth education constitutes a basic element favourable to the permanent strengthening of peace.

23. Any long-term analysis of mankind's social, cultural and economic development should take due account of national and international tourist and recreational activities. These activities now form an integral part of the life of modern national and international societies. Bearing in mind the acknowledged values of tourism which are inseparable from it, the authorities will have to give an increased attention to the development of national and international tourist and recreational activity, based on an ever-wider participation of people in holidays and travel as well as the movement of persons for numerous other purposes, with a view to ensuring orderly growth of tourism in a manner consistent with the other basic needs of society.
24. The States and other participants in the Conference, together with the WTO, are strongly urged to take into account the guidelines, viewpoints and recommendations emanating from the Conference so that they can contribute, on the basis of their experience and in the context of their day to day activities, to the practical implementation of the objectives set with a view to broadening the process of development of world tourism and breathing new life into it.
25. The Conference urges the WTO to take all necessary measures, through its own internal machinery and, where appropriate, in cooperation with other international, inter government and non-governmental bodies, so as to permit the global implementation of the principles, concepts and guidelines contained in this final document.

## CONCEPT OF TOURISM

The concept of tourism adopted by the International Association of Scientific Experts in Tourism was put forward by the Swiss Professors Hunziker and Krapf as follows:

> "Tourism is the sum of the phenomena and relationships arising from the travel and stay of non-residents, in so far as they do not lead to permanent residence and are not connected with any earning activity."

Since then the basic concept has been broadened to include various forms of business and vocational travel because their economic significance is the same.

On an analysis of the above definition, we find the following features of tourism:

1. Tourism arises from the movement of people to, and their stay in, various destinations.
2. There are two elements in all tourism—the journey to the destination and the stay.
3. The journey and the stay should take place outside the normal place of residence and work.
4. The movement to destinations is of a temporary character with the intention to return within a few days. A tourist is expected to spend a minimum of 24 hours and a maximum of six months in the destination.
5. Destinations are visited for purposes other than taking up permanent residence or employment.

Gunn feels that tourism includes all travelling except commuting.

Tourism is a leisure activity which involves a discretionary use of time and money and recreation is often the main purpose for participation in tourism. As already pointed out, all tourism includes some travel but all travel is not tourism. The temporary short-term character of tourism distinguishes it from migration, which means a long-term population movement with a view to taking up permanent residence. In tourism money earned in one's normal domicile is spent in the places visited.

There are three main aspects of tourism. The first is the purpose of travel or visit which expresses a particular motivation. Second, it is usually necessary to define the time element. The minimum and maximum period have to be established for a particular purpose. Thus travel for a period shorter than 24 hours may be excluded. Also, a foreigner who comes and works in a country to make a living or to study in its universities is not a tourist. Thirdly, much tourism is characterized by seasonality or periodicity (the high concentration of visitor activity at particular times of the year).

## QUESTIONS FOR ANSWER

1. *Define the term 'Tourism' and enumerate the Indian concept of tourism as per three word in Sanskrit literature.*
2. *Define tourism and tourist as per the concept of Nassau Bahamas Development Board and S.L. Sand.*
3. *Write a note on the declaration of World Tourism Conference, 1980.*
4. *Write a short note on the Concept of Tourism.*

# 3

# Nature and Classification of Tourism

The study of the basic concept of tourism as discussed in the previous chapter clearly states that tourism is multi-disciplinary with human dimensions and it is considered as one of the largest and fastest growing industries of the world as well as in socio-economic phenomenon and such an instrument of social change and economic growth. Hereunder, we will consider various aspects concerning the nature and scope of tourism, very briefly.

## BASIC NATURE

Tourism as a socio-economic phenomenon has evolved into one of the largest and fastest growing industries of the world. The multiplier effects of tourism in terms of employment generation and income re-distribution are unique. Moreover, its extensive backward and forward linkages make it particularly potent as an instrument of economic growth.

Its value addition in terms of earnings hard foreign exchange is exceptionally high. Its spread in developing countries would provide a natural channel for significant resource transfers from advanced countries to backward economies. Interestingly, the growth path for international tourism has been more stable than for international trade.

In India too, tourism has emerged as a key factor in the national effort to augment foreign income, attract overseas investment, foster competitive efficiency and take other steps with the aim of securing a respectable place for India in the globe in the 21st century. Importantly, tourism is a socio economic phenomenon with vast economic activity.

The main factors which have been responsible for the vast expansion of tourism are the influence of people in the industrialized nations of the west, increase in leisure time, advance in transport technology besides the rising curiosity about people in other lands.

Interestingly, tourism has reached significant dimensions in many countries and it has been referred to as the 20th century migration of nations. Some nations are moving from an industrial leisure and, consequently, more desire by its people to travel and accumulate experiences. But the potential for growth in this field has been hardly tapped and realised. Several factors point to a bright future for tourism in the 21st century.

Conceptually, tourism is defined as 'the sum of the phenomenon and relationships arising from the travel and stay of nonresidents in so far as they do not lead to permanent residents and are not connected with any earning activity. Broadly, the concept of tourism is characterized by (*i*) a movement of people to various destinations and has two components—the journey and the stay—both of which take place outside the normal area of residence and work; (*ii*) the movement is of a temporary nature and for a short duration which distinguishes it from migration; (*iii*) it gives rise to activities at the destination place visited; (*iv*) the main motive for participation in tourism is largely recreation and the visit is made for purposes other than seeking permanent residence or employment remunerated from within the place visited and, lastly, (*v*) tourism, in the real sense, is essentially a pleasure activity and involves a discretionary use of freely disposable incomes and of free time.

Tourism has to be regarded as an 'industry' although, strictly in accordance with the classical definition of the term, like recreation, it is not an industry. From the receiving country's view point, however, tourism would be regarded as an industry which contributes to its economic and social development and activates many productive sectors. In economic terms, tourism 'creates a demand or provides a market for a number of quite separate and varied industries. In some areas tourism represents the major part of market, in others a complementary, but frequently highly profitable, demand for accommodation, catering, transport, entertainment and other services designed largely, perhaps even primarily, for a residential or industrial community.

Tourism has been also conceived and described in some other ways. For instance, Lundberg has described it as a business. He is of the opinion that tourism is the business of the transport, care, feeding and entertainment of the tourists. Mill and Morison have treated it as a system consisting of interrelated parts and expressed the view that tourism is not an industry. Moreover, tourism is conceived as a medium of human communication.

According to this view, tourism must not be regarded merely as business. It is a means of communication between individuals and between people's. The tourists' interests should not be exploited exclusively because of his consumer potentialities but also to communicate a positive message which will foster cultural development and mutual understanding. Tourism creates a dynamic system of communication among individuals, states and nations, it retains the perspective of the traveller as a human being without losing sight of the economic impact of the tourist phenomenon. This new focus accentuates the fundamental values which should guide official policy and not limit or completely disregard possible benefits of vast value.

## NATURE OF TOURISM: LEIPER MODEL

Tourism is characterized by two main concerns: It is multi-disciplinary with the human dimensions of tourism attracting the attentions of geographers, historians, behaviour scientists. While the nature of tourism as a commercial activity appeals to those engaged in economics and business activities. Second, it is a young area of study—almost 70 years old—without the antecedents of a nature subject.

International organisations support tourism for its contributions to the world peace, the benefits of mixing peoples and cultures, the economic advantages which can ensure and the fact that tourism is a relatively 'clean' industry.

Tourism, however, is surrounded by a number of myths (which have contributed to the glamour) and these should be broken:

1. Tourism in the world is dominantly domestic (people travelling in their own country), not international.
2. Most tourism journeys are by surface transport (mainly car), not by air.
3. Tourism is not purely for the purpose of leisure. It also includes business tourism, pilgrimages and tourism for health purposes.

We shall approach tourism by adopting the model suggested by Leiper. There are three basic elements in *Leiper's model.*

### Tourists

The tourist is the actor in the system. Tourism is a human experience enjoyed and remembered by many as a very important aspect of their lives.

### Geographical Elements

Leiper outlines three geographical elements in his model:

(*i*) Traveller-generating region,
(*ii*) Tourist destination region, and
(*iii*) Transit route region.

The traveller-generating region represents the generating market for tourism and in a sense provides the 'push' to stimulate and motivate travel. It is here that the tourist searches for information, makes the booking and makes the departure.

The tourist destination region represents the 'end' of tourism. At the destination, the full impact of tourism is felt and planning and management strategies are implemented. The destination is also the *raison d'être* for tourism. The 'pull' to visit destinations energizes the whole tourism system and creates demand for travel in the generating region. It is, therefore, at the destination where the most noticeable and dramatic consequences of the system occur.

The transit route region represents not only the short period of travel to reach the destination but also the intermediate places which may be visited en route.

### Tourism Industry

The third element of Leiper's model allows the locations of the various industrial sectors to be identified. For example, travel agents and tour operators are predominantly found in the traveller-generating region, attraction and the hospitality are found in the destination region, while the transport industry is located in the transit route region.

The fact that tourism is also an industry of contrasts is illustrated by examining two major elements of Leiper's model.

Demand for tourism in the generating region is inherently volatile, seasonal and irrational; yet this demand is satisfied by a destination region where supply is fragmented and inflexible—surely a recipe for the financial instability of tourism.

Tourism is a multidimensional, multifaceted activity which touches many lives and many different economic activities. Not surprisingly, tourism has, therefore, proved difficult to define, yet Leiper has suggested following definition:

> "The tourist industry consists of those firms, organisation and facilities which are intended to serve the specific needs and wants of tourists."

It is difficult to define leisure. Leisure can be thought of as a combined measure of time and attitude of mind to create periods of time when other obligations are at a minimum.

A number of official proclamations have affirmed every individual's right to demand tourism. In 1980 the Manila Declaration on World Tourism stated that the ultimate aim of tourism was the improvement of quality of life and the creation of better living conditions for all peoples.

## VARIED BENEFITS OF TOURISM

As already mentioned, tourism is unique because it involves industry without smoke, education without classroom, integration without legislation, and diplomacy without formality.

The importance of tourism was highlighted when the UN General Assembly designated 1967 as the International Tourist Year. It recognised that tourism is a basic and desirable human activity deserving the praise and encouragement of all people and governments.

The so-called Manila Declaration supports the view that tourism is an activity essential to the life of nations because of its direct effects on social, cultural, educational and economic sectors of societies.

The world tourism can contribute to the establishment of a new international economic order that will help to eliminate the widening economic gap between developed and developing countries and ensure the steady acceleration of economic and social development and progress, in particular of the developing countries.

Tourism is the world's largest export industry. Tourism provides a major contribution to foreign exchange earnings of several developing and even developed countries. In 2000 world tourism generated 16 per cent of world GNP. Domestic tourism is assumed to be nine times greater than international tourism.

Today, tourism is a major item of international trade—perhaps the biggest international business activity after all. International tourism is the largest single item in the world's foreign trade and for some countries, it is already the most important industry and earner of foreign exchange.

The economic gap between rich and poor countries has widened over the past decades. To create new industries and to transform rural life of a developing country like India is a gigantic task. The relevance of tourism in this situation is that income from international tourism can bring the foreign exchange essential for major investments.

By appreciating other people's ways of life and institutions, tourism may create goodwill for a country. Tourists travel to participate in many events like conferences, exhibitions, etc.; their visits also provide an opportunity to improve cooperation as well as to project an image of a country to the outside world. When tourists come in contact with other people, social exchange takes place. Tourists often carry back home with them new ideas and a new outlook on life.

Tourism has an educational significance. It has a beneficial effect which is brought about through contact between people of different races and nationalities. Tourism is a form of culture contact between peoples of different countries. Tourism involves cultural exchanges and results in cultural enrichment of those who travel as well as of those at the receiving end.

Cultural factors attract tourists to destinations: architecture, historical monuments and birthplaces of famous men are often visited by tourists. Culture is tourism's main attraction. Without culture to make the difference, every place would seem blandly the same. Without different cultural heritage, places around the world would have little to offer that would attract for purposes of tourism. World heritage sites are nothing but cultural sites, such as the Pyramids in Egypt, the Tower of London, the Taj Mahal of India, the Great Wall of China.

In bringing together people of different backgrounds from

different countries, tourism has a political and social significance. Domestic tourism promotes similar interaction between people and places and contributes to that knowledge which may enhance understanding. The main economic significance of tourism—money earned in places of normal residence is spent in places visited—is common to all tourism. The outstanding economic effect of tourism lies in the purchasing power generated in receiving areas through the expenditure of visitors who tend to spend at a much bigger rate than when they are at home.

International tourist expenditure introduces an additional aspect of economic significance as different countries have to balance their transactions with the rest of the world. International tourism enters into the balance of payments accounts of individual countries and is of major significance in international trade. Globally tourism constitutes a major item in world trade which is growing at a much faster rate in recent years than world trade in goods.

Tourist expenditure increases the income of the destination by an amount greater than itself. The expenditure is amplified and this is known as the multiplier. The multiplier itself is the numerical coefficient indicating how much income will increase as a result of tourist expenditure. If the tourist expenditure is Rs. 10 crores and the value of the multiplier is 1.9, the income will increase to Rs. 19 crores.

Tourism is an integral part of modern life. As a force for social change tourism has had an impact of the same order as the industrial revolution. In the last three decades, tourism has transformed the way the world looks and works.

No place in the world is isolated. The realms of space have been conquered and many remote corners of the globe are now accepted holiday centres. Distance is no longer so much costly. This has transformed not only world economics but also human lifestyles.

## ADVERSE ENVIRONMENTAL IMPACT OF TOURISM

On the negative side, tourism may have direct environmental impacts on the quality of water, air and on noise levels. Sewage disposal into water will add to pollution problems, as will the use of powered boats on inland waterways and sheltered seas.

Increased usage of the internal combustion engine for tourist transport and oil burning to provide the power for a hotel's air conditioning and refrigeration units add to the diminution of air quality, and noise levels may be dramatically increased in urban areas through discos and nightclubs and by increased road, rail and air traffic.

Campfires may destroy forests, ancient monuments may be worn away or disfigured and damaged by graffiti and the improper disposal of litter can detract from the aesthetic quality of the environment and harm wildlife.

Physical deterioration of both natural and man-made environment can have serious consequences. Hunting and fishing have obvious impacts on the wildlife environment; sand dunes can be damaged and eroded by overuse; vegetation can be destroyed by walkers.

## CLASSIFICATION, FORMS OR TYPES OF TOURISM

There are different criterias of classification of tourism. These criterias are based on the purpose, place, nature, distance of visit etc. etc. Hereunder, we will discuss these aspects, very briefly:

### Purpose of Tourism

On this basis the tourism has been classified in six classes:

1. *Recreational Tourism*: which is what most people have in mind when tourism is mentioned. This is where mass and popular package tours seek mainly sun-see-sand and fresh air or sporting activities of various kinds. These groups are mainly seeking a change and rest.
2. *Cultural Tourism:* Here the aim is to experience new cultural activities *i.e.* folklore, art, music etc.
3. *Historical Tourism*: This involves visit to heritage locations, museums, churches, temples etc.
4. *Ethnic Tourism*: This involves contact with unusual or quaint customs in remote areas, visiting the family's country of origin and relatives and friends.
5. *Environmental Tourism*: When the higher income groups in particular are interested in visiting remote environment.
6. *Adventure Tourism:* This is geared to promote mountaineering, trekking and adventure activities.

Tourism does not lend itself to a single form. It is a generic term which includes several types of travel and stay depending upon the motivations that impel people to move from one place to another. People travel for various reasons and the main purpose of travel determines the form of tourism. Accordingly, tourism as a phenomenon is presented under various forms and classified on the basis of factors such as geographical location, the purpose served by travel, the means of transport used, the number of persons travelling etc.

## Domestic Tourism

The basic distinction in tourism between domestic and international tourism is place of travel. The travel by people, outside their normal domicile, in other areas within their own country, constitutes domestic or internal tourism. It represents the tourism movements of citizens and residing foreigners inside the country. There are no language, currency or documentation barriers or restrictions associated with domestic tourism and, consequently, it has no balance of payments implications.

## International Tourism

International Tourism involves the movements of people between different countries in the world. The travel by people to a country other than that in which they normally live, and which is a separate national unit with its own political and economic system, constitutes international tourism. Foreign travel and tourism necessitates its two essential requirements of documentation and currency. The former regulates and controls of the flow of visitors by means of passport, visa, entry permits and the latter has important bearing on the balance of payment.

### *Distinction between Domestic and International Tourism*

In domestic tourism, people travel outside their normal domicile to other areas within the country. They do not cross national boundaries. In this case there are no language or currency or document barriers. A tourist is any person visiting a place for a period of at least 24 hours. Persons travelling on holiday for a period of less than 24 hours are to be treated as excursionists.

When people travel to other sovereign countries, they are involved in international tourism. In this case there are different languages, different currencies and documentation in the form of passport and visa which stand in the way of free movement of people. The Manila Declaration of World Tourism Conference held at Manila in September 1980 declared:

> Within each country domestic tourism contributes to an improved balance of the national economy through a redistribution of the national income. Domestic tourism also heightens the awareness of common interest and contributes to the development of activities favourable to the general economy of the country. Thus the development of tourism from abroad should be accompanied by a similar effort to expand domestic tourism. Thus regional redistribution of income and political unification are two vital spirits of domestic tourism.

To most people, tourism does not appear as a basic need or even as a priority good. Rather, it appears to them as a mere luxury good. To a great extent this is the legacy of the earlier association of tourism for recreation with the leisure class. The days of elite tourism is over and tourism has a role to play for better international understanding as well as for national integration.

According to World Tourism Organisation, a foreign tourist is a person visiting a country other than that in which he usually resides, for a period of at least 24 hours.

The following are to be considered tourists:

(*i*) Persons travelling for pleasure, for health, etc.
(*ii*) Persons travelling in a representative capacity of any kind;
(*iii*) Persons travelling for business reasons;
(*iv*) Persons arriving in the course of a sea cruise, even when they stay for less than 24 hours.

The following are not to be regarded as tourists:

(*i*) Persons arriving to take up an accommodation or engage in any business activity in the country;
(*ii*) Persons coming to establish a residence in the country;
(*iii*) Students and young persons in schools;
(*iv*) Any person domiciled in one country and working in an adjoining country;
(*v*) Travellers passing through a country without stopping, even if the journey takes more than 24 hours.

## Intra-regional and Inter-regional Tourism

Intra-regional tourism refers to tourist flows between countries of the same region. A region refers to and includes the countries belonging to a specific World Tourism Organisation, Regional Commission, together with the non-member countries of the same regions. The World Tourism Organisation regions are: Africa, America, East Asia and Pacific, Europe, Middle East and South Asia. Inter-regional involves tourist flow from one region to another country in another WTO region. The term Regional Tourism denotes tourist movement between countries forming one tourist region, *e.g.* tourist traffic between countries of western Europe.

## Holiday Tourism

According to the purpose of visit, broad distinction is made between holiday, business and common interest tourism. Holiday takes many forms such as recreational tourism, health tourism, sport tourism, cultural tourism. Recreational tourism aims at the reformation and rejuvenation of the physical and mental capacities of the individual tourist.

Likewise health tourism, satisfies the need for improving health and vitality of visitors in other countries or places which offer an invigorating climate, spas, hot springs and curative facilities like mineral water treatment etc. Cultural tourism sources to enrich knowledge about other countries and people and includes visits to places of historical, artistic and cultural interest.

Sport tourism relates to satisfying people's hobbies such as fishing, animal hunting, sea diving etc. It also includes activities like skiing, hiking, trekking, mountain climbing and rafting which are also considered part of adventure tourism.

Moreover, the holiday tourists have a freedom of choice about where to go and, to a greater or lesser extent, when to go. They decide for themselves whether they should apply a part of their income and a part of their leisure time to participate in tourism.

## Eco-tourism

Eco-tourism is a logical component of eco-development. It is a complex and multidisciplinary phenomenon and has a tremendous role to play in the interpretation of nature and natural resources, as well as in the understanding of human history and its interaction with the rural environment, and the diffusion of environmental knowledge and awareness. It can serve as an important tool for environmental education and for raising ecological awareness, both in tourist and local people, and government officials.

Interestingly, eco-tourism has been defined by the world conservation union as environmentally responsible travel and visits to relatively undisturbed natural areas, in order to enjoy and appreciate nature (and any accompanying cultural features both past and present) that promotes conservation, has low visitor impact, and provides for beneficially active socio-economic involvement of local populations. Importantly, eco-tourism respects the environment and encourages and promotes the well being of local people.

Nature tourism may or may not do this. Eco-tourism is also not to be confused with adventure sports or even snow skiing, amusement parks etc. which in fact might have a negative impact on the environment. Eco-tourists like to go around in a 'low impact way'. Adventure tourists are not necessarily eco-tourists. However, eco-tourism certainly needs a spirit of adventure, especially when negotiating bad roads. Eco-tourism covers a broad spectrum—plants, forests, animals in the wild, under water life, coral reefs, national parks, etc.

The World Heritage Convention of UNESCO has declared world heritage. When the nature and culture are present together, it is an attractive combination, like we have at the Ajanta and Ellora caves, Mr. Hector Ca Lascurain is of the view that 'regulated eco-tourism can have several positive effects on the environment.

Since tourist operators have a vested interest in maintaining the environmental quality of tourist destinations, they are becoming increasingly interested in collaborating with those who work to protect the environment. Income from tourism can also assist in the development, and improvement of facilities such as sanitation systems, for residents and tourist like.

### Business Tourism

Business tourism has become very significant. There are three constituent elements of business tourism—incentive travel, conference tourism and business travel.

The per capita spending power of the business tourists is considerably higher than that of the leisure tourist.

Of the three main types of international business tourism, incentive travel is the least important. Incentive travel is an employment perk used to motivate employees.

Conference tourism represents big business at both the national and international level. By 1980, there were 14,000 international conferences each year. Within Europe, the major international conference centres are Paris, London, Madrid, Geneva and Brussels. Outside Europe, the main centres are Sydney, Singapore, Washington and New York.

International business travel has expanded considerably in recent years as a result of the globalisation of the world economy.

There are a number of important features of international tourism. First, the international tourist movements are highly polarised. The moves are mainly among the more developed countries. Second, most of international movements are regionalized and are especially concentrated within Europe. Third, the overall dominance of Europe continues but is in relative decline. International tourism rapidly expanded in Europe but subsequently it has declined.

**Cultural Tourism**

Cultural tourism is one of the important features of tourism in India. Our historical and archaeological monuments continue to be the biggest draw in attracting international tourists. Cultural tourism plays a major part in increasing national and international goodwill and understanding. Thousands of archaeological and historical monuments scattered throughout the country provide opportunity to learn about ancient history and culture.

India has a great variety of typical cultural, historic and natural attractions. By upgrading the level of and access to these attractions, the island and other places will gain cultural prestige and may offer more interesting places to visit. The level of service and quality of museums and other archaeological monuments might be improved. Organisation of art exhibitions or other cultural manifestations may also be an interesting possibility. Moreover, cultural traditions such as folk songs, dances, folk music, folk crafts and folk arts of a region attract tourists.

### Adventure/Sport Tourism

Tourism can roughly be defined as an activity of travelling and staying in places outside for business, pilgrimage, leisure and other purposes. The history of adventure tourism in India can be traced back to the Vedic times. Our great Indian rivers and mountains have always been considered as holy places and centres of pilgrimages. The geography of our country is sufficiently endowed so as to attract tourists with an adventurist's zeal. Adventure and sports tourism consists of many activities such as trekking, rock climbing, skiing, mountain climbing, skating, hang gliding, paragliding, golf, horse riding, cycling, etc.

### Sea and Island Tourism

India has a strong comparative advantage in sea and island tourism, because it has an abundance of surrounding waters and habitats. The sea lends itself to wind surfing, water skiing, snorkeling and sailing. Establishment of modern water sports facilities may be established at some tourist resorts. Moreover, sea beaches are most attractive for tourists both domestic and international. Interestingly, ecofriendly beach resorts in eco-villages, water sports etc. are also attractions for tourists.

### Sustainable Tourism

One of the important prerequisites for attracting tourists to an area is the beauty of the natural environment. But if such an attraction force becomes successful, it has to be recognised that too large a number of tourists will damage or even destroy the natural environment, thus eroding the very base of tourist activity. A new concept which has begun to dominate the tourism debate in recent years is that of 'sustainable development'.

The idea of sustainable tourism development is now a popular concept and refers to allowing tourism growth while at the same time preventing degradation of the environment, as this may have important consequences for future quality of life.

In this context, Buchalis and Fletcher quote Goodall who has suggested that sustainable tourism requires that the demand of increasing numbers of tourists is satisfied in a manner which continues to attract them whilst meeting the needs of the host population with improved standards of living, yet safe guarding the destination environment and cultural heritage.

With sustainable tourism development we mean that tourism development is both in volume and in direction of development evolving in such a way that the pressure on the natural environment remains below the level of the carrying capacity for both the present and future generation. One way of analysing this is by r ans of appropriate indicators.

Sustainable tourism development indicators can help determining whether or not the development of tourism is damaging the natural environment, and to what extent. Some examples are: quality of the surface water, the level of noise in a certain area etc. Impact of tourism on the local environment can be assessed on the level of air pollution, water pollution, pollution of sites, noise pollution, loss of natural land scape (agricultural and pastoral lands), destruction of flora and fauna, degradation of landscape and historic sites and monuments, conflict and social tension, congestion and stress on civic services/facilities etc.

### Exclusive Tourism

Exclusive or top-class tourism is aimed at the arrivals of high income tourists. Exclusive tourism can be developed through improvement and addition of more luxury facilities, better service provision and higher standards of environment. The improved standards of quality should be applied to restaurants, transport, travelling and their support facilities.

### Health Tourism

The sea beaches and islands may also develop facilities for curative tourism. For example, thermal waters (which are characteristics for the island) are recommended for people with rheumatic problems, bronchitis, back aches, skin diseases etc. Bath facilities, accommodations around the spa's and access roads way then be improved or established.

### Common Interest Tourism

Common interest tourism includes visitors who travel for specific purpose and objectives other than that of holiday and business. It includes visits to friends and relatives, or for study, health, religion and other miscellaneous purposes. The return of people to the country of their origin, sometimes labelled as ethnic tourism, falls in this category. The flow of immigrants to pay a nostalgic visit to the old country is an important part of such traffic. It is reflected in the large scale movements between United States of America, U.K. and European countries.

### Wildlife Tourism

India has several places which have fascinating beauty and abode of wildlife. Our sanctuaries, national parks and zoo provide an opportunity to such wildlife and nature lovers. A wildlife tourist visits these areas looking for typical Himalayan wildlife including Thar, Boral and Snow Leopard. Moreover, hunting of wild bear, Cheetal, Nilgai, Patridges and Quails etc. fishing, sea hunting, etc. attract tourists.

### Educational Tourism

Tourism may also be developed on the basis of meetings, conferences, congress of symposia. Extension of University, academic centres and colleges may provide opportunities to develop educational tourism. For such objectives, short-term cultural and languages courses and sharing the research experience may be proved best approaches.

### Agro-Tourism/Rural Tourism

Agro-tourism is a kind of tourism which favours the economic activities in the agriculture sector at the same time. An important aim is to stimulate these activities in relation to the agricultural potential so that the economy of the state/area will not become solely dependent on tourist activities. Agro-tourism contains, for instance, the construction of tourist accommodations and facilities at farmer's places, besides, tourists may watch the processing of farm products.

Handicrafts, leather industry, fruits and vegetable processing industry etc. are popular traditional activities to which agro-tourism may also be applied. Interestingly, the stress and strain of modern life in the industrialised countries of the west are such that a large number of holiday markets have turned to the countryside for tranquility, rest and reoperation. The peace and quiet of nature is perceived as having effect on body and mind. Rural tourism is an escape, a return to saving and an environment for rejuvenation.

## OTHER FORMS OF TOURISM

In addition to the above tourism is also classified on the following basis:

1. According to the duration, short trips which do not involve an overnight stay are described as day trips or excursions and should be differentiated from journeys and stays at destinations for at least 24 hours which are described as tourism. These involve an overnight stay.
2. Tourism may be divided into individual and group travel and into independent travel and inclusive tours. The first classification is self-explanatory. The distinction between independent travel and inclusive tourist based on how the individual elements of a trip are bought by the tourist. In the former case, transport, accommodation, etc., are arranged separately by the tourist himself or through the travel agent. In the latter case, the tourist buys a trip for which he is unable to distinguish the prepaid cost of his fare from the cost of accommodation and other elements; this arrangement is also known as the package tour. The tourist may move about as an individual or as a member of a group.
3. Mass tourism refers to the participation of a large number of people in tourism. In this sense the term is used in contrast to the limited participation of people as in elite tourism. Mass tourism is essentially a quantitative notion based on the volume of tourist activity.

## INDIAN CONCEPT OF CLASSIFICATION OF TOURS/TOURISM

Broadly, tourism can be divided into three main categories:

1. *Thirthutun*—travelling for religious purposes.
2. *Deshatan*—travelling for trading or commercial purposes.
3. *Paryatan*—travelling for curiosity, knowledge and leisure.

Leisure holidays, in recent times has become the most publicized form of travel. Peoples' curiosity and love for adventure has led to a range of specialized holiday packages. To name a few:

1. Health based holidays—(yoga, meditation and relaxation). This has been gaining a lot of importance nowadays in this stress-filled world.
2. Sports based holidays—which include skiing, surfing, swimming, under water activities like snorkelling, etc.
3. Wildlife holidays—exploring the wildlife of the country. India has a wide range of wildlife sanctuaries.
4. Beach resorts—This remains one of the main attraction for tourists—the sun and the sea.
5. Heritage holidays—explores historical and cultural heritage of our country. In India; we have innumerable historical monuments, forts and palaces coupled with numerous festivals and carnivals which highlight our handicrafts, dance and music.
6. Hill station/resorts—popular for its calm scenic beauty, where people can relax in the lap of nature and the adventurous ones can go on long nature walks or treks.

India as a destination can offer all these and so much more! Coupled with our innate hospitality, friendliness and warmth, India should become one of the most sought after destinations in the South East Asia region in the years to come.

### Types of Tours

Tours are classified into three main groups:

1. *Inbound Tours*—which promotes and brings tourists from foreign countries. This type of tourism brings in foreign exchange and is the most preferred by any tour operator.
2. *Outbound Tours*—which promotes foreign tours of local nationals through various packages. Since it involves outflow of foreign exchange, it is strictly regulated by the Department of Tourism and RBI.
3. *Local or Domestic Tours*—promotes tours within the country for the local population. This type of tourism has been on the increase recently, as more and more people are becoming aware that our own country is a rich storehouse of religion and cultural heritage.

**Categories of Tours**

Tours can be broadly divided into the following categories:

1. *Pleasure Tours*—most sought after type.
2. *Promotional Tours*—for travel agents or middlemen involved in trade or commerce.
3. *Incentive Tours*—mainly for middlemen in trade sponsored by their principals as a reward for attaining sales or set targets.
4. *Religious Tours*—promoted to places of religious interest.
5. *Study Tours*—promoted for studies in specific areas, history tours, science tours, archaeological tours, etc., also known as special interest tours.
6. *Sports Tours*—promoted for sportsmen in different fields like football, cricket, tennis, chess etc.
7. *Conference Tours*—(*i*) promotion of conferences, congresses and business meetings, (*ii*) post conference tours—promoted for conference participants after the conference.
8. *Adventure Tours*—promoted for adventures like mountain climbing, trekking, river rafting, aqua-sports, skiing, etc.

## BASIC REQUIREMENTS

For a country to become a major tourist destination, it must have the following basic requirements:

1. *Tourist Attractions*—For a place to become a tourist attraction, it should be able to offer something unique. This can be natural like hills, beaches, mountains, sun, lakes, river, sand, wildlife, jungles etc., or man-made like caves, temples, culture, traditional festivals, customs, costumes, etc.
2. *Accommodation*—This mainly determine the city's or country's ability to attract visitors. Without this basic infrastructure, tourism cannot be promoted. Accommodation available should be affordable, clean with basic amenities like water, power supply, proper drainage and sewage systems. It should be easily accessible by good roads and have commercial facilities like currency exchange counter, parks and recreational facilities,

healthcare facilities, proper security measures and hygienic food and dining facilities.

3. *Other Support Services—*
   (*a*) Local day tours
   (*b*) art galleries and museums
   (*c*) duty free shops
   (*d*) guide service
   (*e*) recreational facilities like horse riding, swimming etc.
   (*f*) sports, theatres, and clubs
   (*g*) restaurants, bars and pubs
   (*h*) festivals on local customs
   (*i*) services like laundry, petrol, bookshops
   (*j*) ethnic shops selling local made handicrafts
   (*k*) safety and security for tourists
   (*l*) local hospitality.

## QUESTIONS FOR ANSWER

1. *Discuss the nature of tourism. What is the product of tourism?*
2. *Explain the nature of tourism in terms of Leiper model.*
3. *Explain the concept of tourism. What are the different types of tourism?*
4. *Discuss the different classifications of tourism.*
5. *Discuss the importance of tourism from different stand points.*
6. *Write a note on the Indian concept of classification of tours/tourism.*
7. *Discuss the benefits and adverse effects of tourism.*
8. *Write short notes on the following:*
   (*a*) *Distinctions between domestic and international tourism.*
   (*b*) *Basic requirements of tourism.*
   (*c*) *Eco-tourism.*
   (*d*) *Business tourism.*

# 4

# Tourism through the Ages: A Brief History

Sporadic travels by the nomads in earlier days has now termed into world's most flourishing industry, namely tourism. In this chapter we will discuss the nature of tourism through ages, because the history of tourism is as old as the history of human civilization. Hereunder, we pen a brief account of historical development of tourism.

History reveals the harsh realities of travel in ancient times and civilizations. The search for basic necessities of life—water, food, shelter and safety—kept early hunters constantly on the move from one settlement to another. This often meant dangerous and difficult travel for individuals, families or the entire communities. In the absence of any organised roads, people travelled by foot or on animal backs over open fields, forests, and marshy lands often facing great dangers. Thus it was a virtual adventure that required caution and skill.

## TRAVEL IN PREHISTORIC TIMES

Travel in the prehistoric times Paleolithic Age (30,000 B.C. to 10,000 B.C.) suggests that all human activity, as also movements, revolved upon day-to-day survival. Gradually, when the regions were explored, fire was discovered and tools were made, people were able to settle down in shelters. The ability to make and use tools and build shelters enabled prehistoric man to travel to new hunting grounds even in very extreme and inhospitable weather. Subsequently, during the Neolithic Age, which began about 10,000 B.C., primitive people settled in more permanent regions and formed themselves into some kind of agricultural communities.

During the Neolithic Age, several innovations in the field of transport changed the very nature of travel. In Egypt, sailing vessels were built around 4000 B.C. This resulted in conscious travel in order to explore and see the world. The invention of wheel and money by the Sumerians (Babylonia) around 3500 B.C. marks the beginning of the modern era of travel. All the above factors and inventions greatly affected travel. The money invented by the Sumerians was used by them in their business and travel dealings. Many traders could pay for transportation as well as accommodation either with money or by exchange of goods. Shulgi, the ruler of ancient Babylonia, claimed to have protected roads and built resthouses at various places. These were forerunners of modern day accommodation. These resthouses were the ideal places of rest for the travellers of those days.

From the earliest times, travel has fascinated man. Much of travel in the beginning was largely unconscious. The cumbersome procedures that we witness in travel today were not to be found in olden days. No travel formalities existed. The traveller of the past was a merchant, a pilgrim, a scholar in search of ancient texts, or even a curious wayfarer looking forward to new and exciting experiences. Trade and commerce was, however, the strongest force in the ancient times; it made people to travel to distant lands in order to seek fortunes.

Gradually, opening of the new trade routes gave a big boost to travel. With the opening of the trade routes, travel became easier and more regulated. At the marketplaces, travellers made contacts with each other resulting in increased flow of trade and commerce. Trade relations matured into cultural relations and better understanding of each other's way of life.

From the third century B.C., Greek tourists travelled to visit the sites of healing gods. Since the independent city-states of ancient Greece had no central authority to order the construction of roads, most of the tourists and merchandise travelled by water, the seaports prospered. The Greeks, too, enjoyed their religious festivals. By the fifth century BC, Athens had become an important destination for travellers. Innkeepers of this period were unfriendly. Courtesans trained in the art of music and dance were the principal entertainers.

Much of what we know of travel during this early period is due to the writings of Herodotus, who is the world's first significant travel writer. Guidebooks made their appearance as early as the fourth century BC covering Athens, Sparta and Troy. Advertisements in the form of signs directing visitors to wayside inns, are also known from this period. It was under the Roman Empire that international travel first became important.

With the seas safe from piracy due to the Roman patrols, conditions favouring travel had arrived. Roman coins were acceptable everywhere and Latin was the common language of the day. Romans travelled to Sicily, Greece, Rhodes, Troy, Egypt, and to the Holy Land.

It is, at this stage, the growth of travel bureaucracy developed. An exit permit was required to leave many seaports and a charge was paid for this service.

Domestic tourism also flourished within the Roman Empire's heartland. Second homes were built by the wealthy within easy travelling distance of Rome, occupied during the springtime. The most fashionable resorts were to be found around the Bay of Naples. The rapid improvement in communications, which coincided with Roman conquests, aided the growth of travel.

Classical scholars have shown that wealthy Greeks and Romans travelled to Egypt on holiday, sport the summers in second homes in locations such as the Bay of Naples and visited spas—more often for leisure than for health reasons. Ancient Greece was the destination for those attending the Olympic Games and other major festivals.

Early travel in the Orient, particularly in India and China, was also largely based on trade and commerce. Travel to the Orient, especially to India, was undertaken by travellers from all over the world. This was done for a variety of reasons—the most important among them being trade and commerce. India and China enjoyed the reputation of being countries of fabulous wealth. It is on record that long before the Christian era, travellers visited India in search of fortune. This trend continued and became more marked in course of time with Europeans heading towards the Indian shores for the sole purpose of trade and commerce.

Not only did India attracted series of invaders starting with Alexander of Macedonia, but also great travellers like Vasco da Gama. Many foreigners. Arabs and Europeans alike came to India to establish trading posts. The great explorer, Christopher Columbus, set out to find a new route to India and in the process discovered the New World. India always held a great fascination for foreign travellers. Mark Twain described it as a fabulous world of "Splendour and rags, the one country under the sun with an imperishable interest, the one land that all men desire to see".

## TRAVEL IN THE MIDDLE AGES

History thus reveals that trade and commerce remained a strong force for many travellers to undertake long journeys to distant lands. This was followed by an urge to explore new lands and to seek new knowledge in ancient and distant lands. There are many references to great explorers who spent many formidable years of their lives in search of knowledge. The great explorers can perhaps be credited with the distinction of being the pioneers who subsequently paved the way for modern travel. When Alexander the Great reached India, he found well-maintained roads lined with shady trees. Along one royal highway, 1,920 kilometres long and about 19 metres wide, people travelled in chariots, palanquins, bullock carts, on horses, camels and elephants.

Young Marco Polo left Venice in the year 1271 with his father and uncle. They travelled through Persia and Afghanistan to the "roof of the world", the then unknown Pamir Plateau. After crossing the wind swept Gobi Desert, he reached Kublai Khan's palace and remained in China for over twenty years. On his way back home, he stopped in Sumatra, Java, India, and Ceylon.

The first medieval traveller to reach the Orient was probably Benjamin of Tudela, a Jewish scholar who left Saragossa in A.D. 1160. He wrote a detailed account of his thirteen-year journey through Europe, Persia and India, giving information on the Jewish communities, and the geography of the various places he visited. Yet another famous traveller who recorded interesting accounts of his travel experiences was Ibn Batuta. Ibn Batuta wrote a detailed diary of his travel experiences. He was born at Tangier (Morocco) in A.D. 1304.

In A.D. 1325, he left his home, and passing through various countries in Africa and West Asia, crossed the Indus (also Sindhu) in A.D. 1333. The travels took him as far as Indonesia and China. Out of a total of more than 17,000 miles, he covered over 14,000 miles through India, Maldives and Ceylon.

There are also accounts of some European travellers who

visited India during the period described above. The Franciscan friar, John of Monte Corrino, visited India on his way to and back from China during the last decade of the thirteenth century.

Mention may also be made here of the famous Portuguese chronicle—the commentaries of the Great Alfonso D'Albuquerque. Later on in the sixteenth and seventeenth centuries many more European monks, travellers, and adventurers visited India and many other places in search of knowledge.

The expeditions of these great travellers rewarded them with new ideas and also with fabulously rich treasures from rich and highly advanced civilizations of Asia and other parts of the world. The actual number of individuals who participated in various explorations as travellers in search of knowledge, however, represented only a small proportion of the total population.

Travel was considered difficult and not a thing of pleasure. Transport and communication systems of today were non-existent. Land migrations were done by foot and on horseback, elephant, camel and river craft in Europe, Asia and Africa, and the very limited exploration by rafts and primitive vessels moved by tides, oar and sail.

In brief, we may understand the development of tourism in Middle Ages as follows:

After the collapse of the Roman Empire and the onset of Dark Ages, Travel became less attractive, more dangerous, difficult and synonymous with *travail* (a painful and laborious effort, and the origin of the world). The result was that most pleasure travel was undertaken close to home but international travel was available in a small scale. Adventurers sought fame and fortune through travel, and merchants travelled extensively to seek new trade opportunities.

Holidays played an important role in the life of the public and from earliest times religion provided the framework within which leisure was spent. To perform a religious duty, pilgrimages would be undertaken to places of worship.

Before the sixteenth century, those who sought to travel had three modes in which to do so; they could walk, they could ride a horse or they could be carried on a litter or a carrier's wagon. The journey was unsafe because highwaymen abounded on the major routes posing a threat to wayfarers.

The development of stage coach was a great advance for travel.

In the eighteenth century the introduction of turnpike roads, for which tolls were charged, added to the development of travel in UK and USA.

Travel of some distance requires accommodation. By 1820s, the horse-drawn omnibus was a common sight in London and Paris.

### The Grand Tour

From the early seventeenth century, a new form of tourism developed as a direct outcome of the freedom and quest for learning heralded by the Renaissance. Under the reign of Elizabeth I, young men seeking positions at court were encouraged to travel to the Continent to finish their education. This practice was soon adopted by others in the upper sections of society and it eventually became customary for the education of a gentleman to be completed by a Grand Tour of the major cultural centres of Europe accompanied by a tutor and often lasting for three years or more. The Grand Tour gave a further boost to the educational tour.

### Political Hindrance to Travel

Travel outside the boundaries of one's country had always been subject to restrictions. Few people travelled a great distance.

Passports have their origin in the medieval *testimonial*. A letter from an ecclesiastical superior was given to a pilgrim to avoid the later's possible arrest on charges of vagrancy. Later, papers of authority to travel were more widely issued by the state, particularly during periods of war with neighbouring countries. The introduction of compulsory passports as a permanent requirement of Britain is of recent origin, dating from AD 1916.

## EPOCHS OF TOURISM

Three major epochs of tourism may be distinguished. Tourism is a matter of being elsewhere and to be elsewhere implies the use of transport. Transport is the necessary precondition of tourism and the three epochs are to be identified with particular modes of transport. Mechanised transport has made travel possible for a significant proportion of the population of the developed countries, at least.

The first epoch is the early days of the railway age, that is up to 1840. The second epoch covers the railway age itself. The years between two world wars which witnessed the significant development of the private motor car and of the bus the coach, and the period after the Second World War, when civil aviation together with private motor car assumed principal transport in tourism, form the third epoch.

Travel before the Industrial Revolution was largely for pilgrimages and for business or official purposes. There was no private travel in the medieval period.

## TRAVEL IN THE INDUSTRIAL AGE

The concept of modern tourism came into being in the second half of the nineteenth century hand in hand with the development of the industrialized societies of Western Europe and North America. Development of industrialized societies of Western Europe and North America can therefore be considered as responsible for growth of modern tourism.

Development of industrialized societies was a direct result of Industrial Revolution in the West. The Industrial Revolution brought in its wake tremendous changes in society. As has been mentioned earlier, travel before the Industrial Revolution was mainly a matter of seeking knowledge, engaging in commerce and trade and undertaking pilgrimage.

The Industrial Revolution was responsible for the change in the economic and social systems. It threw up great factory towns, big and small. The working class was in the beginning burdened by long working hours and poor working and living conditions. For a large number of people there was little relief from routine of putting in long hours of work in difficult conditions in the factory set-up of those days.

Sudden concentration of population in towns and cities created unhealthy social conditions. As the industrial momentum gathered and the cities and their populations increased at an enormous rate, the need for escape became even more acute. The prosperous and well-to-do proceeded to various resorts. Industrialization also brought in an increase of material wealth and certain improvements in transport and communications during the second half of the nineteenth and early twentieth century.

The factors, like increasing need to find relief from workday routine; the city dweller's yearning for physical adventure, comforts and pleasure; and development of resorts and spas for health and relaxation produced a fertile ground for the development of pleasure traffic on a big scale. Many resorts owe their present day popularity to their original discovery by wealthy minorities during the Roman Empire. The nineteenth century saw the development of large-scale pleasure zones in various parts of tourist areas.

## Rail Transport

The introduction of railways in the nineteenth century was yet another crucial landmark in travel history. Passengers were first carried by rail in 1830 in England. The newly completed railway track between Liverpool and Manchester in England featured special provisions for carrying passengers in addition to freight. However, the birth of organised rail travel came in the year 1841.

A Baptist preacher of Derbyshire was on his way to a temperance meeting in Leicester when he struck upon the idea of engaging a special train to carry the friends of temperance society from Leicester to Loughborough and back to attend a quarterly delegate meeting. The man behind this was Thomas Cook. He broached his idea to his friends. A few weeks later 570 passengers made the journey by the Midland Countries Railway at a specially reduced fare. This venture was followed by various excursions to beauty spots. 3,000 school children were taken on a trip from Leicester to Derby in the year 1843. From 1848 to 1863 Cook conducted circular tours of Scotland, with 5,000 tourists a season.

The success of the Liverpool and Manchester railway encouraged many other countries in Europe to open railway lines. Railway tracks were laid in France, Austria and in Switzerland. Across the Atlantic the tracks were laid in America. This revolution in transport technology produced an immediate expansion in European tourism. In the year 1881, the railways carried over 600 million passengers over lines operated by one hundred odd companies.

The railways were now keen to stimulate travel and to improve the system. There was also now an element of competition and the various railway companies tried to make travel as comfortable as possible. In the early 1870s, first-class railway travel was introduced by an American, G.M. Pullman, who developed the Pullman coaches with their luxury furnishing and dining facilities. Long distance travel could now be undertaken in comfort and with pleasure.

The Pullman cars manufactured in America were imported by some railway companies in England and other countries in Europe. The cars, which were very comfortable for long journeys, were first introduced in America. The longer distances in America necessitated assurance of greater comfort for passengers. By the year 1872 the Pullman Company had 700 cars working over 30,000 miles of railway under contract with over 150 different companies.

The introduction of railways thus vastly increased the opportunities for escape from the rigours of city life as a result of urbanisation. The railways can be considered as one of the most powerful motives for mass travel in nineteenth as well as early twentieth centuries. The railways carried and continue to carry millions of passengers from all over the world, mostly from large urban centres.

**Sea Transport**

Like the railways, shipping also made significant contribution to travel during the nineteenth century. While railways were responsible for inland travel especially in Europe, the steamship crossed the boundaries and made strides in intercontinental travel. Shipping technology made a number of innovations in the nineteenth century. In America, a number of sailing ships were built which were considered to be superior to those built in England or elsewhere.

The English felt a great need for improved communications across the Atlantic with America for the purpose of trade and commerce and passenger transportation. As a result of this, there were great strides in the development of deep-sea shipping. The history of the Cunard Steamship Company in England demonstrates important features in the growth of North Atlantic Shipping. A subsidy in the form of the award of mail contract represented a recurring theme in the development of passenger transportation.

With the passage of time, toward the last quarter of the nineteenth century, emigrant traffic became an important factor in North Atlantic travel. America was considered at that time the New World full of opportunities and fortunes for people in Europe. A great number of people from the Continent started going to America in search of fortune.

Great Britain and Germany, along with other countries, became the principal generators of emigrants to the New World. Many travelled as tourists to see this new land. The opening of the Suez Canal in 1869 brought about the possibility of a much shortened route between the West and East and in turn stimulated the introduction of better steamship carriage to the Far East.

The use of chartered ships for cruising and operation of cruises on a limited scale dates from the mid-nineteenth century. One of the earliest cruises perhaps was that described by Mark Twain in his first book, *The Innocents Abroad*, published in 1869. Cruising, however, did not play a significant part in the world of shipping until the beginning of the twentieth century.

The period just before the First World War can be considered the heyday of passenger-liner service. It was an era of large and comfortable fast ships operated by relatively small number of companies in various countries. The glamour of the deep-sea travel was, however, reserved for the wealthy Europeans and Americans.

In the luxury liners, a big space reserved for the not too wealthy was used by the emigrant traffic. In fact, the biggest volume of transatlantic passenger trade was the emigrant traffic.

In the first half of the twentieth century, the descendants of those migrants must have formed a large part of the transatlantic tourist movement. Transport by water makes a significant contribution to the development of travel on land and by air. Scheduled liner transport, formerly used for intercontinental travel, has presently almost vanished. The expansion of international tourism has, however, led to an increasing use of ferry boats by tourists on short-sea crossing. Tourist sea transport on the whole does not seem to have a promising future. Long distance sea travel may continue to contract, although there will always be a limited demand for sea cruising, since this leisurely and attractive mode of travel has great appeal. In the recent past one of the most important developments in sea traffic has, in fact, been that of holiday sea cruises, especially in the Mediterranean and Caribbean and also in South-East Asia.

By the turn of the twentieth century all the main characteristics of modern tourism were evident in its embryonic form. Changes in mental attitudes towards pleasure seeking, the recognised value of travel for education, an increase in material wealth and improvements in transport, social prestige, the growing need to find relief from working routine—all these factors produced a fertile ground for the development of excursion traffic on a large scale.

Up to the first quarter of the twentieth century, tourism was essentially a luxury commodity within the reach of only a privileged few having both plenty of free time and considerable purchasing power. Admittedly, such tourism had a charm all its own, associated as it was with elegant luxurious hotels, such long-distance trains as the Orient Express and the blue-riband transatlantic liners like the *Queen Mary*. Although all the main characteristics of modern tourism were evident by this time, only the privileged few managed to indulge in this luxury.

### Paid Holidays and Growth of Tourism

It was in the last quarter of the nineteenth century that increasing attention was paid to the desirability of holidays with pay or at least of cheap holidays for working class people. During this period a few factories gave paid holidays to their workers in some countries in the West. The introduction of annual paid holiday is very largely of English origin and this had important repercussions on development of mass tourism.

The annual paid holiday was established during the inter-War years as a reality for a considerable part of the working population. By the year 1939, in UK, some eleven million people were covered by the Holidays with Pay Act (1938). Introduction of paid holiday had led to greater mobility of the population, created new industries, resulted in the creation and growth of many towns of distinctive function and broadened the horizons of millions of people. In fact, the introduction of paid holidays can truly be associated with development of modern mass tourism.

In the year 1936, modern tourism really got under way when, at the instigation of its trade union representatives, the International Labour Organization (ILO) adopted the first convention that was to support serious movements to promote paid holidays and, in turn tourism. That convention on paid holidays was an innovation well ahead of time, when only fourteen countries, mostly European, had enacted general legislation on paid holidays. Soon afterwards tourism experienced an extraordinary growth. Paid holidays are now established all over the world, and in most countries a minimum duration of one to three weeks is specified either by law or by collective agreements, between the employer and the workers.

Today the right to paid holidays has universal recognition. The trend is to grant longer holiday periods. The employers have realized that the paid holidays have not affected industrial production. The legal minimum in many countries at present is three weeks. Some countries have even gone beyond this and granted four weeks of paid holiday.

Rise in the standard of living of the working and the middle classes in America and in certain European countries was yet another factor responsible for growth in tourism. Soon after the War the tourists began to appear in countries where tourism had been practically unknown a few years earlier.

The early traveller had advanced from the scholar and the pilgrim of the past to the pleasure seeker of today. The major tourist countries enjoyed an unprecedented boom in the late twenties. In the year 1929 there were nearly one and a half million visitors to Switzerland, over one million visitors to Italy and about two million to Austria. Great Britain also received a considerable number of visitors.

## DEVELOPMENT OF MODERN TRANSPORT SYSTEMS

Development of road and air transport, especially the former, is the major factor which was largely responsible for and continues to be so far the great spurt in modern tourism. Transport is the necessary precondition of travel. The greater part of contemporary tourism, transport means airlines and the private cars.

As a broad generalization it can be said that holiday-makers travelling away from home to a foreign country spend the major portion of their total holiday money on transport and travel. Travel costs as much as about 40 per cent of the total holiday expenditure. This fact has been brought about by a number of studies. Tourist traffic, as we know it today, could not have developed without relatively inexpensive and efficient modes of transportation.

## Road Transport

Up to the beginning of the twentieth century, people travelled almost exclusively by rail and steamship. With the invention of the new transport medium, travel by a private car and coach received its first great impetus in the ten years which preceded World War I. The entire shape of tourist industry was therefore transformed by the invention of this new transport medium. The growth of the private car may be identified as a major cause of the decline of the railways. In both USA and the United Kingdom, passenger rail traffic almost halved in the first ten years or so after the First World War. The motor car gradually came to be the alternative means of transport for both short- and medium-range journeys. Subsequently, with the growth of a fine network of fast and superfast national and international highway systems, long journeys were also performed by motor car and motor coach.

There are large-scale highway programmes in the pipeline at present in different regions of the world. When completed, these will cater to the ever increasing demands of the tourists. Mention may be made of the following highway programmes:

(*i*) *The Trans-African Highway*: This highway, 6,596 kilometres long, will cross Kenya, Uganda, Zaire, the Central African Empire, Cameroon and Nigeria. Several feeder roads are also planned particularly in Gabon, Democratic Republic of Congo and Tanzania.

(*ii*) *The Trans-West African Highway*: This road will link Dakar and N'Djamena running through Senegal, Mali, Upper Volta, Nigeria, Cameroon and Chad for a distance of 4,771 kilometres.

(*iii*) *The Trans-East African Highway*: The Trans-East African Highway will link Cairo in Egypt with Gaborone in Botswana, passing through Sudan, Ethiopia, Kenya, the United Republic of Tanzania and Zambia. The Trans-East African Highway will be little over 9,000 kilometres long. There will be 20,000 kilometres of feeder roads.

Apart from the above four other major projects are on in various parts of the world and former Prime Minister A.B. Vajpayee was trying his best to develop road in India in a big way.

## Air Transport

The role of air transport in the development of international tourism is becoming increasingly important. Air transport has certainly been a key factor in the growth of international tourism especially in respect of long-distance and intercontinental travel. Although commercial travel took place before the Second World War, air transport for the masses has essentially been a post-War phenomenon. The main period of growth was during the 1960s when overseas holiday became a symptomatic benefit of a society experiencing rising living standards.

In Europe, the years immediately after World War I witnessed the attempts to create commercial airlines. The war itself had a direct bearing on the development of air transport in a similar way as had with motor transport. Certain commercial civil air services were inaugurated and developed in this period. Besides Europe, air transport, however, was developed in many other countries including in India during this period.

Although international air travel was born at the end of World War I and slowly grew between the two wars, it was only at the end of World War II that it made a tremendous breakthrough. It emerged into a practical mode of transport over long distances only in the late forties when the aircraft industry in America applied the technical and manufacturing resources it had developed during the war.

This period saw the development of large pressurised civil aircraft like the Douglas Corporation's DC-6s and the Lockheed Constellations followed by the DC-7s and the super-constellations operating at twice the speed and flying attitudes of their predecessor war planes.

The removal of wartime restrictions on international travel and the tremendous increase in speed, safety and comfort provided by the new aircraft released the long pent-up wanderlust of the people, the world over. In the year 1952 the two-class travel was introduced which was made possible by the larger capacity of the new aircraft. The larger capacity of the new aircraft resulted in lowering air fares.

The steady fall in the real cost of flying has been chiefly productive in traffic across the Atlantic and within the USA, stimulated by the introduction of tourist fares in the year 1952. This period also saw the first post-War attempt to build a "package holiday" around air transport, the model for most of today's global tourism. The growing willingness of tourists to take to air travel during this period was responsible for the annual flood of North Americans across the Atlantic to Europe. This trend continues even today. Within Europe, there has been the spectacular growth of the Mediterranean resorts.

### Advent of the Jet

The advent of jet travel in 1958 was the most dramatic event which introduced an entirely new dimension of speed, comfort and efficiency to air transport and brought mass travel to its present level. As a result of the introduction of jets, air travel from 1960 grew tremendously. The most decisive development during this period was, however, the development inclusive tours in which travellers are carried on charter flights at rates substantially below those of normal scheduled services. It only slowed down after 1973 because of the worldwide oil crises which resulted in widespread recession and galloping inflation. In spite of this, the volume of world air travel today is several times more than what it was in 1960s.

Despite rising fuel costs and inflation, the industry was able to control successfully the fare levels; as a result of the economies of scale provided by the very big aircraft. The improved fuel efficiency of later model of jet engines and the ingenuity and marketing expertise of the airlines, travel agencies and tour operators are other factors. The latter is illustrated by the North Atlantic route—the golden route of tourist traffic—which saw the successive introduction of excursion fares in 1948, coach fares in 1952, family fares in 1955, economy class fares in 1958, affinity group fares in 1963, group inclusive tour fares in 1967, youth fares in 1972 and apex fares in 1975. As a result of these innovations in air travel, fares per seat mile declined in real terms, between 1963 and 1975.

Great advances have been made in air travel in the recent years, more particularly for overseas holiday making. Tourism in turn has had a significant impact on the aircraft industry and on the carriers. Factors like comfort, speed, and safety influence the tourists' choice of mode of transport. New wide bodied jets such as Boeing 747, the McDonnell Douglas DC-10, the Airbus A300 and Lockheed TriStar L-1011 are all parts of response to the requirements of the ever-growing travel market.

Transport thus is the single key factor which has largely been responsible for the spurt in tourism, especially modern tourism. Tourist traffic, as we know it today, could not have developed without the development of various modes of transport from time to time. Early travel in the nineteenth century was dominated by the railway and the steamship. Up to the beginning of the twentieth century tourists travelled almost exclusively by rail, internally and by steamship, overseas.

World War I witnessed the development of motor and air transport, and in the years which preceded the War, private car and coach travel made much progress. However, the years between the two world wars mainly witnessed the significant development of the private motor car and also of the bus and coach travel. Post-World War II period saw the great development of civil aviation. It was the aeroplane—the most glamorous of all modes of transport—which came into its own in the fifties and gave international tourism a real shot in the arm. International tourism as, we know it today, has been largely shaped by air travel.

## Advent of High-Speed Trains

A recent and interesting development in the field of transportation is the advent of high-speed trains. The energy crisis since 1974, which resulted in widespread recession and galloping inflation, had adversely affected travel by air and the private motor car. It was becoming increasingly expensive to travel by air and by the private car and coach. The fuel consumption per passenger kilometre is two to four times more in automobiles and ten times more in aeroplanes as compared to trains.

This factor of increase in oil prices was responsible for the remarkable achievement in recent years in the growth of faster and cheaper rail transport. Besides the cost factor, the railways also have an advantage over the airlines in that the terminal stations are often located in the heart of the cities and the train timing are generally more convenient. To add to this, the growing congestion on highways and airports has given a further impetus to the trend.

All the above factors coupled with advanced technology and increasing needs for mobility are leading to a renaissance of the rail transport. The railways, which were pioneers in the growth and development of early mass travel and were relegated to a secondary place with the introduction of motor and air transport, are once again assuming an important role. In almost all the European countries, the United States, the countries of Asia and elsewhere, revolutionary ideas for achieving higher speeds and comfort are being conceived and put into practice.

In the United States of America, the combination of rail cruise and railbus offered by Amtrak (American Travel by Track) resulted in 1974 in a rise of 11.2 per cent over 1973 in the number of passenger kilometres performed. Long-distance trains running on the Amtrak system between New York and San Francisco have been lately modernised. Amtrak is adding new double-decked Pullman coaches gradually on the system with a view to encourage more rail travel. High speed train services now connect the highly populated Washington—Baltimore—Philadelphia—New York—Boston corridor in the United States.

In Asia, it was Japan which took the epoch-making decision, to use the latest technology and convert the rail line between Tokyo and Osaka, covering a distance of 515 kilometres into a high-speed track. This ambitious project was completed in the year 1964. The super-fast train known as Hikari Express (is popularly known as Bullet Train) travels on the new Tokaido line at a crashing speed of 210 kilometres per hour cutting the journey time to less than three hours against six and a half hours taken earlier.

Encouraged by the success of its bold venture, it went further and built the new Sanyo line, 565 kilometres in length on which trains travel even faster at a maximum speed of 260 kilometres per hour. Elsewhere in Asia, new and faster rail tracks are being introduced. The number of passengers carried by rail have been increasing in Malaysia, Philippines and Thailand.

In India railways have made great strides in technology, resulting in increased speed, comfort and carrying capacity. Efforts were initiated as early as in 1964 to increase the speed of some trains in 120 kilometres per hour. The tests enabled the railway authorities to introduce the first high-speed train, Rajdhani Express, between New Delhi and Calcutta (Kolkatta). It was originally meant to run at a cruising sped of 120 kilometres per hour to cover a distance of 1,441 kilometres in 17 hours and 30 minutes.

A fully air-conditioned comfortable train now runs at 130 kilometres per hour reducing the running time to 16 hours and 20 minutes. The special coaches for the train have been manufactured in India. In 1972, another such train was introduced between New Delhi and Bombay (Mumbai) at a speed of 120 kilometres per hour to cover a distance of 1,384 kilometres in 16 hours and 50 minutes. Trials have already been successfully conducted over small sections on both these routes to run the trains at 160 kilometres per hour. Taking advantage of improvements in track for the Rajdhani Express trains, a number of other important trains on trunk routes were designed as super-fast trains and the speeds were increased up to 120 kilometres per hour. A number of new high-speed trains have been introduced linking large metropolitan cities with important tourist centres.

Some experts today even visualize potential speeds of 500 kilometres per hour on rails. The day is not very far off when trains will cruise at such high speeds. The new technology aims at dispensing the conventional rails. It aims at providing an air cushion to replace the conventional run on the rails. The projected aero-trains will not only be fast but also relatively sleek looking, noise and pollution free and, above all, will cause no wear and tear on the track because they never touch it. In France and Japan many such trains are already operating.

## LEISURE DEVELOPMENT AND STATE INTERVENTION

It has been pointed out already that tourism is characterised by a positive income elasticity of demand, *i.e.*, the demand for holidays rises proportionately with increases in personal income.

### Leisure Development

It is a fact that because of institutional changes in tourism (cheaper air travel, package tours and holiday camps) it has become accessible to large sectors of society. Access to leisure both for men and women has improved considerably by increased disposable income.

At the informal level, access to holidays has been improved through the activities of Church organisations and youth movements such as YMCA which often provide subsidized holiday centres. Similarly, labour and trade union organisations have sought to provide cheap holiday centres for their members, while in some countries (Germany and Japan), a number of companies make contributions for the cost of their employees' holidays. Brazil has holiday camps run by worker's associations while Israel has holiday chatels operated by both trade unions and employers.

Historically, the creation of package holidays is associated with Thomas Cook. Cook's first foreign holiday was arranged in 1855 but within 10 years he had a thriving international business. By 1872, Cook was able to offer round-the-world holidays. Its main rival in the USA was American Express which offered financial and other services, too, to travellers. Eventually other tour companies entered the market which was boosted by popular mass tourism.

**State Intervention**

While tourism enterprises are mostly owned by private capital in capitalist countries, the state is usually involved in this sector. There are the following reasons for state intervention:

(*a*) *National Economic Goals:* The main attraction of tourism for national policy makers is that it is an agent of economic development. The ratio of labour to capital and the rapidity of development compared to agricultural and manufacturing sectors make tourism particularly attractive to national policy. The state may intervene directly as in Spain or indirectly via infrastructural investments in these industries.

International tourism offers an added attraction of earning foreign exchange. For these reasons most governments have become involved in the promotion of their tourism attractions.

(*b*) *Political Legitimation*: Tourism can be used as an instrument of political legitimation. There are many examples of governments which have used tourism as a means of improving their international political standing. Spain, Israel and the Philippines have all consciously used tourism in this manner. The reverse position can be observed and a prohibition on tourism can be used to record opposition to a particular Government. For example, for many years USA banned travel to China and Cuba and at present, the same policy has been applied to Libya.

(*c*) *Equity and Social Needs*: If access to tourism is left to itself, the distribution of income in society will be very uneven.

The state intervenes, reallocating access in order to bring about greater equity.

(d) *Externalities and Social Investment*: Investment in airports or roads may not be profitable investments for individuals. Since there are positive externalities to be obtained from such investments, the state may undertake these investments.

(e) *Regulation and Negative Controls*: Tourism services may be developed in such a way as to be harmful to the consumers or to the long run interests of the industry itself, *i.e.* a series of large hotels may be built with poor standards in a beauty spot. The state has to intervene to regulate the production and delivery of tourism services.

(f) *Regional Development*: Tourism development tends to be unevenly distributed especially because of the uneven spread of attractions. Tourism has been used as an instrument of regional development policy. In 1975, master tourism plan for Malaysia attempted to decentralise tourism from the urban areas of the west by developing tourist regions on the eastern coast.

## QUESTIONS FOR ANSWER

1. *What are the different epochs of tourism? What are their characteristics?*
2. *Discuss the reasons for state interventions in tourism.*
3. *Write a note on travel in Prehistoric Times.*
4. *Discuss the nature of Travel in the Middle Ages.*
5. *How has the development of Rail Transport and Sea Transport boosted Tourism? Explain.*
6. *Concept of Paid Holidays greatly contributed in the growth of tourism. Explain.*
7. *Write short notes on the following:*
   (a) *Impact of the Advent of the Jet Air Transport on tourism.*
   (b) *Impact of the Advent of High Speed Trains on tourism.*

# 5

# Basic Constituents of Tourism Industry

The constituents of Tourism Industry are varied ranging from small scale businessmen operating at local level to multinations. There are different components/constituents of the industry which are closely linked with each other, but there is an element of competition within our set of components only. The constituents of tourism industry may be divided in two categories which we discuss hereunder:

## PRIMARY OR MAJOR CONSTITUENTS

These are essential components as discussed, hereunder, very briefly:

### Transport

Well, you need a mode of transport to travel or to suggest one to your client if you are a travel agent or a tour operator. Further, the travel depends on the availability of seats etc. Today, the travel industry is a highly developed industry with its various branches in the areas of road, rail, air and water.

### Accommodation

A tourist not only travels but also stays somewhere. And here comes in accommodation. It could be of different types, *i.e.*, from cottages or tourist lodges to a house boat or a five star hotel.

### Catering, Food and Entertainment

Well, a tourist has to eat also and here comes the role of catering and food. Restaurants, fast food joints and *dhabas*, all play a role in this regard with different cuisine to offer. Different forms of entertainments are provided as attractions at the destinations.

## Intermediaries

The intermediaries constitute the travel agency, tour operator and guide services.

The constituent which co-relates all the components of tourism is the travel agent/tour operator who has accumulated knowledge, expertise and contacts with providers of services. He is a useful and invaluable intermediary between the traveller and the suppliers of tourist services, *i.e.*, airlines, transport companies, hotels and auto-rental companies.

The functions of travel agency depends upon the scope of activities it is involved in and also the size and the location. The agency has specialised departments each having to perform different functions such as:

1. Providing travel information
2. Preparing itineraries
3. Liaising with providers of services
4. Planning and costing tours
5. Ticketing
6. Providing foreign currency
7. Insurance, etc.

Some of the travel agents are also tour operators who manufacture tourism products. They plan, organise and sell tours. They make all the necessary arrangements, *e.g.*, transport, accommodation, sight seeing, insurance, entertainment and other allied services and sell this 'package' for an all-inclusive price. A package tour may be a special interest tour, mountain tour, adventure tour or a pilgrimage tour. These tours are escorted and include transportation, meals, sight seeing, accommodation and guide services. The escort or the group leader is responsible for maintaining the schedule of the tour and for looking after all the arrangements.

The guide services play a vital role in tourism, as a tourist feels comfortable when the essence of the culture is explained, especially when it is done in his own language.

## Government Departments/Tourist Information Centres/Tourism Organisations

Many national and international organisations related to tourism form part of the Tourism Industry.

## SECONDARY CONSTITUENTS

Today there are a variety of services (formal and non-formal) that constitute the tourism mix or are directly and indirectly related to tourism. For example, banks don't come under the Tourism Industry but they cater to tourists through traveller's cheques or credit cards. Similarly, insurance companies offer short-term safety or accident policies tourists. Here we list certain such constituents:

1. *Shops and Emporiums*: These sell various products to tourists. Many state governments have opened the emporiums in other states also. For example in Delhi practically all state emporiums have their showrooms.
2. *Handicrafts and Souvenirs*: Certain handicrafts and souvenir shops today are totally dependent on tourists for their sales.
3. Local taxi/Transportation (*e.g. Rickshaw, Tonga* etc.)
4. Hawkers and Coolies
5. Communication services at the destination (*e.g.* STD booth)
6. Touts and Brokers
7. Advertisement agencies
8. Publishing industry, *i.e.*, publishers who publish travel guides, brochures, magazines, postcards etc.
9. Artist, performers, musicians etc. who perform for the entertainment of tourists.

In the United Nations study on "The Economic Impact of Tourism in India". The segments having receipts from tourism employment due to tourism are mentioned as:

1. Hotels and restaurants
2. Railway Transport services
3. Transport services
4. Shopping
5. Food and Beverages
6. Wool, silks, synthetic fibre, textiles
7. Wood and wood products except furniture
8. Leather and leather products
9. Metal products except machinery and transport equipments
10. Miscellaneous manufacture industries
11. Trade
12. Other services

Hence, we can say that Tourism Industry has a very wide range and the governments in the Third World are giving incentives for its development.

*Note*—In addition to the above Tourism Marketing is a very vital component of Tourism Industry, which we will discuss in a separate chapter.

## QUESTIONS FOR ANSWER

1. *Write a note on the primary constituents of Tourism Industry.*
2. *Explain the role of secondary constituents of Tourism Industry in making tourism comfortable.*
3. *Write short notes on the following:*
   *(a) Catering, Food and Entertainment.*
   *(b) Role of Intermediaries.*

# 6

# Tourism Planning: The Basic Concepts

Tourism is the most rewarding modern industry and considered by many advocates, as a panacea for solving an area's developmental problems but this view is unrealistic because benefits may be accompanied by detrimental consequences as already discussed elsewhere in this book. Therefore, there is a need for proper tourism planning. A review of the advantages and disadvantages of tourism development will indicate why careful planning is necessary, because proper planning must aim at reducing damage, which might be caused by tourism while ensuring the maximum benefits of tourism for socio-economic development of the nation. Hereunder, we mention advantages and disadvantages of tourism, in brief.

## Major Advantages of Tourism

1. Provides employment opportunities, both skilled and unskilled because it is a labour-intensive industry.
2. Generates a supply of needed foreign exchange.
3. Increases income.
4. Creates increased gross national product.
5. Requires the development of an infrastructure that will also help stimulate local commerce and industry.
6. Justifies environmental protection and improvement.
7. Increases governmental revenues.
8. Helps to diversify the economy.
9. Creates a favourable worldwide image for the destination.
10. Facilitates the process of modernization by education of youth and society and changing values.

11. Provides tourist and recreational facilities that may be used by a local population who could not otherwise afford developing facilities.
12. Gives foreigners an opportunity to be favourably impressed by a little-known country or region.

**Some Disadvantages of Tourism**

1. Develops excess demand.
2. Creates leakages so great that economic benefits do not accrue.
3. Diverts funds from more promising forms of economic development.
4. Creates social problems from income differences, social differences, introduction of prostitution, gambling, crime and so on.
5. Degrades the natural physical environment.
6. Degrades the cultural environment.
7. Poses the difficulties of seasonality.
8. Increases vulnerability to economic and political changes.
9. Adds to inflation of land values and the price of local goods and services.

Consequently tourism is not always a panacea. On the contrary, overdevelopment can generate soil and water pollution and even people pollution if there are too many visitors at the same place at the same time. It can lead to traffic congestion, inadequate parking and displacement of local community leading to degradation of the quality of life rather than improving it. A beautiful landscape can suffer through thoughtless and unwise development.

These responsibilities cannot be really blamed on tourism, but rather on over commercialization. Tourism is one of the world's greatest and most significant social and economic forces. But government officials and business people must weigh the economic benefits against the possible future degradation of human and natural resources.

## NEED FOR TOURISM PLANNING

Planning in Tourism is an essential activity for every destination area because:

Firstly, planning is paramount to avoid situations caused by haphazard developments. It is required to ensure that the natural and created assets are conserved and protected to maintain their tourist appeal. A number of tourist destinations have experienced a cycle of intense building activity and capital investment, witnessed a tourist boom, hit a hay day and then began to decline. To avoid eventual decline responsible planning and management are essential.

Secondly, there are numerous examples which show the consequences of the unplanned development of destination areas. These relate to the negative impacts of the lack of planning particularly on the physical environment leading to the permanent damage, alteration or degradation.

Thirdly, tourism development involves heavy outlays and investments. The resources of the state are, in most cases, limited and also required for several other competing development activities. The developing countries have scare resources and, therefore, particularly need to undertake tourism planning in order to ensure the proper utilization of the finances so that maximum economic and other benefits may be derived.

Fourthly, both the public and private sectors have important roles in the development of tourism which is not always clearly demarcated. The success of tourism development to a large extent depends on the availability of the appropriate facilities at the right time and in the right place. The tourism planning aims to arrive at such a balanced growth of demand and supply.

Fifthly, most countries, to a lesser or greater degree, have planned economies. Tourism development can be most effective if it is undertaken within the context of a plan and forms a part and parcel of the national economic development programme designed to lead to the optimum growth of the economy of the country as a whole.

Hence, the tourism sector of the economy should also be subject to planning. In brief, as observed by Pearce, planning is necessary to coordinate and synchronize the development of the different sectors, to balance competing and sometimes conflicting claims on the same limited resource base, to maximize the positive impacts of tourist development and to minimize its adverse effects.

## ESSENTIALS OF PLANNING

Tourism development must be guided by a carefully planned policy, a policy not built on balance sheets and profit and loss statements alone, but on the ideals and principles of human welfare and happiness. Sound development policy can have the happy result of a growing tourist business and preservation of the natural and cultural resources that attracted visitors in the first place.

Viewed comprehensively, the relationship between tourism and the community, state, regions and countries requires consideration of many difficult issues: the quality of architecture landscape, and environment design; environmental reclamation and amenity, natural conservation; land use management; financial strategies for long term economic development; employment transportation; energy conservation; education; information and interpretation systems; and more.

These are the reasons why sound tourism planning is essential to ensure that tourism development has the ability to realize the advantages of tourism while reducing the disadvantages.

## EIGHT-POINT PLANNING PROCESS

1. *Define the System*—what is the scale, size, market, character and purpose?
2. *Formulate Objectives*—the objectives must be comprehensive and specific and should include a timeplan for completion.
3. *Data Gathering*—fact-finding and research provides basic data that are essential in developing the plan. This can be done by preparing fact books, conducting market research and analyzing existing facilities and competition.
4. *Analysis and Interpretation*—once information is collected, it must be interpreted correctly so that the facts gathered will have meaning. From this step results a set of conclusions and recommendations that leads to making or conceptualizing a preliminary plan.
5. *Preliminary Planning*—alternate solutions are considered and tested.
6. *Approving the Plan*—the parties involved now can look at plans, drawings, models, estimates of cost etc.
7. *Final Plan*—this phase includes a definition of land use, plans for infrastructure facilities such as roads, airports,

bike paths, horse trails, pedestrian walkways, sewage, water and utilities, architectural standards, landscape plans, economic analysis and financial programming.

8. *Implementation*—implementation carries out the plan and creates an operational tourism development. It follows up and evaluates. Good planning provides mechanisms that give continuous feedback on the tourism project and the levels of consumer satisfaction achieved.

## AIMS OF TOURISM PLANNING

Good planning should eliminate problems and provide user satisfaction. The final user is the judge in determining how successful planning process has been.

Tourism development should aim at:

1. Providing a framework for raising the standard of living of the people through the economic benefits of tourism.
2. Developing an infrastructure and providing recreation facilities for visitors and residents alike.
3. Ensuring types of development within visitor centres and resorts that are appropriate to the purposes of those areas.
4. Establishing a development programme consistent with the cultural, social and economic philosophy of the government and the people of the host country or area.
5. Optimizing visitor satisfaction.

## DEVELOPMENT OF TOURIST POTENTIAL

A tourism body or organization should be created to keep abreast of the socio-economic developments in the various market countries or areas to provide a reasonably early forecast of the size, type and structure of probable tourism demand.

Since tourism is such a complex phenomenon, distinct ministerial departments are responsible for finding solutions to developmental problems.

Publicity campaigns should be organized and implemented every year according to the forecasts. These should be to the point, detailed and constructive.

Customs facilities should be as lenient as possible while ensuring control and maintenance of order and avoiding fraud and crimes.

Necessary improvements must be made with regard to transportation, accommodation and finance.

The quality of tourism planning and development will determine the ultimate success and longevity of any destination area. Thus, time, effort and resources devoted to planning are essential investments.

Tourism developments almost always involve both government and private developers. Each sector can best contribute to certain parts in the project. Government typically provides the infrastructure, such as roads, water supply, sewers, public transportation terminals and parks. Private developers supply superstructure, such as hotels, restaurants, recreation facilities and shopping areas.

## SIGNIFICANCE OF PLANNING

Tourism is a highly fragile and competitive industry and calls for people's involvement at all levels. If the climate is not conducive to tourism, it can never grow and flourish. The growth in market share to India still remains considerably lower than other destinations such as Malaysia, Thailand, Singapore and Egypt. The two main reasons for this appear to be perceptions and expectations clients have of India, and the value of money.

Planning for tourism is important due to the following reasons:

1. The lack of publicity is primarily responsible for India occupying a dismal position in the global tourism scenario, and not the lack of infrastructure development, as envisaged by the Indian Tourism industry.
2. Tourism is still not developed in India to the required extent. Both the government and private sectors can help in developing tourism.
3. Tourism is a multisectoral activity involving other sectors such as agriculture, fisheries, manufacturing, historic parks and recreational facilities, transportation and other infrastructure facilities. Therefore policy planning of and coordination of development products are needed to ensure that all these projects are properly developed and integrated to serve tourism and benefit from tourism activities.

4. Tourism is essentially selling a product of an experience to consumers and there must be careful matching through the planning process, but without compromising on environmental and socio cultural integrity in meeting market demands.
5. Tourism can bring various direct and indirect economic benefits which can be optimised through careful and integrated planning; without planning these benefits may not be fully realized.
6. Tourism can generate various socio-cultural benefits and problems and planning can be used as a process for optimising the benefits and for integrating tourism into the local society.
7. The development of tourist attractions, facilities and infrastructure and the tourist movement, generally have an effect on the natural environment and so careful planning is required, so that desirable environmental impact is reinforced and environmental problems are not generated from tourist development.
8. Tourism development requires particular employee skills and capabilities for which there must be appropriate educational training. Satisfying these education and training needs, requires careful programming and in some cases development of specialized training facilities.
9. Achieving tourism development requires special organisational structure, educational and fiscal measures which must be considered in the planning process.
10. Tourism is presently India's third largest export industry after readymade garments and gem and jewellery.

## BASICS OF ITINERARY PLANNING

Itinerary planning is a creative exercise and is tailored entirely to meet the needs of group of individuals. Each set of travellers have their own specific requirements and care must be taken to ensure the following:

1. Adequate time is allowed for sight seeing/excursions in each city and place.
2. Choose appropriate class of hotels, meal plan and transport depending upon the type of travellers comprising the group.

3. Avoid back tracking and don't overstretch the tour programme.
4. Offer optional excursion during the period of tour programme. Optional pre and post tour programmes enhance the value of the tour for the group members.
5. Since check-in and check-out time at all hotels is normally at 12 noon, block hotel accommodation from previous day in case of early morning arrivals *i.e.* for a group arriving at (0400 hrs.) until following day in case of late night departure *i.e.* group departing at 2300 hrs.
6. In the case of group/s on visiting a restricted area, please obtain prior permission from the Ministry of Home Affairs or consult government department.
7. Specify clearly the service included in the tour price as also the services not included in the tour price.
8. Hotel tariffs in India are generally revised with effect from 1st October every year and are valid until 30th September of the following year.
9. For tour groups operating beyond 30th September keep a suitable margin (15 to 20%) increase in tariff. There is approximately a 50 per cent surcharge or rates for A.C. cars/coaches at all places where these are available. At Mumbai and Jaipur the surcharge is (100 to 115%).
10. Transfer and sight seeing rates includes porterage and guide fees. In case foreign language speaking local guides are required advance notice should be given to the concerned sub-agents at stations where they are available.
11. Spanish, French, Italian, German and Japanese speaking guides are available in larger cities.
12. Ensure that airline reservations within India or outside are confirmed well in advance with the domestic and international carrier. Domestic airlines require the passengers list at least 30 days prior to group travel.
13. For groups, obtain a complete passenger list/room list along with passport details of group members to facilitate quick registration at hotels in each city.
14. Whenever a flight, hotel or resort is wait listed due to prior bookings, ensure alternate reservation on another flight or hotel.
15. While planning a tour programme check if there are any

festival or cultural events taking place during that period. These can be included at an extra cost. For example Republic Day Parade, Crafts mela at Suraj Kund, Diwali, Desert festival, Pushkar festival, Taj Mahal by moonlight, etc.

16. Bear in mind environmental factors such as cultural, social, economic and political factors.
17. Bear in mind that all flights or train timings are subject to change without prior notice. Therefore, 45 days before the commencement of the tour, please re-check new timings and ensure the flights arrival time and departure timings don't affect the sight-seeing schedule in any city.

## DRAWING A TOUR ITINERARY

For tour operators, it is important to consider the following:

1. *Interest*—Interest of the person/s for whom the tour is being planned is very important, *i.e.* if the theme is sight-seeing, cultural, religious, historical, architectural, wildlife, trekking, adventure, sport or leisured, etc.
2. *Time of Visit*—When the person wants to visit this is important for season flights, tariffs, etc.
3. *Duration*—Duration of the tour is important. This helps in planning the areas to be visited, shopping, entertainment, etc.
4. *Pace*—This is important as different nationalities and different age groups like to move differently. Some might like to spend one day in each place and visit the maximum number of places possible, whereas some others would like to spend 2-3 days or even more.
5. *Budget*—This is important as this will determine the quality of hotels, amount of travel and other variables like meals, special party, theatre or shows, special visits, etc.

Once the above information is available, you need to find out the following:

1. The proposed points of visit, their location and accessibility by road, train and flights.
2. Facilities available *i.e.* types of hotels, local transport, local agent, telephones, etc.

3. Entrance formalities and other rules.
4. Any permits if required and who will issue it and what are the requirements.
5. Any holiday during the period of the tour. Since it may happen that the place of visit may be closed on that particular day. For example, most museums are closed on Mondays.
6. Fairs and Festivals. This always adds to increasing the value of the tour. For example, Goa Carnival, Holi, Diwali, etc.
7. Any special event taking place may be included to enhance the usefulness of the tour like Book Fair, Handloom Exhibition or a special craft-mela etc.
8. About the time of operation *i.e.* what is the season and any problems that go with it such as heat, snow, floods, etc. One should also see it accessibility is there, as a few National parks are closed for 3-5 months in a year and Ladakh cannot be accessed by road except between July and September.
9. The time taken to travel. It varies depending on the road conditions. For example a distance if say 100 k.m. may take 1.30 hrs in one state, 2 hrs. in another state, etc. The type of transport will also determine the travel time since buses are 20 to 25 per cent slower.
10. The time required to visit a monument temple, National Park or a particular event and the timings.
11. The availability of guides and what languages they can speak.
12. The details of shopping, etc.

## GUIDELINES FOR PLANNING AN ITINERARY

What your customer wants is the most important criteria in planning a tour. There are some basic points to be kept in mind while planning a tour. You should put yourself in your clients shoes and think about the things that you would like.

1. *Comfort*—people like to be comfortable so you should ensure that:

    - the vehicle used for transportation is not too hot or too cold

- scats are not too hard
- driver drives smoothly
- visitors should have the opportunity to use a clean toilet at least every 2 hrs.
- take along small items which will help with comfort and offer them to the group, (cost them into the tour), things such as insect repellent, umbrellas or sun-shades, travel wipes, sick bags, peppermints etc. are advisable.

2. *Create Interest*—clearly places of historical, political or geographical interest are in this category, but visitors also like to know where familiar foods or products come from. Show them how tea is grown or how cotton is woven or whatever else from that area and you will notice that they are keen to see and buy too.
3. *Have Fun*—People mainly want to enjoy themselves and have fun. Young people may enjoy water rafting, hot air ballooning or bungee jumping.
4. While booking car/coach from the operator, check all the licences and road taxes which have to be paid.
5. Do not make the itinerary too tiring at any point of travel.
6. Select places to be visited in such a way so as to give maximum variety of places to the tourist, so that the tour does not become monotonous.
7. It would be preferable to keep photographs of the places being visited along with the tour programme.
8. Keep train/airline timetables for ready reference and always check for arrival/departure delays. Always reconfirm reservations to avoid last-minute confusion.
9. Covei the hil! stations or beach resorts preferably at the end of the tour to give relaxation.

## TOUR PACKAGE COSTING

Tour development is a highly creative position requiring concentration, innovation, resourcefulness, experience, organization, and a thorough knowledge of the market. A group is made up of 15 to 50 persons who are travelling on a specific itinerary. The itinerary can last from one day to more than three weeks, depending upon the scope and price of the tour.

Second, a group tour package is a saleable travel product which would otherwise be purchased separately by a traveller. A group package may include any or all of the following: transportation, accommodation, sight seeing, local guides, food, etc.

Group tours can be the perfect way to start an agency in the group travel business. Before a travel agency commits to group business, however, it must plan and organize the staff to handle it. Most of the time, this kind of captive-group business is handled or mishandled by an agency employee who is confident enough to think that she can handle groups. That employee will soon learn by experience that the group travel business is a specialised field. Unfortunately for tour operators and clients, the learning experience often involves a few and sometimes many mistakes.

Most travel agencies use their present staff to work with groups. Such a move may be adequate if the agency only gets a group now and then provided one person has total responsibility for meeting deposit dates, ticketing, invoicing and mailing deadlines. Several employees trying to handle one group can be disastrous. The intricacies connected with handling a group tour can be shared, but one person should have total control.

An efficient group tour specialist who is not burdened with sales calls or marketing, responsibilities should be able to handle fifteen to twenty tours of twenty to forty participants each. Starting out, a travel agency probably only needs (and can only afford) one staff member to start a group travel department. The success or failure of this specialized department will depend on the staff member employed. If an agency doesn't want to waste sales effort on an inefficient group operations unit, the manager should be very careful in the employee selected. The better qualified the employee, the better job will be done for the agency.

## GROUP TOUR—THE PLANNING GUIDELINES

A thorough knowledge of how to cost group tour correctly is essential for a travel agency that wants to make a profit in this market.

Before beginning the planning stage of a group tour, there are some terms which a group travel counsellor must fully understand. What constitutes a group tour? First, a group is usually made up of 15 to 50 persons who are travelling on a specific itinerary which has been purchased through a travel agency.

The itinerary can last from one day to more than three weeks, depending upon the scope and price of the tour. Second, a group tour package is a saleable travel product which offers, at an inclusive price, several or more travel elements which would otherwise be purchased separately by a traveller.

A group tour package may include any or all of the following: transportation, accommodation, sight-seeing, attractions, meals and entertainment. This package will have a pre-determined inclusive price, a number of features and will cover a specific period of time.

It is a long and winding road from the conception of a new tour idea to the successful marketing and operation of a tour package. Another key point to keep in mind is the potential market for the tour. The more market research available to an agency, the better will the agency be able to pinpoint what kind of tour will sell. In a word, know your markets.

There are various methods of organising a tour and whichever method works best for the individual planner should be used. What works best for one may not work for another. Some planners work primarily from their office, while others must make an inspection trip of their own in order to consider the key points of a tour itinerary.

The most concise and current guidelines for group tour planning are as follows:

Keep an ongoing file of potential tour ideas; even if you can't follow through them immediately, they may be developed later.

Make good use of information from tourist office, for background information, literature, route planning, fame tours etc. Keep an open mind; good ideas for new tours can come from anywhere a movie, visiting with friends, newspapers, magazines etc.

While on a site inspection trip, keep a diary (written or taped) of reactions to what is seen, to use later in writing the brochure.

Take along a camera while on the road; photos of attractions, scenery, and properties can be used for group presentations, brochures, and escort briefings.

Make a specific plan for each day of a site inspection trip this hotel, that attraction etc. or you may be overwhelmed with too many possibilities, and accomplish little.

Call on people in various areas of the country; sometimes a local person will have a unique perspective, that will lead to a new tour idea.

Don't try to sell everyday of a new tour; pick-out one or two destination highlights and focus the planning and marketing on them.

Don't give up on a new tour idea if it doesn't sell the first time out; give it a reasonable chance to catch on.

Make tour planning a company priority and give someone the freedom and time to do it well. Tour development can be the key to future success for your company.

## Group Tour Components

Before one can actually start tour costing, a great deal of work and thought are required. To book each of the components start from the beginning. A travel agent needs a sophisticated set of current reference material, experience in dealing with suppliers and the ability to cost every detail of the tour.

The cost is the most important factor for the persons who is buying the tour. Similarly for a tour operator, it is important to analyse how much profit can be made over the cost. The cost will depend on the following:

- Duration of the tour
- Transport type—AC or Non-AC cars, Jeeps Mini coach or large coach, charter of boat or seat in a boat etc., air or train travel
- Number of persons travelling together (as big groups get discounted rate on fares, accommodation, etc.)
- Category of hotels required
- Type of rooms required
- Type of service required—all meals or part of meals or no meals, excursion and sight-seeing required
- Time of operations—change of tariff; peak season or off season rates would be applicable
- Guides and their allowances and expenses
- Tour Manager's allowance
- Tips
- Service charges

QUESTIONS FOR ANSWER

1. *"Tourism Planning aims at reducing damage which might be caused by tourism while ensuring maximum benefits for the socio-economic development of the nation" Justify.*
2. *Write a note on the need, aims, essentials and significance of tourism planning.*
3. *Discuss Itinerary Planning and its guidelines.*
4. *Explain the term Group Tourism and write a note on the guidelines of group tour planning.*
5. *Write short notes on the following:*
   (*a*) *Major advantages of Tourism.*
   (*b*) *Disadvantages of Tourism.*
   (*c*) *Explain five needs of tourism planning.*
   (*d*) *Eight-point planning process of tourism planning.*

# 7

# Modern Global Tourism Scenario (Mass Tourism)

Tourism as a concept in day to day life is a modern phenomenon. The word 'tourism' did not appear in the English language until the nineteenth century, but now it is the most flourishing industry in the world and as a contributor to the global economy tourism has no equal. Following facts and figures justify this observation.

- Tourism employs 204 million people worldwide or one in every nine workers, 10.6 per cent of the global workforce.
- Tourism is the world's leading economic contributor, producing an incredible 10.2 per cent of the world's gross national product.
- Tourism is the leading producer of tax revenues at US $655 billion.
- Tourism is the world's largest industry in terms of gross output approaching US $304 trillion.
- Tourism accounts for 10.9 per cent of all consumer spending, 10.7 per cent of all capital investment and 6.9 per cent of all government spending.

Furthermore, despite economically and politically induced setbacks and threats of terrorism from a variety of global hot spots, recession in Europe, and economic upheaveal in Japan, and the once Communist Eastern Block, the future of tourism is brighter than ever.

Expectations for growth tourism are 6.1 per cent, 23 per cent faster than the world economy. Travel and Tourism will create 144 million jobs worldwide between now and the year 2005 (112 million in the fast growing Asia Pacific.) "In the 21st century" says Geoffrey Lipman, President of the World Travel and Tourism

Council, "there will be a surge of Asian travellers in markets around the world, and Asian countries will be the premium destinations.

## TOURISM INDUSTRY—THE MULTICOMPONENT

Tourism is a multicomponent industry, many parts of which are inextricably linked to other economic sectors such as airlines to transportation; souvenir shops, concession stands and restaurants to retail or service; hotels and other accommodation to commercial development.

"Broadening the Mind". A survey of the World Travel and Tourism published in the "Economist" offers the following rationale. The size of the travel and tourism business is difficult to comprehend for at least three reasons. First there is no accepted definition of what constitutes the industry, any definition runs the risk of either overstating or understating economic activity. Second, tourism is a business, many of whose activities (like tour guides and souvenir sales people) and much of whose income (tips) are well suited to practitioners of the underground economy. In countries with foreign exchange controls (which are always evaded) every official figure on expenditure will be wrong. Third, international travel is bedevilled by astounding differences in the data of different countries. While efforts are underway to bring uniformity to data collection and analysis worldwide, it will likely to be sometime before a consensus is reached on the scope and impact of the tourism industry. However at least two organisations are dedicated to the task of giving travel and tourism its due as the world's largest industry.

The Brussel based World Travel and Tourism Council (WTTC) is a coalition of 65 chief executive officers from all sectors of the industry. Its goal as stated in WTTC reports is "to convince governments of the enormous contribution of travel and tourism to national and world economic development, to promote expansion of travel and tourism markets in harmony with environment and to eliminate barriers to growth of the industry."

The "World Tourism Organization" (WTO), on the other hand, is an agency of the United Nations Development Programme WTO's membership comprises 113 of the world's government and boasts over 170 affiliate members from the travel and tourism industry. It is the only inter-governmental organization open to the operating sector. Its mission is the promotion and development of travel and tourism as a means of stimulating business and economic development and forecasting peace and understanding between nations.

## WORLD TOURISM SCENARIO

People in general now view tourism as a way of life rather than a luxury item reserved for the affluent and the elite. Tourism has emerged as the largest service industry globally in terms of gross revenue as well as foreign exchange earnings. The present annual global income from tourism (international and domestic) is nearly US $13 trillion, an amount more than the GNP of all countries except the United States.

According to the World Tourism Organisation (WTO), the number of international travels has risen to more than 500 million per annum which means that one out of every ten inhabitant of this planet is a tourist. With rapid developments in the field of transport and communications, the global tourism industry is likely to double in the next decade.

WTO forecasts that there will be 702 million international arrivals in the year 2000, that arrivals will top one billion in the year 2010 and that by 2020, international arrivals will reach 1.6 billion—nearly three times the number of international trips made in 1996 which was 592 million.

The 21st century will see a higher percentage of the total population travelling, especially in developing countries, and people will be going on holidays more often, sometimes two, three or four times a year. Travellers of the 21st century will also be going farther and farther. The "Tourism 2020 vision forecasts predicts that by 2020 one out of every three trips will be long-haul journeys to other regions of the world. Long-haul travel is expected to increase from 24 per cent of all international tourism in 1995 to 35 per cent of all international traffic arrivals by the year 2020.

Tourism is the industry of industries and has a great multiplier effect on other industries. Tourism serves as an effective medium for transfer of wealth because here income earned in places of "residence" is spent in places "visited". It is the highest generator of employment. A total of 212 million persons are now being employed globally through direct and indirect opportunities generated by this industry.

This means that out of every nine persons, one person earns a living from tourism. For every million rupees of investment 13 jobs are created in manufacturing industries, 45 jobs in agriculture and 89 jobs in hotels and restaurants. Tourism is therefore considered to be an important area for intensive development for all governments. As the fastest growing foreign exchange earner, specially in developed countries, it is being given priority attention.

## THREE BASIC ELEMENTS OF TOURISM

The anatomy of the phenomenon reveals that it is basically composed of three elements, namely, man (the human element as the creator of the act of tourism), space (the physical element to be necessarily covered by the act itself), and time (the temporal element which is composed by the trip itself and the stay at the destination).

The time element varies according to the distance between the points of departure and the destination countries or areas, transport means used and the length of stay and destination etc. These elements constitute the essential conditions for the existence of the phenomenon of tourism. There could be no tourism act without them.

The other factors which characterize tourism, and distinguish it from a simple act of travelling, are mainly factors that have to do with the purpose, the temporary nature of displacement, utilization of facilities and the underlying notions of pleasure or recreation.

## DEVELOPMENT OF MASS TOURISM

The following observation is the clear indication of mass tourism. All those who plan for a professional career in the tourism will join an industry that employs more people worldwide than any other enterprise; an industry that will be the world's largest by the year 2000. An industry of this size obviously has a tremendous impact on the lives of individuals and the economics of nations. The explosive growth of the tourism industry has created a demand for new professionals; persons who are committed to professional careers in the industry.

### Indications of Continued Growth

Whether for pleasure or for business, travel demand is rapidly growing. Higher incomes, more leisure time, changing lifestyles, increased overseas visiting, and a growing number of people reaching retirement age, all indicate that the tourism industry will continue to expand. The industry has responded to this increased growth opportunity with new air, land, and sea transportation networks, with new hotels, resort destinations, and convention centres; as well as growing local service industries which support the needs of the tourist.

Tourism is a service industry. Today's tourists and travellers need and expect service, whether related to trip planning, reservations handling, efficiency in transportation, or the services available at their destination. Tourism is an industry of competing firms whose clients have become increasingly cost conscious.

The tourist has the right to expect professional service. The quality of our leisure time is becoming increasingly important to us, and the demand for expert, professional service in planning that leisure time is growing even more important.

In various ways, modern societies increasingly provide their citizens with the opportunity to reach their fullest potential. For many people, this opportunity is satisfied during free time rather than at work. The tourism industry, therefore, affects us not only because of its tremendous size, but also because of the crucial role it plays in improving the quality of life for millions of people.

In such an important industry the potential for jobs is enormous. As the industry becomes more complex, it demands the services of well-trained, enthusiastic, and responsible individuals. The future growth and competitive strength of each of the elements that make up the tourism industry depends on how well each entity cares for the safety and comfort of the traveller, or the value tourists get for their money, and on how well their expectations are met.

## BASIC COMPONENTS OF TOURISM INDUSTRY

Since our purpose here is to discuss the importance of the tourism sector as a whole, we must see the traveller from the industry's point of view. It perceives the traveller as a visitor and classifies him or her according to the reason for the visit and other factors characteristic of the visit, such as the traveller's mode of transport, point of origin, and level of spending.

The traditional tourist may represent an important proportion of the total visitor population, but we cannot equate the tourism section with tourists or pleasure related activities alone. The existence of a tourism industry is primarily from the traveller's desire to experience a change and willingness to spend money in the pursuit of the experience.

The tourism industry is composed to those sectors of the economy providing services such as accommodation, food and beverages, transportation and recreation, as well as the associated distribution and sales services. It is supplemented by public and private concerns organizing and providing a broad range of events and attractions.

The industry operates on profit motive and its promotional efforts are aimed primarily at increasing "tourist" travel. However, it also seeks to serve those who contribute to tourism revenues without being defined specifically as tourists. For example, the business traveller may use the same facilities as "the tourist". Local residents frequent recreational and cultural facilities that often serve the tourist trade as well.

The economic health of the tourism industry depends on the value and pattern of its customers, use of a large variety of facilities and services, and it counts both local residents and all classes of visitors among its valued customers. The tourist, or pleasure traveller, is but one of the classes of visitors catered to by the industry.

Tourism, then, is the business of attracting visitors and catering to their needs and expectations. The following is an overview of the major components of the tourism and travel industry.

**I. Tourist Destinations**

(*a*) Government promotion offices
(*b*) Regional promotion offices
(*c*) Resort areas, convention centres.

**II. Transportation**

(*a*) Airlines.
  (*i*) Major
  (*ii*) National
  (*iii*) Regional

(*iv*) Nonscheduled/charter.

(*b*) Ground Transporter

(*i*) Rent-a-car

(*ii*) Motor/coach

(*iii*) Railroad.

**III. Accommodation**

(*a*) Hotels

(*b*) Motels

(*c*) Resorts

(*d*) Cruise lines.

**IV. Tourist Attractions**

(*a*) Attractions

(*b*) Theme parks

(*c*) Museums.

**V. Travel Brokers**

(*a*) Travel agents

(*b*) Travel wholesalers

(*c*) Tour and charter operators

(*d*) Ground operators

(*e*) Travel incentive companies.

**VI. Travel Related Services.**

(*a*) Financial (credit cards, travellers cheques, travel insurance).

(*b*) Travel publications guide books.

Our world is diverse. It is composed of countries with a variety of cultures and customs, rural areas and urban centres, each with its own distinct flavour, and so on. The activity we call tourism, with its great economic and social benefits, provides citizens of all countries with an opportunity to explore new places, to meet new people, to learn new things, and, perhaps in the process, learn more about themselves.

Travel is a bridge between people. It makes a valuable contribution to the world's economy, employs more people than any other industry and affects the lives of all in one way or another.

Today, the terms *tourism and travel* have become almost interchangeable. However, when we look at the history of transporting people, we see that in the early days travel was a far from a pleasurable activity. The word "tourism" a relatively new addition to the English language, introduced only in the nineteenth century. It connotes the act of travelling for *pleasure*, as well as the industry that developed to service that activity.

Tourism also connotes the ability of people to escape from familiar surroundings and everyday routine. It is no wonder, then that the history of tourism is the history of those who broadened the horizons of transportation.

It was those who dreamed and those who dared, including Henry Ford and the Wright brothers, who gave us our present day transportation system which harmoniously links speed, safety and economy. While travel has been a human passion since the dawn of history, tourism only became possible as technological improvements provided comfortable, safe, and, above all, enjoyable ways to travel.

The modern tourism industry is composed of numerous separate industry segments. Sometimes competing, yet more often providing services supplementary in nature. Each segment of the industry developed as a result of different historical forces.

A study of the tourism industry, its development, current issues, and future opportunities can best be introduced by a closer look at the major historical developments, as discussed in earlier chapter.

## CONCEPT OF MODERN MASS TOURISM

Mass tourism is the product of mass leisure (*i.e.*, rest from work). The World Tourism Organisation (1984) estimated that between 1960 and 1980 the proportion of countries in which the average working week exceeded 40 hours fell from 75 per cent to 56 per cent. There has also been an increase in the number of people who are excluded from the formal economy, for example, there are more people living beyond the retirement age who are able to enjoy tourism.

Mass tourism depends not only on the growth of leisure time

but also the structure of free time and on the economics of tourism industry. The World Tourism Organisation estimated in 1994 that there were 800 million workers globally who received paid holidays from work. The lifetime distribution of free time has also been an important influence on mass tourism. The ageing of the population and the growth of active groups with disposable income has added to the demand for tourism. Perez estimates that in Europe, the proportion of tourism demand coming from 65+ group, increased from 15 per cent to 25 per cent between the mid-1960s and the mid-1980s.

The demand for tourism is influenced by the image markers who effectively create tourist attractions. This is a diverse industry and includes designers of hotels and attractions as well as media and travel writers. Together they generate "the promises of the paradise sellers".

The economics of the tourism industry has played an important part in the emergence of mass tourism. Changes in transport technology—by air as well as by land and sea—have accelerated travel at reduced costs.

The virtuous circle of mass tourism has five main phases, to begin with, mass tourism emerged in the USA in the twenties and thirties. Two important conditions were: the spread of paid holidays and the extension of car ownership. The growth of motel chains also provided the necessary accommodation infrastructure for the emerging tourism industry. The destinations of most tourists were coastal area and spa resorts. Later artificial attractions become popular. There was some working class tourism in Europe at this time directed at the coastal areas.

In the second phase—in the fifties domestic mass tourism emerged in Europe fuelled by leisure time and car ownership. The coast was the main destination although rural tourism was also important in some countries.

In the third phase—the late fifties and sixties mass tourism developed another dimension, being increasingly internationalised. Between 1950 and 1988, the number of international tourists increased from 25 million to 389 million. The USA and Canada topped the list.

In the fourth phase—there was a Europeanization of international tourism from the 1960s. According to the World Tourism Organisation, globally there were 405 million international tourists in 1989, and the destination for 64 per cent of these was Europe. Of these, the movements were mainly within that continent. The growth of mass tourism was facilitated by the easing of travel regulations and by the growth of the international air travel industry. The financial, legal and practical barriers to foreign travel within Europe was an important precondition of mass international travel.

In the last phase—in the late twentieth century—there has been a globalisation of the tourism industry. Globalisation has occurred as more and more countries have become locked into international travel tourism from Japan, Europe, North America, Australia, India and the Middle East have become increasingly internationalized. At the same time, the range of destinations of mass tourism has increased.

The factors responsible for mass tourism are as follows:

(*i*) Sustained prosperity and consequent rise in the income of the people;
(*ii*) Increase in paid leisure time;
(*iii*) Rise in educational standard;
(*iv*) Reduction in the size of family;
(*v*) Development of good communication system;
(*vi*) Growth of travel agents;
(*vii*) Monotony of work life in an industrialised society;
(*viii*) Growth in the number of International Conferences.

## CHARACTERISTICS OF MASS TOURISM

The nature of mass tourism as a form of mass consumption has a number of characteristics.

***Spatially Polarised***: Mass tourism tends to be highly spatially polarised. The contemporary tourist gaze is increasingly signposted. There are markers which distinguished things and places worthy of our gaze. Such signposting identifies a relatively small number of tourist nodes. In the later half of the twentieth century, the tourist image creators in North America and Europe have mainly promoted beach and ski holidays as the objects of the tourist gaze. As a result, most tourists are concentrated into a small number of areas. Eventually diseconomies of scale arising from spatial polarization has led to the decline of particular resorts and development of tourism urbanisation. Tourist cities have evolved during the late twentieth century as sites for consumption.

***Segmented Markets***: Mass tourist destinations also tend to have segmented markets. To minimize costs, there is a historical tendency for high level of movements between adjoining places. Thus in UK in the early twentieth century, Southend developed as the resort for East London, Blackpool as the resort for Lancashire and the Skegness as the resort for the East Midlands. At the international level there are several examples of similar processes; German tourists dominate in Austria, while Japanese tourists dominate in South East Asia and North Americans in Mexico.

***Dependency***: Dependency on particular market segments brings certain economic relationships. Destinations are more vulnerable to external influences. This is particularly pronounced with respect to international tourism. Fears of terrorism in Kashmir valley have led to dramatic fluctuations in the number of foreigners as well as domestic tourists. Gorkhaland movement in Darjeeling has led to a drastic fall in the number of tourists there. It took Portugal four years to recover the tourists number lost following the 1974 military coup. Economic conditions in external markets is also an important factor affecting the flow of tourists. The number of American tourists in the international market have also fluctuated from year to year as the dollar has fluctuated dramatically in value after the abandonment of fixed international exchange rates since the early seventies.

***Price***: Mass tourism involves the movement of large number of tourists with relatively little surplus income. Price is the most important factor. In other words, demand for tourism services is highly elastic with respect to price and income. Hence there is a strong downward pressure on prices for the tour companies.

***Seasonal***: Mass tourism is necessarily highly seasonal. The tourists purchase access to particular seasonal environments or 'space-time packages'. The main objects of the mass tourist gaze—snow or sunny beaches—are temporal attractions. While snow exists in high mountain ranges all the year round, and some coastal areas are warm always, there are seasons in which conditions are optimum. Very few destinations are able to develop year-round tourism.

***Environmental Pressures***: Mass tourism by assembling large numbers of tourists in small areas creates intense environmental pressures. There is a real threat to environmental balance. Infrastructures are required to cope with a large volume of tourists during the busy season but they will remain underutilized during the remaining part of the year.

While coastal resorts had been popular in elite tourism in the nineteenth century, in the twentieth century they became the focus of mass tourism. There are many reasons for this—the emergence of paid holidays, the arrival of mass transport through the railways and the desire to escape the harsh living conditions in industrial capitalism. The attraction was sea and sand and the contrast to home provided by the absence of industry. In the twentieth century, the arrival of mass car ownership modified this pattern. In North America improved accessibility reinforced the attraction of 'the great outdoors'. In Europe, while it gave some boost to rural tourism, it mainly led to a dispersion of tourism along the coast rather than away from the coast. International coast mass tourism has developed into a major industry. The beaches of Europe, Australia, Mexico, the Caribbean and the Black Sea have been attractive to mass tourists from many countries.

## URBAN TOURISM

Urban areas act as tourism destinations, attracting domestic as well as international visitors. Capital cities and historic towns and cities attract holiday makers as well as those on business and conference trips. This is quite natural as towns and cities offer a wide range of attractions. Tourists visit urban areas for various reasons—for night life and entertainment, for enjoying historical and cultural attractions, for attending major sporting events or for shopping. Tourists share these attractions with local people. Conferences and special events draw many visitors. Commerce and industry, museum or castle attract a large number of business travellers. Sometimes visitors come to the cities to meet friends and relatives.

Tourism in urban areas is an extremely diverse phenomenon in three ways. The first is the heterogeneous nature of urban areas themselves, the other two dimensions are associated with the variety of facilities offered. The facilities refer to 'different types of city'. Thus, there are 'tourist city', 'the shopping city', 'the culture city' and the 'historic city' within an urban area.

Urban tourism is also characterized by the fact that cities very often exist within distinctive spatial networks which function at two different levels. The first level concerns urban areas operating regardless of their regional and national contexts, with particular cities forming parts of important tourism circuits. At west European level, Paris, London, and Rome may operate as part of an international tourism network. At national level, within India, the overseas visitor circuit encompasses Delhi, Agra and Mumbai which are linked by strong historical and cultural factors. At the second spatial level, the tourism activities of cities from the viewpoint of domestic tourists exist within a strong regional framework. In this context, cities act as an important focal point for a region's tourism industry.

The urban environment itself can be considered as a 'Leisure product'. An urban tourism product can offer three main levels of facilities—primary elements covering major tourist attractions which in turn are supported by retail and catering facilities and a general tourist infrastructure. In many cities the so-called secondary elements of shops and restaurants may well be the main attractions for certain groups of visitors.

All tourists visit cities with definite expectations of its sights and attractions. The urban tourists can be distinguished from other visitors by two criteria, their place of residence, situated outside the urban hinterland and their motives for visiting.

Tourism in large and historic cities is not a new trend for example, Paris, London and New York all have long-standing tourism industries. In India, Delhi, Agra, Mathura, Gwalior, Mussouri and Indore all have long-standing tourism industries. While tourism was traditionally recognised in historic cities, within large cities and industrial centres. The significance of tourism had been neglected until 1980s; since then it has been perceived as having important roles in economic and environmental improvements. Urban tourism has strong international dimensions relating to the transfer of ideas. The ideas behind using tourism as a spur to economic and environmental regeneration were initially experimented in North America. Tourism was selected because it was a growth industry, provided jobs and could lead to environmental improvements. The idea was that the visitors will be attracted to the city, thus generating income and jobs. Moreover, as tourism develops, new facilities will helps create a better urban environment, some of the benefits of which will be passed on to local residents and there will be a general improvement in the image of the city to potential investors.

## RURAL TOURISM

Rural areas have long played an important role in tourism and leisure within the developed world. It has been estimated that in 1990, 75 per cent of the population of England visited the countryside at least once.

Various factors attract tourists to rural regions—natural features such as rivers, lakes, forests or cultural ones such as picturesque features. Tourists spend their holidays in the countryside as a change from urban areas seeking peace and relaxation which a rural environment can offer. Others come for more active pursuits—fishing, walking, boating, etc. The country has come to be defined in terms of qualities which are absent in urban life.

There is a rural opportunity continuum in the countryside as the location of a wide range of outdoor leisure and tourist activities, although over time the composition of these has changed.

The dominant mode of transport is the private car. Tourists development in rural regions is characterized by multiplicity of small-scale developers.

The construction of the countryside as a tourist zone necessarily results in a number of sharp contradictions. The first of these is that in most developed countries, the vast majority of rural lands are in private ownership which severely constrains accessibility.

Second, there are many social constructions in rural areas—as pastoral idylls, as areas of recreation and as production zones. All of these may come into conflict with each other. There is a potential for host-guest conflicts. Finally, there is the question of the rural residents' own access to recreation.

### Second Homes

One issue in the use of the countryside is second homes. In the developed countries second home ownership is widespread. For people living in London, New York and other large cities, a rural home is used at the weekend as a complement to a city apartment. Parisian families own second homes in the South of France and German families own second homes in Austria. In such cases visits may be made less frequently and may involve seasonal long stays.

**Farm Tourism**

Whereas second home development generally involves a transfer of land and buildings from rural to non-resident ownership, farm tourism represents continuing ownership and active participation by the farmer in small scale tourism ventures. In farm tourism, the tourist activity is closely intertwined with farming activities. In Europe, the term 'farm tourism' applies only to operations, where besides the hospitality function, active agriculture is also providing income to the host family. 'Vacation farm' is the term used in the USA to refer to an active, working farm on which extra rooms in the home or extra houses on the farm are rented to guests.

In Europe, farm tourism takes two main forms—the provision of accommodation in farm premises or the supply of accommodation on the farmer's land in the form of cottages and camping grounds. The most widespread is the letting of accommodation (bed and breakfast) with the second form being more characteristic of northern Europe. Austria is generally recognised as being the country where farm tourism is the most extensive with 100,000 guest rooms on 30,000 farms being made available in 1970.

Four main factors influence the farmers, decision to provide accommodation—to increase income, to offset falling income from agriculture, to utilize disused resources and to enjoy the visitors' company. While farm tourism depends mainly on individual initiatives, farmers in many countries are supported by the State by way of development grants.

The farm tourism market is already substantial but it is also subject to strong growth. On the demand side, this is stimulated by the growth in the short-break holiday market, by the demand for more activity-based holidays, and by the growth of number of critical consumers reacting against mass tourism. On the supply side, the global crisis of agricultural over-production is contributing to a drive to farm diversification with tourism being one of the more significant options available to farmers.

## Ethnic Tourism

Ethnic tourism consists of the return of people to the country of their origin. Much of the flow of American tourists to England is made up of immigrants of British origin paying a nostalgic visit to their old country. In India a large number of people come from Pakistan and Bangladesh to visit the country of their origin. Visiting friends and relatives (VFR) is an important motive behind much of the inbound tourism in India.

## Culture and Tourism

A knowledge of the culture of a country is important to understand how people will behave within that country. Culture refers to a set of beliefs, values, attitudes, habits and forms of behaviour that are shared by a society and are transmitted from generation to generation.

Culture affects society in different ways. First, values of the culture determine which goals and behaviour will gain social approval. People gratify their needs in socially acceptable ways. Second, culture affects the social backdrop through the established conventions and practices of society. Society adopts various practices relating to which foods can be taken, which entertainment is good and which gifts are appropriate. For example, beef is acceptable in Europe and USA but not in India, horse meat is acceptable in France but not in USA. When servicing a market from a different cultural standpoint, it is necessary to know the established practices to avoid undesirable behaviour.

The effect of culture is felt by the individual in two ways. First, culture affects the daily life patterns of individuals in society. An afternoon siesta is common in many south European countries to cope with high midday temperatures. But in USA afternoon siesta is not liked by the society. Concept of time varies from culture to culture. In USA time is money, other cultures attach less importance to time. Second, culture affects the way emotions are expressed. In Indian culture, kissing is not permissible but in western culture it is quite common.

A knowledge of how culture affects the individual, the social groups to which that individual belongs and the society as a whole will better enable the marketer to sell a travel product.

The cultures of different countries can vary greatly. To attract people from a particular country, it is important to know cultural differences.

## QUESTIONS FOR ANSWER

1. *What is Mass Tourism? Describe the factors responsible for mass tourism.*
2. *Write Notes on:*
   (*i*) *Urban tourism,*
   (*ii*) *Rural tourism,*
   (*iii*) *Farm tourism,*
   (*iv*) *Ethnic tourism,*
   (*v*) *Second homes.*
3. *"Tourism is the most flourishing industry in the world and as a contributor to world economy it has no equal." Justify.*
4. *Write a note on multicomponents of tourism industry.*
5. *Discuss the world tourism scenario in detail.*
6. *Write a note on the basic components of mass tourism.*
7. *Discuss in detail the concept of mass tourism.*
8. *Write a note on the basic characteristics of mass tourism.*
9. *Write short notes on the following:*
   (*a*) *Environmental pressures.*
   (*b*) *Culture and tourism.*
   (*c*) *Factors responsible for mass tourism.*
   (*d*) *Three basic elements of tourism.*

# 8

# Planning Aspect of Tourism in India

India, in ancient times was a major destination for the tourists, but as per dimensions of modern tourism, in India, tourism planning has been a late starter due to low priority to the tourism sector in resource allocation even after independence. Having understood the basic concepts of tourism planning, this chapter is devoted to examine the nature of tourism planning in India. The goal of tourism planning is to decide on the objectives of tourism development and on ways to achieve the latter by maximizing the overall economic, social and cultural advantages of tourism while respecting the dynamics of balanced tourism supply and demand.

Before drafting the tourism policy, goals for tourism have to be set up and these goals should be in conformity with the broad national interest and complement the specific objectives of the national, state and local bodies in the related fields. Thus, the tourism policy represents an amalgam of the principles upon which a nationwide course of action for tourism is based.

Interestingly, it provides a set of guidelines and forms the basic foundation to determine which specific goals, strategies and objectives are to be carried out in the interest of the destination. Krippendrof has observed that a careful tourism policy has become necessary for the following reasons: (*a*) the special vulnerability of the rural environment, (*b*) the irreversibility of certain processes, (*c*) the special importance of the environment as the raw material, the basis of tourism and its economic driving force, (*d*) the lack of evidence and uncertainty experienced in respect of measurement of damage to environment etc. and (*e*) the sensibilities of the local people.

## TOURISM PLANNING IN INDIA

We have read history of Indian tourism in an earlier chapter, therefore, hereunder, we will consider only the modern aspect of tourism planning in India. After five years of independence. Government of India tourist offices were set up at New York and London in 1952 and 1953 for promoting tourist traffic to the country. Moreover, the first Hotel Management Institute was set up at Bombay in 1954 to make available manpower resources for tourism. The second plan refers to tourism but only in relation to a few schemes. The schemes are of two categories, namely:

(*a*) Schemes for the development of facilities at a limited number of places visited largely by foreign tourists and;
(*b*) Schemes intended primarily to provide facilities for home tourists of low and middle income groups at a number of places of regional and local importance.

The Third Plan Programmes concentrate largely on the provision of facilities for accommodation and transport. The plan document also makes an important destination between Central and State schemes. While schemes in the Central sector provide for facilities which are important from the point of view of foreign tourism, those in the state plans are intended mainly for home tourism. Interestingly, Fourth Plan looks at foreign exchange earnings as the prime objective of tourism development while employment generation is also considered as an additional benefit. It states tourism is an important means of earning foreign exchange. It also provides employment and promotes international contacts and understanding. During the Fifth Plan, tourism is confined to a few programmes and financial allocations.

## Sixth Plan

Sixth Plan marks the beginning of a new thinking on tourism in India. The emphasis also shifts from schemes to strategies and from foreign exchange earnings to wider issues of economic development. The plan document refers to:

1. Social and economic benefits like promotion of national integration and international understanding;
2. Creation of employment;
3. Removal of regional imbalances;
4. Opening up of new growth centres in the interiors of the country;
5. Augmentation of foreign exchange earnings;

6. Support to local handicrafts and cultural activities;
7. Source of tax revenues for government both Central and State.

## Seventh Plan

Seventh Plan includes a refreshingly, clear enunciation of the role of tourism and a review of the development of the tourism in India. It also sets the objectives for tourism sector as follows:

1. Faster development of tourism.
2. According the status of an industry to tourism.
3. Redefining of the role of public and private sectors to ensure that the private sector investment is encouraged in developing tourism and the public sector investment is focused mainly on development of support infrastructure; and
4. Exploiting tourism potential to support local handicrafts and other creative arts and to promote national integration.

During the Seventh Plan, some thrust areas were also identified for action. Some of such identified areas are:

1. Development of tourist circuits;
2. Diversification of tourism products and expanding the base from cultural tourism to other forms of holiday tourism;
3. Development of non-traditional areas such as treckking, winter sports, wildlife tourism, beach resort etc.;
4. Restoration and balanced development of national heritage products;
5. Exploration of new tourism related markets;
6. Launching of a National Image Building and Marketing Plan in key markets jointly with the private sector.

## Eighth Plan

The Eighth Plan document makes a few very significant and valid observations about the future strategies. The issues identified can be summarised as follows:

1. The future growth of tourism should be achieved mainly through private initiative.

2. The state should confine its role to planning broad strategies of development, providing fiscal and monetary incentives to create a dynamic private sector and devising regulatory and supervisory mechanism.
3. The strategy for development must be based on cost efficiency, higher productivity, efficiency and quality in provision of infrastructure.
4. In view of the fact that capital is scarce, a selective approach, as was identified in the earlier plans, should be adopted for the development of tourism. The Eighth Plan introduces the concept of 'Special Tourism Areas'—areas which will be provided full fledged infrastrutural facilities.
5. Tourism marketing and publicity should be properly focused, strengthened and should be 'dynamic in terms of spread innovation, imagination, new techniques and coordination'.
6. Access to information and proper use of information technologies should be the basis of future development.
7. Tourism development programmes for backward areas should be integrated with area development programmes.
8. To achieve a balanced infrastructural development, all the states should be encouraged to formulate Master Plans.
9. Human Resource Development should be vital importance for the development of tourism.

## Ninth Plan

The Ninth Plan Policy framework on tourism, however, introduces a few new elements of policy. Firstly, it emphasises the importance of looking at infrastructure development for domestic tourism and, therefore, the role played by the respective states. It also elaborates the need for effective coordination of all the relevant agencies involved in the development of proper infrastructure and in the development of the tourism products. The Ninth Plan also brings out the importance of people's participation at the grassroots level for development of tourist facilities, and for creating a tourist friendly atmosphere. Keeping in tune with the overall government policy of balanced development, the plan for tourism also makes a special reference to regional development and in particular, to the special measures to be undertaken for development of the North East region of India.

## INDIA'S NATIONAL TOURISM POLICY, 1982

In 1982 India formulated its one and only National Tourism Policy. The objective of this policy is to so develop tourism that it:

1. Becomes an unifying force nationally and internationally fostering better understanding;
2. Helps preserving Indian heritage and culture and projecting the same to the world.
3. Brings socio-economic benefits in terms of employment, income generation, revenue generation, foreign exchange etc.;
4. Gives direction and opportunity to the youth of the country to understand the aspirations and view point of others and helps in greater national integration;
5. Offers opportunities to the youth of country, not only for employment but also for taking up activities for nation-building and character building like sports, adventure, etc.

Interestingly, the new tourism policy in the changed scenario, has:

1. Placed tourism as a central input in the economic development process because of its role in resource generation and employment creation;
2. Focused on the role of tourism in socio-economic development of the backward areas, weaker sections, women and artisans;
3. Allowed these goals to be pursued in tune with the goal of the enrichment of the environment and the ecosystem; and
4. Recognized the role of tourism as a potent global force for national and international understanding and for creating awareness for sustainable development.

Any policy for sustainable development will naturally revolve around the following cardinal principles:

1. That there is need for striking a balance between development and conservation;
2. That there is need for commitment of the nation as a whole to the goals of sustainable tourism development.

3. That adequate, effective and pragmatic control systems are devised and are efficiently put into place; and
4. That the policy incorporates and motivates cooperations of the local community who must perceive the benefit of such participation and should be able to partake the same.

## NATIONAL TOURISM ACTION PLAN, 1992

This plan contains following aspects:

1. Assessment of the ground realities.
2. Based on such an assessment, making effective plans which in management terms will imply:
   (*a*) Setting down the objectives;
   (*b*) Taking stock of the organisational capabilities to achieve these objectives; and
   (*c*) Assessing the physical, financial and human resources available to implement the objectives.

The following ground realities will also have to be kept in view:

(*a*) Inadequate and poor quality of infrastructure;
(*b*) Carrying capacity by air, roads and railways;
(*c*) Clean and comfortable lodging facilities at reasonable price;
(*d*) Trained guides and tourist amenities of international standard;
(*e*) Adequate entry points;
(*f*) Positive image building abroad;
(*g*) Publicity; and
(*h*) The need to preserve the heritage and natural attractions for posterity.

The future action programmes will revolve around creating adequate infrastructure of international standard to make arrivals easy and a pleasurable experience. Some of the areas where action can be taken are:

(*i*) Eco-friendly sustainable development;
(*ii*) Importance of generating awareness and seeing people's participation;

(*iii*) Improving the quality of services;
(*iv*) Improving building image;
(*v*) Making travels a pleasure;
(*vi*) Ensuring basic facilities/amenities;
(*vii*) Beautification and preservation of heritage;
(*viii*) Beautification of heritage places;
(*ix*) Establishing clear and visual signs;
(*x*) Effective information dissemination,
(*xi*) Easy access of transport and travel facilities; and
(*xii*) Improving/developing infrastructure.

## FIVE KEY STEPS IN TOURISM PLANNING PROCESS

National, regional and local are the three levels of tourism planning which involves following steps or phases: (*a*) assessment of tourist demand and supply; (*b*) establishing objectives; (*c*) territorial planning; (*d*) basic infrastructure; (*e*) financial planning; (*f*) human resource planning; (*g*) administrative structure; (*h*) marketing and promotion; (*i*) monitoring progress; and (*j*) the time factor. However, following five phases of tourism planning are essential and deserve mention.

The first phase is concerned with an analysis of the existing situation and produces the direction for the succeeding phases. It takes into consideration the policies and plans of other public sector bodies which have an impact on tourism and identifies the existing tourism related programmes and activities. This analysis results in assessment of the tourism resources components of the area and the preparation of their inventory.

In the second phase, detailed research and analysis is carried out in respect of the resources and markets. On the basis of the inventory prepared in the first phase, key resources are identified and located and their capacities are assessed. Besides, activity analysis is also undertaken to determine all those things or activities in which tourist can participate while visiting the destination area. Moreover, resources are graded and classified in terms of the scope of their appeal for the international, national, regional or local market. In this phase, a detailed study related to existing and potential markets of an area is suggested for comprehensive planning for tourism development. Moreover, preparation of master plan is another important step in planning for completing and detailing additional work on the portions of the conceptual plan which are approved for further development.

The third phase is regarded as one of the most important and creative stages in the tourism planning process. The major conclusions derived from the research and studies in the first two phases are formulated at this stage. The conclusions mainly relate to 5 distinct subjects *viz.* (*a*) tourism development, (*b*) tourism-marketing, (*c*) tourism industry organization, (*d*) tourism awareness and (*e*) other tourism support services and activities. The synthesis of present situations and the desired future situation in a destination area, provides the basic future directive for the development of tourism in the area.

In the fourth phase, the tourism planning goals, strategies and goal related plan objectives are decided and formulated. These must be complementary to the goals and objectives of the tourism policy. The planning goals are achieved through a variety of approaches or strategies. The tourism plan objectives are directly related to the strategy adopted for achieving the goals. The planning goals, strategy and plan objectives are closely interlinked.

The development of the plan itself constitutes the fifth phase of the planning process. At this stage, the plan details, the actions and programmes required to achieve the plan objectives, implement the strategy and satisfy the planning goals. It specifies the roles and responsibilities of the public and private sector, describes the specific developing and marketing concepts in respect of the objectives. Further, it specifies the requirements of funds, time table for carrying out the various programmes and method of monitoring the progress of the plan.

## PLANNING TOURISM PROJECTS

Different methodologies are used in the preparation of tourism planning projects. Kaiser has formulated 10 key steps to guide the planning of a tourism project. These are: (1) establishing understanding, (2) preliminary position statement, (3) commitment for tourism study, (4) market research and analysis, (5) conceptual planning, (6) plan approval, (7) master planning, (8) final commitment, (9) staged implementation programme, and (10) evaluation and direction. Most of these steps propounded by Kaiser are already covered in the planning process discussed earlier.

### Factor Influencing Planning

During last decades, several new trends dramatically influenced planning applications to tourism. The strong preoccupation with promotion by nation, provincial, state and city tourism agencies is now being modified.

The following are the leading factors fostering change in the tourism planning sector. For a long time, new tourism development was largely planned according to land and building patterns of the past and generalized assumptions regarding markets. More recently, supply side imitation has been modified greatly in an attempt to meet new market needs.

New market trends are creating new challenges, cultural and natural resource interests, better human relationships and desire for specialized travel products. Creative and innovative planning and design approaches are now changing in order to develop attractions, facilities and service that better reflections of segmented market needs. Interestingly, tourism related business is growing, demanding comprehensive services.

Moreover, environmental concerns are stimulating greater interest in tourism planning. Tourism destinations are facing environmental threats from all sources. Municipal and industrial wastes continue to cause air, water and land contamination. Depletion of forests, reduction of wildlife, air pollution and soil erosion continue to destroy resources potential for tourism. Gradually tourism proponents are beginning to recognize these threats and are expressing their concerns in political and physical plans.

It is now well proved that tourism can produce its own negative impacts on society and economy. So the major challenge is to minimize the negative impacts and maximise the positive impacts of tourism. Importantly, sustainable development is advocated by specialists and economists. Therefore perspective planning regarding tourism destinations development is called for.

## THREE LEVEL TOURISM PLANNING

### Planning at National Level

At the national level, a geographical perspective is necessary for tourism planning. Priority areas must be defined and their relation and development needs to be based on factors which influence tourist development. Therefore, national tourism plan should formulate policies and guidelines for the public and private sectors to enable them to meet future tourism development requirements. Moreover, tourism product development should be market oriented and emphasis should be on the development of the country's unique assets.

Pearce has rightly observed that to make investment economically viable and to prevent disturbance of traditional way of living, dispersed concentration of facilities is imperative. Infrastructure and super-structure should be as much multipurpose as possible serving also other sectors of the economy. Strike regulation should control environment.

## Planning at the Regional Level

The national plans incorporate tourist development at the regional level. A tourist region, identified at the national level, is usually defined in terms of spatial associations of specific tourist resources and their associated facilities. It is also conceived in physical terms or an administrative zone in which tourism forms an important factor of regional development.

Regional planning can be effective in seeking to achieve the appropriate balance of use and pressures in rural areas where multiple use is a common phenomenon and the potential for conflict between agriculture land scape, conservation, and the tourism is very high.

Significantly the preservation of the natural environment and its protection from degradation are the important aspects of planning at the regional level. Regional planning provides probably the best opportunity for achieving environmental protection goals, and the coastal and alpine environments can benefit significantly from it.

## Planning at the Local Level

At the local level, tourism planning is very much concerned with the provision of the requisite services and facilities required by the tourist at his destination points. Interestingly, planning relates to the physical organization of the elements of tourist supply attractions, transport, accommodation, infrastructure and other supporting facilities.

The emphasis at this level should be on infrastructural components and their integration with the resources of the locality. It is at this level that detail is required to ensure essential facilities, and measures such as the prevention of water courses or the sea from being polluted by the sewage system. Importantly, the planning activity at the local level centres around the primary attraction whether natural, historical or cultural.

The development will vary in respect of each of these but, as a general rule, the basic principle to guide planning at the local level is that the original form and features of the tourist attraction must not, in any way be affected and altered, either physically or usually, by obstructive or incongruous constructions or provision of facilities. The constraints of the site should be taken into consideration and it should be developed harmoniously.

## QUESTIONS FOR ANSWER

1. *Explain why careful tourism policy is necessary?*
2. *Write a note on tourism policy as outlined of the Planning Commission in Sixth, Seventh and Eighth Five Year Plans.*
3. *Write a note on India's National Tourism Policy, 1982.*
4. *Discuss five key steps in tourism planning process.*
5. *Write short notes on the following:*
   - (*a*) *National Tourism Action Plan.*
   - (*b*) *Factors effecting tourism planning.*
   - (*c*) *Planning Tourism Projects.*

# 9

# Tourism Scenario in India: Potentials, Problems and Prospects

## INTRODUCTION

Tourism has been in practice from time immemorial. Centuries back, the king of Babylon, Sheelaket, protected roads, rest houses and gardens for travellers. Prior to it India also has a glorious past for travel facilities. When Alexander the Great reached India, he found the well maintained roads, guest houses, wells and even police stations. Chinese and European travellers who visited India in earlier days also appreciated the travel facilities in India. It is also noted that there were large scale visits from India to foreign countries. All the prominent religions in the country like Hinduism, Buddhism, Islam and Christianity contributed a lot towards wide travel. In most of the cases travel was effected for pilgrimage, trade and commerce.

The World Tourism Organisation lays down the following objectives for tourism: (1) poverty alleviation, (2) environmental regeneration, (3) job orientation, both skilled and unskilled, (4) advancement of women and other disadvantaged groups, (5) preservation of monuments and heritage sites. Interestingly, travel and tourism is expected to create employment for 262 million people of 10.5 per cent of the global work force, growing to 383 million people by the year 2007.

Presently India is trying its best to become one of the top destinations in world tourism. Former Prime Minister Atal Bihari's stress on the development road infrastructure in India will prove to be an important step in this direction, because we have great potential for tourism development as discussed hereunder:

## INDIA'S RESOURCE POTENTIAL FOR TOURISM

Tourism is a very complex industry that includes a variety of economic activities, services, facilities, human relations and demand supply patterns. While tourism development in any area depends on the type of facilities and services offered to the consumers (*i.e.*, tourists), what is more important is the availability of a strong recreation resource base. To put it differently, potential for tourism development largely depends on the variety and richness of tourist-resource(s); the more unique and varied the resources better the prospects for tourism development.

The term potential broadly means something existing but not yet fully exploited. Thus it symbolizes the sum total of qualitative and quantitative values on which the degree and the extent of exploitability depends. It is difficult to explain or assess the potential in numerical terms as it involves many factors in the context of tourism.

Besides, this phenomenon is very complex by nature. Hence, tourism deals with physical, psychological and sometimes even spiritual demands of the people from diverse geographical, socio-cultural and economic background who travel under different motives, interests, preferences and immediate needs. Furthermore, in view of recreation, entertainment, stay, transport, shopping and the like, the demand patterns and desire lines of the tourists, recreationists or the pleasure hunters ought to vary in transit and at destinations.

In fact, potential for tourism development in any area largely depends on the availability of recreational resources in addition to factors like climate, seasons, accessibility, attitude of the local people and the tourism planners towards the nature and the extent of tourism development, the existing tourist plan facilities and the degree to which they can be further developed within the prevailing limitations of natural, cultural and financial environments.

The term tourist resource again is complex and comprehensive as tourism potential and therefore, equally difficult to define. As such, any natural or cultural object. Ranging from a mountain peak, river, lake, waterfall, dam, forest, wildlife, bird, historical monument, an object of an art fair or festival, beach, a vantage point, to even a person can be a tourist resource.

Different people have different perceptions, interests and tastes, and accordingly, they are interested in different aspects of nature or culture. The resource potential however, considerably depends on the way a resource is developed and, more important, how it is sold. Thus, we can say that in tourism, resource is that which can become an attraction.

India abounds in tourism potential in all spheres, be it historical or cultural, be it hills and forests or other places of scenic beauty, be it wildlife, be it hot springs, be it fairs, festivals and people. For the tourists, India has two special attractions which few other countries can offer—rich and varied wildlife and a wealth of ancient monuments. The remains and relics of the prehistorical civilization, the temples, sculptures and holy sites associated with Buddha, the Hindu temples and caves at Ellora, Elephanta, Khajuraho, Khandagiri, Udaygiri and Tanjore; the monuments, palaces and forts of Muslim rule—the exquisite Taj Mahal—and the remains of European rule like the Portuguese forts and churches at Goa, Diu and Bandel and the British forts and residencies at Chennai, Surat and Lucknow and the beauty spots on the Himalayas are all tourist attractions.

There has been widespread awareness of the potential benefits of tourism, but very little has been done in practice to tap this vast potential. Guidelines to develop our potentials to stimulate tourism in India will be discussed later.

## BRIEF HISTORY OF TOURISM IN INDIA

For centuries India has been a centre of attraction for different people for different reasons in the outside world. The ancient invaders viewed it as a golden bird with abundant wealth accessible to plunder; the learned were fascinated by its mystic spiritualism and profound philosophy, the uninitiated saw it as a land of naked fakirs, snake charmers and rope trick performers, while the others were simply charmed by the sheer beauty of its natural attractions and amazing variety of its flora and fauna.

The lure of the snowclad mountains, grandeur of the mighty rivers like the Ganges and Bhramaputra, awe inspiring sand dunes of the Thar, beautiful beaches of Goa along with exotic beauty of various medieval forts, architectural elegance of holy temples and ageless charm of heritage monuments like the legendary Taj have in their own inimitable ways been beckoning the wonders since long. The diverse climatic conditions too have made it possible for the tourists to visit our country round the year.

India has an ancient tradition of tourism. It has existed as an industry in the informal sector since ancient times and was indulged in by all classes of people. The travels were made by business class and also for paying pilgrimage and attending ceremonies in the neighbouring states. The tourists or travellers had rest houses like *Dharamshalas, Sarais* and *Havelis* at tourist places or on the way for comfortable rest and stay. However, as organised industry of tourism is a twentieth century phenomenon and came into existence mostly for catering to foreign tourists who wanted to live in style during their visits to India.

The Alexander the Great of Macedonia with huge army invaded northern part of India. He was followed by many explorers like Vasco-d-Gama and Christopher Columbus, who actually set out to find a new route to India. Young Marco Polo also visited India on his way back from China. During 1333 Ibn Batuta visited India.

During 16th century English traveller Sir, Tomas Ro and William Hawkin visited India and it made possible the establishment of British India Company. Thus India's glorious traditions and rich cultural heritage made India a major attraction for foreign tourists and travellers in the past. The climatic conditions and geographical features provide varied interests to the visitors.

If seen in retrospect of just a few hundred years to the third century A.D., since the first exploration of Alexander the Great, or only about 700 years since Marco Polo and his amazing explorations crossing many lands fascinating accounts of these persons are found.

These great explorers can be credited with the distinction of perhaps being the pioneers who subsequently paved the way for modern travel. When Alexander arrived in India, he found well maintained roads covered with shady trees. Along one royal highways, 1920 kilometres long and about 19 metres wide, people travelled in chariots, palanquins, bullock carts, on horses, camels and elephants.

Despite our early history in tourism where in most of the cases travel was effected for knowledge and education, pilgrimage, trade and commerce; tourism declined during medieval era for want of proper educational system in our country on account of rulers apathy, but we preserved our cultural heritage, which is a great natural resource to boost tourism in India, therefore, even before World War II Government of India made some efforts to ensure proper tourism development, as discussed hereunder:

## RECOGNITION BY GOVERNMENT

In, India the importance of tourism was recognised even before the Second World War. However, the War put a stop to the tourism promotion activities of the government. The first conscious and organised effort to promote tourism in India was made in 1945, when a Committee was set up by the Government of India under the Chairmanship of Sir John Sarjent. The main objectives of the Committee were:

- To review the nature and extent of Tourist traffic in India both from within the country and from overseas which existed before the War.
- To examine what scope there was for increasing tourist traffic during the post-war period.
- To suggest ways and means of creating, both in India and overseas, the desire for touring including visits to holiday resorts, good climate stations, scenic places, places of pilgrimage, of historical, and of archaeological interest in India.
- To suggest what facilities should be provided at places to be developed and advertised for (*a*) Indian visitors; and (*b*) foreign visitors. The facilities to be considered should include means of travel from nearest railway station, residential accommodation, supply of literature and guide books, provision of authorised guides, etc.
- To recommend what action should be taken for providing the necessary facilities by (*a*) Indian States or local government; and (*b*) various departments of the Central Government.
- To deal with other aspects of tourist traffic not covered by the terms of reference.

The Sarjent Committee which submitted it's interim report in October 1946, were unanimously of the opinion that it would be in the interest of India to develop and encourage tourist traffic, both internal and external by all possible means. The Committee was of the opinion that successful steps in the promotion of tourism would result in a substantial addition, both direct and indirect, to India's revenue and that, if properly organised, every aspect of business could benefit greatly by an influx of tourists.

One of the major recommendations of the Committee related to the setting up of separate representative organisation of semi-officials. The Committee recommended that the promotion of tourist traffic was a matter of great national importance and therefore, deserves the whole time attention of separate organisations which should take initiative in such matters as:

(*a*) Publicity both in India and abroad.
(*b*) Production of suitable literature such as guide books, folders, posters, etc.
(*c*) Provision for training of tourist guides.
(*d*) Liaison with other government departments responsible for providing facilities required by tourists, including information with regard to industries and commercial matters.
(*e*) Liaison with the travel agencies which would necessarily remain responsible for the detailed arrangements of tourists.
(*f*) Liaison with the hotels and catering establishments.
(*g*) Collection of tourist statistics.

Some of the major other recommendations of the Committee were:

(*a*) Co-ordination with air and train services with a view to facilitate both air and train journey and to make it comfortable in India.
(*b*) Provision of a chain of first class hotels of international standard for the convenience and comfort of foreign tourists.
(*c*) Starting of Publicity Bureau in London and New York and in the Capitals of other countries from where substantial number of tourists might be forthcoming.

The Committee also recommended that a separate tourist organisation should be set up at the Centre with regional offices in the metropolitan cities of Bombay, Delhi, Calcutta and Madras. The Committee also recommended setting up of tourist publicity cells in the Indian Embassies and Consulates all over the world. As a followup an ad-hoc Tourist Traffic Committee was appointed in the year 1948. This Committee was entrusted with the job of suggesting ways and means of promoting tourist traffic to India.

## TOURISM IN FREE INDIA

One of the major recommendations of the Sarjent committee appointed in the year 1945 was that "the work of development of tourist traffic in India should be undertaken on a methodical basis by a separate organisation". As a result of this recommendation, a separate Tourist Traffic Branch was set up in the Ministry of Transport in the year 1949.

With the increase in its activities the Tourist Traffic Division expanded considerably and during the Year 1955-56 the establishment was increased from one branch to four branches, each having wide ranging duties. The four sections which were looking after various subjects were, viz.,

- Tourist Traffic Section
- Tourist Administration Section
- Tourist Publicity Section
- Distribution Section.

### Tourist Traffic Section

This section was tasked with a large number of travel trade subjects which included development of both internal and external tour traffic, legislative matters, five-year plans, travel agencies, hotels and rest houses, facilitation, tourist statistics and monthly reports. It also dealt with international conferences on tourism and references relating to U.N. and its agencies, coordination with railways, establishment of bureaus in the states, development of tourist centres and the training of guides.

### Tourist Administration Section

This section dealt with administration work relating to tourist offices both in India and abroad, budget, delegation of financial powers to tourist offices, opening of new tourist offices in India and abroad and periodical inspection of these offices.

### Tourist Publicity Section

This section was responsible for publication of the tourist literature such as pamphlets, guidebooks and posters, issue of advertisements and participation in exhibitions and fairs.

### Distribution Section

This section dealt with the distribution of tourist publicity literature in India and abroad.

### Tourist Information Offices

Another important step during 1955-56 was the opening of a chain of tourist offices both in India and abroad. Steps were taken to establish Regional Offices at important points of entry. Tourist offices were opened in Delhi, Mumbai, Kolkata and Chennai. This was followed by the establishment of a chain of information offices all over the country. By the year 1955, nine such offices were opened. They supplied upto date information on places of tourist interests to tourist after they arrived in India.

With a view to attracting foreign tourists to India the Government also decided to open a chain of tourist offices overseas. The first step in this direction was the establishment of the Government of India Tourist Office in New York in December 1952. To arouse interest among Europeans to visit India, a chain of offices were also opened in London in July 1955. Two more offices were opened, one in Paris in February 1956, and the other in Frankfurt in September of the same year.

In order to promote tourist traffic from Australia and New Zealand, a tourist office was opened in Melbourne in September 1956. Also in 1956 an office was opened in Colombo on the occasion of 2500th anniversary of Gautam Buddha.

## FORMATION OF THE DEPARTMENT OF TOURISM

On 1 March 1958, a separate department was created in the Ministry of Transport to deal with all matters concerning tourism on the guidelines of the Estimates Committee. This new department was put under the charge of the Director General who had under him one Deputy Director General and four Directors, each in charge of Administration, Publicity, Travel Relations and Planning and Development.

There was a decline in tourist traffic to India from, 1,39,804 in 1961 to 1,34,036 in 1962. This promoted the government to appoint an ad-hoc Committee on Tourism in March 1963, under the chairmanship of L.K. Jha. Some of the recommendations made by the Jha Committee were:

- Grant of landing permits on arrival to Tourists coming without visa for more than seventy two hours;
- Opening of additional tourists offices abroad;
- Provision of shopping and entertainment facilities;
- Setting up of three government corporations to develop hotel, transport, and entertainment facilities;
- Need to build 5,500 additional hotel rooms within the next five years;
- Official approval of restaurants, shops, and guides;
- Improvement of facilities at airports;
- Provision of adequate facilities by Indian Airlines;
- Introduction of the permit room system in Delhi;
- Import of cars;
- Training of immigration and customs staff;
- Increase tourist publicity;
- Integrated development of a few selected tourist centres;
- Stoppage of leakage of foreign exchange; and
- Establish of a standing committee of main departments of the government dealing with tourism for reviewing inadequacies.

In 1965, as a follow up on the Jha Committee Report, a high level coordination committee was appointed to suggest ways and means to implement the recommendations of the Jha Committee with the help of the concerned department for development of tourist traffic to India. Again, in accordance with the recommendations of the Jha Committee,

- Hotel Corporation of India Limited,
- India Tourism Corporation Limited,
- India Tourism Transport Undertaking Limited.

The three Corporations did not seem to be working well and were, therefore, amalgamated into one corporation with effect from 1 October 1966. The new corporation was called India Tourism Development Corporation Limited. The importance of tourism was further underline when the then Prime Minister of India, Indira Ghandi, convened a Round Table Conference. The Round Table Conference held earlier under the chairmanship of the Prime Minister had dramatic effects on liberalising entry formalities for tourists. For the first time, landing permits were issued to visitors coming without a visa for a period of one week. Advisory Committee was set up by the Civil Aviation Department for four International Airports in October 1966 to discuss matters pertaining to the development of tourism.

## MINISTRY OF TOURISM AND CIVIL AVIATION

On 13 March 1967 a separate Ministry of Tourism and Civil Aviation was created with Dr. Karan Singh as Cabinet Minister. This was a significant step as it brought tourism and civil aviation together under one administration.

Since the formation of the Ministry of Tourism and Civil Aviation, Indian tourism has been developing in spite of limited resources and relatively low priority given to this economic activity. Indian Tourism Development Corporation shaped into a gigantic and dynamic Public Sector organisation implementing programmes and policies laid down by the Government.

The Department of Tourism is under the charge of a Director General of the rank of an Additional Secretary and reports directly to the Minister. Under him, there are Divisions of Planning, Administration, Publicity, Hotels, Marketing Research, Wildlife, Supplementary accommodation, etc.

The activities of the Department of Tourism include:

- Compilation collection, and dissemination of tourist information in India and abroad and attending to enquiries from international tourists, tour operators and travel industry sectors such as airlines, steamship, companies and hotels, production of tourist literature posters, brochures, information directories, tourist guide-maps for wide distribution;
- Cooperation with international travel and tourist organisation at government and non-government levels;
- Facilities work such as simplification of frontier formalities in respect of international tourists;

- Development of tourist facilities of interest to international tourists;
- Publicity at home and abroad with the object of creating an overall awareness of the importance of tourism;
- Regulation of the activities of various segments of the travel trade, such as hotels, youth hostels, travel agents, wildlife outfits, tourists car operators and, shopkeepers catering to tourist's needs; and
- Compilation of statistics and market research on international tourist traffic to India and their utilisation for more effective tourist promotion.

**Organisation Chart of the Department of Tourism**

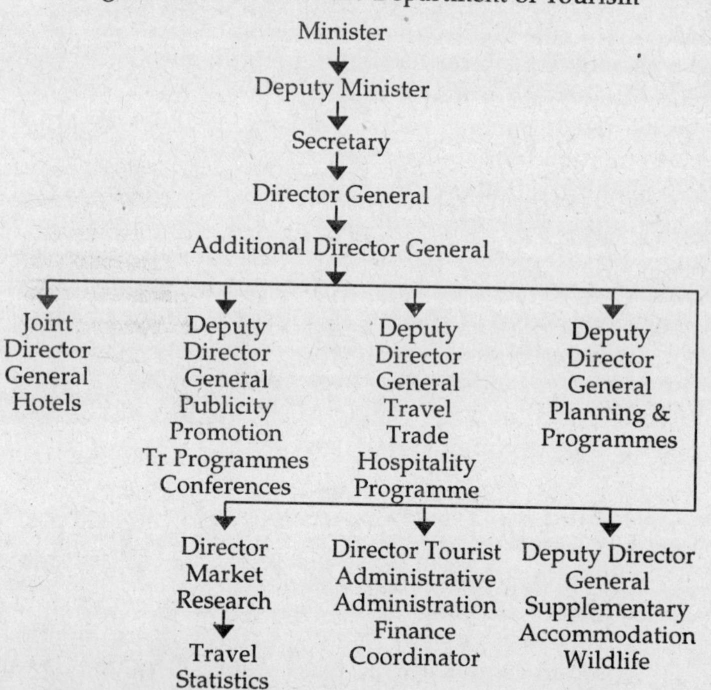


The question of making the tourist organisation a more effective wing of government has been considered by the Government of India from time to time. It was with this objective that the government in 1970 invited a UNDP team led by Dr. Timoth O'Driscoll, former Head of National Tourist Organisation of Ireland, to study the present tourist set-up of India. The study team recommended the establishment of a single tourist authority to deal with tourism matters. The task of making detailed recommendations was assigned to the Indian Institute of Public Administration in 1972. The main recommendation of the Institute was the setting up of a "National Tourist Authority" with a marketing and sales approach to 'sell' the Indian tourist product in the world market and provide encouragement through vigorous incentives such as tax rebates, loans, grants etc., to trade and travel agencies. The Institute also supported the idea of a single tourism authority, suggesting that it continues as a part of the government, with operational authority. The government did not accept the need for creating a tourism authority. However, it set up a National Tourism Agency under the chairmanship of the Minister of Tourism and Civil Aviation to advise him on tourism matters, which stopped functioning soon after the Minister, Dr. Karan Singh who created it, was moved.

It will, therefore be seen that no major change took place in the tourist organisation of India since its emergence as a separate department in 1958, except for minor expansions here and there.

In connection with the formulation of a long term perspective plan for the tourism sector on an integrated basis, it was then decided to set up a National Committee on Tourism under the chairmanship of Mohamad Yunus, Chairman, Trade Fair Authority of India.

## DECLARATION OF TOURISM AS AN INDUSTRY

Tourism is a State subject. The Centre, however, formulated and implemented many schemes for the development of the industry essentially to complement the State schemes.

Tourism has been declared as an industry in 14 states viz.: Meghalaya, Himachal Pradesh, Uttar Pradesh, Andhra Pradesh, Kerala, Haryana, Arunachal Pradesh, Tamil Nadu, Manipur, Bihar, Tripura and Assam and the Union Territory of Andaman and Nicobar Islands. Dadra, Nagar Haveli and Lakshadweep, States like Punjab, West Bengal, Orissa and Rajasthan have declared 'hotels' as an industry. The government of the States and Union Territories have also set up Directorates of Tourism and many have also set up Tourism Development Corporations.

Since the creation of the Ministry of Tourism and Civil Aviation tourism in India in spite of various limitations has grown satisfactorily and now India is a major attraction for the tourists of almost all the major countries of the world. It is worth to be noted that in last five years during Prime Minister Atal Bihari Vajpayee's period the growth of international tourism in India has been almost 50 per cent higher than before and accordingly it has earned maximum foreign exchange to enhance our foreign exchange reserves. This is a clear indication that future of tourism industry in India is very bright, if we correct our approach in this regard and provide this industry desired support, as we are faced with the problem outlined hereunder:

India has not formally liberalised the tourism sector as much as many other countries. However, it is important for India to attract foreign technology investment and expertise in those relatively new and unconventional areas like ecotourism, adventure tourism, camping and related areas so that its share of world tourists grows rapidly and does not decline to the benefit of other countries.

## TOURISM REGULATIONS IN INDIA

Those in the tourist trade should know all the legal and quasi-legal regulations which concern the tourist trade. A traveller who is also a tourist is governed by the laws and regulations in force in the country which he visits.

### 1. Passport and Visa Requirements

It is important for all visitors from abroad to possess a valid passport issued by their respective countries before they enter Indian territory either by land or sea or air.

Visa is an essential requirement for all people of all nationalities for entering India. There are several types of visas available to foreign nationals as follows:

1. Entry Visa
2. Tourist Visa
3. Business Visa
4. Long term Visa (maximum duration of 5 years)
5. Collective Landing Permit (group tourists from abroad).

Indian consular offices in different countries issues Indian Visas. The fee for this visa is US $5 per person. But nationals of Britain pay a Visa fee of £23.

The maximum duration for which tourist visas are issued is 180 days. The requirement is the submission of passport photographs. There is also a provision for the extension of visa beyond 180 days.

Visas can be renewed in all State capitals and district headquarters on an application made to the district Police Chief *e.g.* SP. Visa renewals and extension cases in the cities of New Delhi, Bombay and Calcutta are handled by Foreigners Regional Registration Offices.

The outbound travellers will seek visas from embassies or consulates of respective countries they wish to visit. Most of these offices are located in New Delhi.

### 2. Special Permits

Normally there is no restriction on Indian and foreign nationals for movement within India. But in case of border states and the two groups of island (Andaman and Lakshadweep), a visitor requires a special permit. This permit is valid for 15 days only.

**Andaman and Nicobar Islands.** Foreigners visiting the islands require prior permission. This can be obtained from Immigration officer, Port Blair on arrival. Permits can be obtained in advance from Chief Immigration Officers at Delhi, Calcutta, Mumbai and Chennai.

**Arunachal Pradesh.** All foreign nationals intending to visit Arunachal Pradesh require restricted area permits issued by Deputy Secretary, Ministry of Home Affairs, Government of India, Lok Nayak Bhawan, Khan Market, New Delhi. Indian nationals (domestic tourists) can obtain permits from Arunachal Bhawan, New Delhi, Calcutta, Guwahati and Tezpur.

**Assam.** Only Guwahati, Sibsagar, Halflong and Kaziranga are open for foreigners. To visit these places, permits are issued by Assam State Tourist Information Centres at Delhi and other parts of the country.

**Gujarat.** Border regions of the Runn of Kutch are restricted areas. Permits to visit Banni region and areas beyond the India Bridge are issued for both foreign and Indian nationals by DM, Bhuj.

**Himachal Pradesh.** Lahaul and Spiti and the district of Kinnaur are restricted areas for which entry permits are granted to a group of 4 or above, sponsored by a travel agency for a fixed itinerary. These permits are issued by Deputy Commissioner, Shimla, Kullup, Keylong and Rampur.

**Lakshadweep.** Only the island of Bangaram (which had no habitation) is open to foreign tourists. Permits are issued by Foreigners' Regional Registration officers. For domestic tourists, entry permits and travel arrangements are handled by the Commissioners Office in New Delhi.

**Manipur.** Foreign nationals require an inner line permit from the Deputy Secretary, Ministry of Home Affairs, Government of India, Lok Nayak Bhawan, Khan Market, New Delhi.

**Meghalaya.** Foreigners intending to travel in groups of 4 or more can obtain restricted area permits from Meghalaya House at Delhi, Bombay and Calcutta.

**Mizoram.** Mizoram is a restricted area for foreign tourists. Permits may be obtained from the Deputy Secretary, Ministry of Home Affairs. Indian citizens can obtain inner line permits from Resident Commissioner of Mizoram at Delhi, Calcutta, Bombay and Chennai.

**Nagaland.** Foreigners cannot enter without a special permit which can be obtained from the Deputy Secretary, Ministry of Home Affairs.

**Sikkim.** Foreigners can get permit for Gangtok, Rumtek, Penayangtfe and Thodong from Sikkim Tourist Information Centre at Delhi, Kolkata and Siliguri.

**Tripura.** Tripura is a restricted area. Foreign tourists visiting Tripura are required to obtain a permit from the Deputy Secretary, Ministry of Home Affairs.

**Uttar Pradesh.** Foreigners must have permission from the Government of India to enter the Tehsil Dharchola and Tehsil Muspari areas near the border of Tibet.

**West Bengal.** Parts of Sunderbans area are restricted for tourists. Conducted tours by West Bengal Tourism Authorities require no prior permission.

### 3. Customs Regulations

The usual duty-free regulations of one bottle of liquor and 200 cigarettes apply for India. If the tourist brings in more than $ 1,000 in cash or in traveller's cheques, it must be declared. A tourist can clear goods upto Rs. 2,400 in value duty free. Goods brought in excess of this are chargeable to duty as per prevailing law.

### 4. Economic Regulations

The inbound as well as outbound tourist is subject to the following economic regulations:

*(a) Currency*

Tourists are not allowed to bring Indian currency into the country or take it out of the country. However, there is no restriction on the amount of foreign currency or travellers cheques that may be brought into India. On arrival, visitors should declare all foreign currency above $1,000. They are supposed to exchange currency only at banks and through authorized dealers.

With each exchange of currency, they are issued an exchange certificate which should be retained to re-exchange unused rupees on leaving the country. It is also their proof that they exchanged currency through legal channels. The foreign tourist must not exchange currency in black-market. Foreigners are not allowed to leave India with any local currency. For their convenience, banks at international airports are open 24 hours daily to convert unused rupees.

*(b) Income Tax*

If a person not domiciled in India intends to stay in the country for more than 120 days, an Income Tax Clearance Certificate is required in order to leave the country. This document will prove that the person's stay in India was financed by his own money and not by working or selling his goods.

The foreign sections of the Income Tax Department at Delhi, Kolkata, Chennai and Mumbai issue these certificates on the basis of the person's passport, visa and currency exchange receipts which have been used by the person.

*(c) Foreign Travel Tax*

For international travel from Indian airports Rs. 150 must be paid for travel to neighbouring countries and Rs. 300 for travel to all other countries.

## VIVID BENEFITS OF TOURISM INDUSTRY

As an industry the impact of tourism is manifold. Tourism industry nourishes a country's economy, stimulates development process and restores the cultural heritage. This industry enjoys a major advantage over other industries that of having a unique product which might differ from state to state. For example, Goa is renowned for its sunny beaches and colonial charms, palaces which are reminders of princely era.

Tourism works on the system in following ways:

### Tourism Earns Foreign Exchange

During the 1960's great emphasis was placed on tourism as a source of foreign exchange earner. Tourism is the one industry that earns foreign exchange for country without exhausting natural resources and without actually exporting any material goods.

The income from tourism has tended to increase at a higher rate than merchandise export in a number of countries. There is now almost a continuous flow of income from richer countries to the not-so richer and developing ones, raising the latter's export earnings and rate of economic growth. For example in countries like India and Spain, tourism is the single largest earner of foreign exchange. According to official Spanish sources, in 1981 there were more visitor arrivals in Spain (40 million) than the actual population of the country (36 million). Tourism is thus the most important source of income for many countries.

### Tourism Helps in the Development of Infrastructural Facilities

Development and improvement of infrastructure facilities is another important benefit offered by the tourism industry. Infrastructural facilities such as airport, roads, water supply and other public utilities may be widely shared by the other sectors of the economy.

Development of new infrastructure and improvement in the existing infrastructure may confer benefits upon the resident population which they may have not enjoyed otherwise. Furthermore the provision of infrastructure may provide the basis or serve as an encouragement for greater economic diversification. A variety of secondary industries may be promoted which may not serve the needs of tourism.

Thus, indirectly, tourist expenditure may be responsible for stimulating other economic activities of a country.

## Tourism Helps in the Balanced Regional Development of a Country

Tourism development greatly benefits the underdeveloped regions of a country. These economically backward regions mostly have places of high scenic beauty, which if developed for the tourism industry, will help to bring a lot of prosperity to the local people. Money spent by tourist helps to improve the health of every business in that region. For example, road constructed for use by tourists provides local people access to the market centres as well.

Earlier, there were many backward areas but due to tourism development, these places got international recognition. For example, Khajuraho, a few years back was considered a remote and unknown small village, but today, it is an internationally famous tourist place of interest and also generates employment to hundreds of local people in hotels, restaurants, travel agencies, handicraft shops etc. Without tourism development Khajuraho would have remained a remote and unknown village till today.

## Tourism Helps in Generating Employment

Tourism industry is a highly labour intensive service industry that generates employment for highly skilled, semi-skilled and unskilled labours in sectors like hotels, restaurants, travel agencies, tourism offices, shops etc. One additional room in a hotel helps at least 8 to 9 people in getting jobs. Not only that, tourism creates employment outside the industry as well, for example the basic infrastructure like roads, airport, water supply etc. provided by construction industry creates jobs for thousands of both skilled and unskilled workers.

## Tourism Helps in Preserving Cultural Heritage

Tourism remains basically a cultural phenomena. Tourism has always stood as a unique vehicle for cultural promotion. In the past, travel was based on cultural interest. Even today large number of people travel to foreign countries to know about their culture and tradition. Tourism indirectly preserves environment by discouraging large scale industrialisation in places where natural beauty has to be kept intact. It thus, helps a country to restore its ancient monuments and archaeological treasures. Most of the developing countries which possess an ancient civilization can benefit greatly from tourism. Tourists visiting these countries have a great urge to become acquainted with ancient civilizations.

As a result of cultural shopping, which forms an important part of any tourist itinerary, local handicraft is still surviving. Tourism has also given a new lease of life to the traditional customs, costumes, festivals and dances which generates employment for the weaker section in the remote areas of the country.

Hence, tourism can contribute unique benefits to a nation by exploring its cultural heritage and can serve indirectly to improve the individual cultural levels of both national and foreign tourists.

### Tourism Helps in Maintaining International Peace and Understanding

Tourism plays an important role in promoting international goodwill. It creates awareness and appreciation of other countries' culture and tradition and makes possible cultural exchange and enrichment. Tourism can be a vehicle for international understanding by way of bringing diverse people from different cultures and traditions face to face. The best way of getting to know another country is to go there and when vast number of people travel, the prejudices, barriers and suspicions that exists between different countries breakdown the narrow, rigid boundaries that keep people away from each other, naturally tend to shrink and a positive move towards better international understanding begins to operate. Tourism can greatly enrich and promote friendship between different countries in the world.

Tourism, thus, develops not only the economic condition of a country by earning foreign exchange for it, but also plays a vital role in its social, cultural and regional development and in promoting goodwill and friendship among all nations of the World.

## HOW TO STIMULATE TOURISM IN INDIA

To a large number of people across the world, India is a land of their dreams—exotic, mysterious, full of colour, pomp and pageantry. But that is not enough to attract more tourists to India unless the Government adopts a dynamic, pragmatic and realistic policy.

The cost of travel to a country is one of the major factors determining the share that the country can secure of future world tourist trade as tourists are becoming conscious of "good value for money". Any country wishing to expand its share of the tourist trade needs to make a realistic assessment of the future cost of travel from the main market.

India is a long way from its main sources of tourism. This disadvantage can be neutralised by reducing air fare. Fares should be maintained at as low as a level is economically possible to encourage tourists to visit as many parts of the country as possible. Compared to other countries, India is a relatively inexpensive country to tour.

Second, crime is a great deterrent to the promotion of tourism in the country. As a result of disturbances in Punjab, particularly after the assassination of Mrs. Indira Gandhi, there was a big slump in tourist arrivals. The tourists from UK, USA and Japan are hesitant to come to India because they are not sure that our law and order machinery is strong enough to render them protection. The former Minister of State for Tourism and Civil Aviation, Mr. Ashok Gehlot admitted that there had been a decline in foreign tourist arrivals from July 1984 to May 1985 due to disturbances in the country and the adverse media publicity abroad.

Measures should be taken to create confidence among prospective tourists like reassurance, press campaign by the overseas offices of the tourist department and the Indian High Commission and invitation to foreign travel agents and media persons to visit at government expense to have first-hand information on the normal conditions in the country.

Third, the proportion of outlays on tourism in most developing countries is very low. In our Sixth Plan it is 0.90 per cent of the total outlay; in the Fifth Plan it was only 0.16 per cent. In the Seventh and Eighth Plans share of this sector should be further increased as done in 2003-04.

Fourth, it is widely believed that a country cannot promote international tourism unless its domestic tourism has attained a high level of development. Many Western countries adopted this approach successfully in the post-war era. In the Ninth Plan the

Central Government has laid much more emphasis on domestic tourism than in the past.

Fifth, tourism is not free from evil sides. Rapid and uncontrolled development of tourist facilities can be a factor contributing to inflation by driving up real estate prices, fostering land speculation and creating excessive demand on construction and other industries supplying tourism. Government policy must be such as to counteract such undesirable development.

Sixth, visa and other travel formalities should be simplified to obviate harassment to the tourists. It is happy to note that due to persistent demand by both the media and the travel agents, the Home Minister has agreed to relax the visa restrictions to tourists travelling in groups and to businessmen.

Seventh, there is a vast scope for attracting ethnic tourists, *e.g.*, people of Indian origin living in Indonesia, Fiji, West Indies, Africa etc. With proper promotional efforts, we can tap this new source of international tourism.

India has undoubtedly made substantial progress in promoting tourism since independence. However, we have a long way to go before we achieve our target, *i.e.*, our due share of the huge international tourists traffic. This is a challenging task and it is necessary for the public sector and the private sector to mobilise all available resources to meet the challenge.

## FUTURE PROSPECTS OF TOURISM

Tourism has developed to a level where it has become a major industry, a major force for social change and a major power for good, for evil.

The world is in a period of rapid transition; the traditional tourist generating countries are moving from an industrial stage to becoming post-industrial societies. With this change, lifestyles and values are also changing; the old desire to accumulate material possessions shows signs of abating; this will result in a new desire to accumulate experience as avidly as we formerly collected possessions. This changing lifestyle will influence consumers' demand for travel.

The following variables will shape tourism in the future.

### Demographic and Social Trends

Future demographic and social trends will influence tourism

demand to the year 2000 and beyond. Demographic trends, such as ageing populations in the major generating countries and the declining number of young people, are particularly important. Demographic trends are mixed up with the social trends which lead to late marriage, couples having children in later life and increased number of single child and childless-couple households.

In the Third World, growing labour force will lead to immigration to the developed world and the growth of knowledge and interest in other countries will see a convergence of lifestyles worldwide. With increased level of education, these trends will give people more time, resources and inclination to travel. This will be encouraged by the growth and spread of discretionary incomes and the liberalisation of trade on an international scale. It is beneficial for tourism in India.

## Political Developments

In the late 1980s we saw a change of the political map of the world, and this has a number of implications for tourism. The fall of communism has led to expansion of tourism because huge numbers thronged to see the outside world. The emergence of market economy in eastern Europe and the opening of the borders will pave the way for East European countries to participate more fully in travel movements, particularly to western countries. Already Hungary has become a leading international destination for tourism and other parts of Eastern Europe will become important destinations as travel restrictions are eased. It will benefit tourism in India.

## Transportation Development

Tourism is highly dependent upon transport technology and the consequent improvements in efficiency and safety of travel.

Although it is generally accepted that total deregulation of the international airline industry is not practical, the trend towards deregulation will continue in 1990s in Europe. In the US deregulation has led to domination by a small number of larger airlines—a trend which is emerging in other sectors of the tourism industry.

Forecasts of international transport over the next 10 years predict that technological developments, increased airline efficiency and labour productivity savings will offset any rises in aviation fuel prices and thus fares will continue to fall. This will support the continued trend towards long haul travel. P.M. Atal Bihari Bajpai's project of development of road transport in India will benefit tourism in India.

Despite the focus on air transport, most tourism journeys are by car. Continued development of highway network, developments of car technology and improved fuel efficiency will all make motoring more cheaper and more attractive.

It is believed that by the year 2005 there will be gradual switch away from air to surface transport.

## Other Factors

There are other variables which also influence the future of tourism. These include the changing value systems of the consumers as well as global warming. The raising of the earth's temperature and the consequent rise in sea level will affect tourism to India's advantage because we are adopting environment friendly approach.

Human behaviour too is a threat to tourism as the spread of AIDS may render some otherwise attractive destinations no-go areas; increasing incidence of skin cancer may reverse the fashion for a suntan; and disease in some parts of the world decreasing levels of safety will constrain the uninhabited expansion of tourism. Since we are trying India disease free to stimulate tourism in India.

Advances in computer reservations will allow individual holiday-makers to select their destinations, accommodation and flights, put together their own packages, book and pay for the booking by direct debit to their bank account, all without leaving their armchair. The ability to book from home would suggest a rise in impulse booking, coupled with a decline in traditional patterns of advance booking. If consumers can package their own holidays at home at the push of a button, it could make the task of operator and travel agent redundant. We are progressing very well in this area, therefore, tourism will benefit from it in future.

Some futurologists have predicted that there will be no need to travel away from home in the twenty-first century. Holographs are capable of reproducing an environment artificially, so that we will be able to recreate in the home any environment of our choosing in order to 'experience' foreign travel.

QUESTIONS FOR ANSWER

1. *Discuss India's resource potentials for tourism.*
2. *Give a brief history of tourism in India through ages.*
3. *Describe in brief Indian Government's efforts to promote tourism between 1945 and 1967.*
4. *Give details of the organization of the Ministry of Tourism in India and its working to promote tourism in India.*
5. *Write a note on 'Tourism as an Industry' and its benefit to the society.*
6. *Write a note on tourism regulations in India.*
7. *Write an essay on measures to stimulate tourism in India.*
8. *Discuss vivid benefits of tourism industry in developing national economy and international understanding.*
9. *Write an essay on future of tourism in India.*

# 10

# Role of Human Resource Management in Tourism

## INTRODUCTION

Organisations exist for people. They are made of people and by the people and their effectiveness depends on the behaviour and performance of the people constituting them. Interestingly, people are considered as a resource and as asset rather than a liability. Social obligations, legal aspects and trade union pressures are actively shaping the environment. The environmental trends in terms of five principal environmental aspects viz. economic, demographic, socio-cultural, politico-legal and technological are important variables for shaping the present personnel environment.

Today, there is a growing awareness of the importance of the human side of organisations as a vital factor in overall progress. There is no doubt that people, not science and technology, will determine the future. It is to be noted that preparing for personnel management has been considered more a process of osmosis.

Education, training facilities and practices have been highly fragmented. The growth of unionism, state intervention through a spate of legislation and code of practices, the stress on statutory welfare, and need for broader and consistent policies in large and complex organisations made it easy for personnel specialists to expand their role and enhance their status.

Importantly, with advances in the information technology, the personnel specialists are now increasingly using computers for information system management and resource planning. It is rightly remarked by Michael Riley that every industry thinks it is unique and, in a very real sense, each industry is right.

Interestingly, managerial task running a hotel, restaurant or institutional establishment can be seen as a set of systems and processes common to managing anything.

Interestingly, all managers have direct responsibility for the human assets in an organisation and are responsible for activities and decisions concerning personnel. Still most organisations have a separate personnel department whose main job is to coordinate all personnel activities. There is need for a close interaction between the personnel department which has the responsibility for the administration of personnel and line managers who have responsibility for optimizing the use of their resources, viz., physical, financial and human. The personnel department is then required to maintain personnel information systems and comply with government's legal regulatory framework and union management agreements. Moreover, top management expects personnel specialists to devise ways and means for better utilization of human resources.

It expects them to develop cost effective means to help maintain rightly motivated satisfied and productive human resources. Personnel policy is a statement of what the organisation wishes to do with regard to its employees in order to meet its objectives. It is a general guide to decision-making. The decisions may concern recruitment, promotions, transfers, appraisal, training, pay, benefits, leave and several other aspects. There is need for consistency and uniformity in all these matters in the interest of both the individual employee and the organisation. The policy should clearly state the purpose, and a procedure for implementation. The procedure should indicate:

1. Who has the authority to implement policy;
2. Whether and who has the discretion;
3. The flow of paper work in connection with action; and
4. Records to be maintained for monitoring and control.

## HUMAN RESOURCE MANAGEMENT IN TOURISM DEVELOPMENT

Tourism may be termed as product and also services. Thus, marketing of tourism destinations may be termed as tourism product while facilities related to tourism may be termed as services. In this sector man power involvement is needed and management of man power particularly analysing and designing job, job enrichment, human resource planning, recruitment, training and retention, performance appraisal, working/job environment, industrial relations, employees participation in management etc. are quite relevant in tourism perspective.

## Analysing and Designing Job

Job analysis involves formal study of jobs. It attempts to provide information on both the requirements of a job in terms of time completion, necessary activities and the expected performance standards on the one hand, and also the specific technical and behavioural knowledge, skill and attitudes needed among the personnel to meet those job requirements on the other.

A brief reference of motivation is called for to analyse the job satisfaction, job performance and job enrichment. Maslow has categorized human needs as follows:

1. A need for self acteralization (personal growth);
2. A need for self esteem;
3. A need to belong and be loved;
4. A need for safety and security;
5. A need for food, drink, health, sleep (physiological need).

He argues that these needs emerge as motivations in the hierarchy as listed above so that as the need below is satisfied, the next need emerges as a motivation capable of being fulfilled. Maslow's theory belongs to a humanistic school of thought which is optimistic in its view of human life and which is concerned with human potential.

We need some extra money for family, we might seek part time work or seek an organisation that offers pay for part time work. The basis of our need is for money and convenience. Therefore, motivation stimulation related to these two aspects may be the basis of our performance. In the hotel and catering labour markets a majority of people work as unskilled and therefore have a wide range of unskilled and probably mundane jobs to choose from.

Importantly, the first task of the team is to identify what the knowledge skill and ability are in respect of job analysis. They would come up with something like;

**I. Knowledge**

1. The legal position;

2. The insurance position, including assessment rules;
3. Rules on credit and procedures;
4. Current reservation situation.

**II. Skill**

1. To analyse situations into information collection area,
2. To be able to devise a set of alternative strategies based on The information collected,
3. Tto be able to think through and anticipated client reactions,
4. Personnel assertiveness,
5. Recording formally what is required.

**III. Ability**

1. A general ability to confront difficult social relations.
2. The degree of ability to understand the assigned work/ job and perform effectively.
3. The ability of performing responsibilities.

## MAN POWER PLANNING

Of the three Ms of management—Man, money and material—it is man who is at the centre of the organization. In this light, personnel administration is that part of management which is concerned with people at work and with their relationship within an enterprise. The emphasis is to transform a manpower into human resource. A human resource may be described as the sum total of inherent abilities, acquired knowledge and skills, represented by the talent and attitudes of employees.

Manpower planning, therefore, is concerned with "organising, in systematic fashion, the goals, objectives, priorities and activities of Manpower Development in order to ensure that the right number of staff with the appropriate skills are provided at the right time to meet the requirements of the work to be done.

Manpower planning, thus, is a dynamic process as planning is amenable to modification, review and adjustments in accordance with the needs of an organisation and on the changing circumstances.

Thus the process of manpower planning is one of the most crucial, complex and continuing managerial function which "embraces organisational development, career planning and succession planning". In brief, this process includes various issues such as:

1. Deciding goals and objectives;
2. Estimating future organisational structure and manpower requirements;
3. Auditing human resources;
4. Planning job requirements and job descriptions; and
5. Developing a human resource plan.

The basic objective of manpower planning is to have the right people properly trained and motivated, available for the right jobs. The day-to-day benefits to be derived from fairly straight forward manpower planning are:

1. Determination of recruiting needs;
2. Anticipation of surplus to be corrected by natural shortages rather than redundancies or dismissal;
3. Indication of future training needs;
4. Provision of a basis for management development programme;
5. A factor in industrial relations and productivity bargaining;
6. Monitoring of labour costs;
7. Indication of staff facilities required; and
8. Identification of critical or shortage areas where particular skills or experience will be missing. This is essentially important in business diversification and the introduction of new technologies.

Thus, the objectives of manpower planning are to fulfil individual, organisational and national goals but its ultimate mission or purpose is to relate future human resources to further enterprise needs so as to maximise the future returns on investment in human resources.

Manpower management starts with manpower planning, for which it is necessary to forecast the manpower needs. This is first done by studying three types of forecasts:

1. Economic forecast;
2. Company's sales and expansion forecast; and
3. Employee market forecast.

Such forecasts result in the company's organisational plans. A combination of the forecasts and the plans can result in anticipating the manpower needs.

In terms of this, the staffing function has to be performed by personnel department. It involves recruitment and selection either from outside sources or could include promotion and transfer from within the organisation. The provision of an appropriate organisational climate includes consideration of adequate leadership styles and motivation, with which is connected, the question of wages and salary administration or compensation plans incorporation appropriate incentives. Proper communication is also essential, for the maximum performance.

Further training too should be provided for the existing employees for future promotions. A manpower skills inventory must also be maintained, of the types of skills available presently. Also adequate developmental facilities should be provided for fully utilising the existing potential of the employees.

According to Gordon McBath, "Manpower planning involves two stages: the first one is concerned with the detailed planning of manpower requirements for all types and levels of the employees throughout the period of the plan and the second stage is concerned with the planning of manpower supplies to provide the organisation with the right types of people from all sources to meet the planned requirements. It involves following four steps:

1. Anticipating manpower needs;
2. Planning job requirements and description;
3. Analysing skills, to determine the nature of the manpower needed; and
4. Selecting adequate sources of recruitment.

If the manpower skills inventory is supplemented with the appraisal of the existing performances and assessment of future potential to indicate training and developmental plans for future promotions, the organisation can ensure retention of its best people by securing optimum motivation.

To determine the requirement of personnel, the four methods generally used are:

1. Annual estimation of vacancies;
2. Long-run estimate of vacancies;
3. Fixed minimum man specification requirements; and
4. Specific power estimation.

Manpower planning can basically be done by observing the three steps (*a*) determination of the period for forecasting requirement of manpower and (*b*) from the numbers available at the commencement of the period, deduct the expected wastage through discharges, retirements etc. (*c*) a comparison of the figures arrived at in steps one and two, would indicate shortage or surplus of personnel. The shortage filling procedure could be through fresh recruitment or promotions or through training and developmental facility while the surplus can be dealt with through discharge early retirements, lay-offs etc.

Also, the job analysis has to be made to secure the relevant information for job information and description. The skills required in different jobs must be analysed in terms of job description followed by job analysis.

The steps required in recruitment are generally as under:

1. After job analysis, preparing job description and man specification;
2. Determining the source of recruitment;
3. Conducting the interviews;
4. Putting the applicant through the necessary tests;
5. Checking the responses;
6. Conducting the medical examination of applicant where necessary; and
7. The final selection interview with the applicant ultimately selected.

Planning creates a favourable psychological climate for motivation and helps in identifying the weaknesses of existing manpower so that creative training could be incorporated. Better developmental power results in a relative reduction in the manpower cost. However, manpower planning is a double edged weapon which, if used properly, leads to the maximum utilisation of human resources; reduces excessive labour turnover and high absenteeism, improves productivity and aids in achieving the organisational objective but if faultily used, it leads to disruption in the flow of work, lower production, less job satisfaction, high cost of production, and constant headaches for the management.

**Performance Appraisal**

Everyone wants to know how they are getting on its natural. Therefore, feedback becomes part of the interaction between the subordinate and the superior knowing 'where you stand' and 'if you are on the right lines' are part of every day work and, as such informal appraisal is continuous and part of daily life. An appraisal system attempts to ensure some continuity of purpose by checking the validity of individual goals in terms of organisation goals. An appraisal system can promote effectiveness, job satisfication and better manpower utilization.

Therefore, it is necessary for organisations to development performance analysis and review systems which:

1. Define the specific job criteria against which performance will be measured;
2. Objectively and accurately measure past job performance;
3. Determine rewards based on performance; and
4. Develop programmes to enhance performance on the current job and prepare and also realize the potential for future responsibilities.

The objectives of performance appraisal could be either for evaluation or development. The evaluation objectives include:

1. Provision of feed back to subordinates to know where they stand; and
2. Developing valid data for personnel decisions concerning placement, performance appraisal, promotion, punishment, etc.

The developmental objectives include:

1. Diagnosing individual and organisational strengths and weaknesses;
2. Counselling, coaching, career planning and motivation of subordinates, and developing positive superior subordinate relations. Thus, performance appraisal system can be put to several uses covering the entire spectrum of personnel/human resource functions in an organisation. The illustrative list of uses of performance appraisal to promote a variety of management objectives include:
   (*a*) Systematic efforts to tone up performance based on performance results, appropriate feedback and corrective actions;
   (*b*) Input for an array of personnel decisions such as placement, transfer, promotion and rewards;

(*c*) To identity individuals with high potential;
(*d*) To develop career and development needs;
(*e*) To take decisions on termination;
(*f*) Human resource planning;
(*g*) For diagnosing individual and organisational problems; and
(*h*) To validate selection and recruitment tests and procedures.

By seeking effective use of the performance appraisal system, an organisation may seek to:

1. Improve productivity,
2. Promote internal control through timely detection and feedback on actual performance,
3. Create a positive work environment,
4. Stimulate, recognize and reward achievements,
5. Provide objective measures of performance, and
6. Furnish information for other human resource sub-systems.

**Training and Development**

The effectiveness of career planning in an organisation system will largely depend on the extent to which training and development opportunities are made available to employees to enable them to realize their growth potential and to make contributions towards achievement of organisational objectives.

Training and development activities are the main mechanisms through which individual's goals and aspirations can be integrated with organizational goals and requirements. Such an integration can be achieved only when training and development efforts are linked with the organizational requirements and they are carried out in a systematic manner throughout the organization.

Thus the first phase in the planning process is the identification of specific training and development needs which involves (*i*) organizational analysis,: (*a*) analysis of objectives; (*b*) resource utilization analysis; (*c*) environmental scanning; (*d*) organizational climate analysis; (*ii*) task/role analysis; (*iii*) man power analysis.

**Working Conditions**

Industrialization has brought in its make a reluctant respect for environment. The people in many societies are exposed to certain health hazards. Moreover, workers, employees and staff are very often exposed to additional risks of environmental pollution, occupational diseases and injuries.

These aspects of industrial life, once ignored by employers as a necessary by-product of industrialization, are now being addressed by governments, employers, employees and their unions, besides a host of other public and industrial organisations. Thus working conditions are closely associated with work efficiency and performance. If working conditions are conducive and welfare measures for workers/employees are ensured then productivity will be higher, ensuring high efficiency and employment stability, working conditions include all aspects of work; physical, social, economic, technical, legal and human.

**Grievances and Dispute Management**

Despite the significance of healthy employee relations, there are occasions in the life of every organisations when relationships are strained, particularly between the management and the individual employee. The management has certain expectations of the employees in terms of standards of behaviour and performance, code of conduct, desirable actions and behaviour which are made known to the employees through formal or informal, within or verbal means. Failure to these expectations or deviations from the laid down norms of behaviour on the part of the employees leads the management to initiate action to ensure that an employee's behaviour is in conformity with their expectations.

Similarly, these employees also have certain expectations of the management in terms of their conditions of service, working environment, satisfaction of their variety of needs, freedom of expression and operation, and equitable, just and fair treatment which are often made known to the management through various means of upward communication. Failure on the part of the management to meet those expectations leads to what is called employee grievance. The grievances may relate to:

(*i*) *Promotions*

- (*a*) Supercession,
- (*b*) Acting from others,
- (*c*) Seniority, and
- (*d*) Pay fixation.

*(ii) Compensation*

(*a*) Increments,
(*b*) Payment, and
(*c*) Recovery of dues.

*(iii) Amenities*

(*a*) Inequitable distribution,
(*b*) Entitlement, and
(*c*) Medical benefits.

*(iv) Service Matters*

(*a*) Transfers,
(*b*) Continuity of service, and
(*c*) Superannuation.

*(v) Disciplinary Action*

(*a*) Punishment,
(*b*) Fines, and
(*c*) Victimization.

*(vi) Nature of Job*

(*a*) Job allocation.

*(vii) Conditions of Work*

(*a*) Safety, and
(*b*) Hazards.

*(viii) Leave*

Since hotel and catering industry has a reputation for high levels of labour turnover, diagnosis of the problem related to grievances and stress should be ensured for organisational development and smooth functioning of organisations. The grievances may be caused due to arbitrary behaviour of supervisors and managers; induction crisis and distribution of efforts and rewards. Similarly causes of stress may be related to:

*(i) Extra Organisational*

(*a*) Fast pace of social and technological change,
(*b*) Economic and financial conditions, including inflationary pressures,

(*c*) Code system, ethnic identity, minority issues,
(*d*) Family demands and social obligations, and
(*e*) Relocation and transfers.

*(ii) Organisational*

(*a*) Unfair policies, arbitrary performance reviews, inequity in pay, rigid rules and ambiguous procedures, frequent transfers necessitating relocation;
(*b*) Structures: Centralization and formalization, lack of involvement in decision making, little opportunity for career advancement, high degree of specialization, inter-departmental conflict; live staff conflict; and
(*c*) Processes: poor communication, inadequate feedback on performance, ambiguous and conflict goals, unfair control systems, inadequate information,

*(iii) Group*

(*a*) Lack of group cohesiveness,
(*b*) Lack of social support, and
(*c*) Interpersonal and intergroup conflict.

*(iv) Job Related*

(*a*) Unrealistic job description,
(*b*) Crowding and lack of privacy,
(*c*) Excessive noise, heat or dust,
(*d*) Safety hazards,
(*e*) Routine nature of job, and
(*f*) Presence of toxic materials.

*(v) Individual*

(*a*) Personality characteristics, and
(*b*) Life and career change, management has to handle stress through creating a supportive organization climate, job redesigning and role clarity. Moreover, career planning and individual counselling.

There is concern about the following aspects which have implications for personal/human resources in an environment marked by changes in tourism sector. These implications can be well understood in the context of rapid changes in technologies, changes in employee profile, competition, globalization, growth of services economy, customer oriented marketing, total quality management demand for employment stability and social security and phenomenon of working non-employees (domestic workers, outsourcing etc.).

In the changed context the linkage between HRD and industrial relations needs to be properly appreciated and recognized and trade unions should be actively involved. HRD efforts should not be construed as management strategies to weak the employees away from the union. Therefore, human resource policies should focus on:

(*i*) Horizontal human resource management policies based on trust, openness, equity, consent and consensus than those based on hierarchical control and direction,

(*ii*) Build stake and say for people at all levels in jobs and organizations;

(*iii*) Development objectives performance review and management system;

(*iv*) Restructuring reward systems that are contingent on performance and sustain motivation, and

(*v*) Information storing, grievance redressal and participation.

It may be concluded that HRM perspective in tourism industry has significance since marketing of tourism services as well as destinations require satisfaction of tourists and tourists oriented approach for development of infrastructure and services.

## QUESTIONS FOR ANSWER

1. *Write a note on the significance of human resource management in tourism.*
2. *Discuss the concept of analysing and designing job in tourism industry.*
3. *Write short notes on the following:*
   (*a*) *Man Power Planning.*
   (*b*) *Training and Development.*
   (*c*) *Grievances and Dispute Management.*

# 11

# Tourism and Transportation

Travel developed from the human need to service, desire to expand and the quest to conquer, thus driving forces behind the development of tourism were curiosity about the world to satisfy his desire for knowledge and needs and to escape the stresses of urban life.

## HISTORY OF TRANSPORT AND TOURISM

Tourism involves the movement of people. As a consequence, the relationship between transportation and tourism is a very important aspect of tourism studies. In most cases, tourism has developed in those areas where extensive transportation networks are available. Transportation may be defined as the means to reach the destination and also the means of movement at the destination.

Tourism demand has stimulated the rapid development of transportation. As bulks of tourism expect to be transported safely, quickly and comfortably to their destinations at a reasonable cost.

Transport may be public or private, inland or international and air or surface. In recent years, the fastest means of long distance tourist transport has been the aircraft. By contrast shipping has come to play a more prominent role on sea routes and waterways. Rail represents short and medium distance transport within and between countries. Road transport by bus or car provides regular direct route services for short and medium distances to the destination.

There are four major modes of tourist transport automobile, rail, ship and aircraft.

Tourist's choice of mode of transport is affected by the following factors:

1. Distance and time factor,
2. Status and comfort,
3. Safety and utility,
4. Comparative price of services offered,
5. Geographical position and isolation,
6. Range of services offered, and
7. Level of competition between services.

## ROAD TRANSPORT—THE AUTOMOBILE

Road transport is dominat .d by the automobiles. Car is the most perfect means for providing door-to-door service, providing views of the landscape and a means of transporting recreational equipment.

Development of automobile allowed the freedom to travel. Improvements in road transport facilities stimulated tourism in many European countries. Great progress has been made in the USA by building highways, expressways and superhighways.

Conformable motels on the highways made travel by car easy and exciting. The possibility of taking the entire family on the trip made it a very attractive tourist transport. The development of 'motorail' the carrying of cars and coaches over long distances by train is making it possible for tourists to use their motor cars in holiday areas.

The introduction of the automobile has led to the demise of the train in most developed countries. The emergence of the automobile has spread the benefits of tourism more widely and has provided more and more people with the means to travel individually or in small groups. The automobile has brought about a more random pattern of travel movements, has opened up new destinations and has stimulated the development of new automobile oriented facilities and services along highways and roads.

Car rentals and recreation vehicle (or RV) spurred the development of travel by car. RVs offer the opportunity to combine driving and camping. Camping has become very popular in North America. The USA has more than 14,000 public and private parks and camp grounds.

Road transport has a number of attractions for tourists:

1. The control of the route and the stops en route.
2. The ability of carrying baggage and equipment easily.

3. The ability to use the vehicle for accommodation.
4. Privacy.
5. Low expenses.

## RAIL TRANSPORT

The invention of the railroad in Germany in the seventeenth century revolutionized transportation. The first railroad used wooden tracks. It was not until the early 1800s that the first steel rails appeared in USA.

With the age of the train the mass movement of people began. Thomas Cook is quoted as saying that his planned tours added much to the advancement of human progress. The railways is the most convenient and the most popular mode of travel all over the world.

The railways may be considered as the most powerful means for mass travel in the nineteenth and twentieth centuries. Trains are perceived to be safe and inexpensive. They may also provide view to attractive scenery like the toy train between Siliguri and Darjeeling.

In India, railways provides the principal mode of transportation for freight and passengers. It brings together people from the farthest corners of the country and makes possible the conduct of business, sightseeing, pilgrimage and education.

High speed trains are running in different parts of the world. In 1981, France started operation of its train which runs at a speed of 380 kilometre per hour, even faster than the Japanese Bullet Train which runs at a speed of 225 kilometre per hour. The day is not far off when aerotrains will be introduced which will run at a speed of 480 to 500 kilometre per hour.

The railways systems of six European nations have been integrated to make rail travel convenient for the people of Europe. One can buy a Eurail pass for a specially discounted travel bargain for a week. Indian Railways have introduced Indrail passes on the lines of Eurail pass. The pass has to be bought in foreign currency and only foreigners and non-resident Indians can buy it. The Indrail pass permits unlimited travel, so long as the pass remains valid. To attract foreign tourists, Indian Railways have introduced a new train called the Palace on Wheels.

Although in the USA, trains are considered a second rate means of passenger transportation, in western Europe and in India, trains hold a valuable market share of passenger traffic.

## Indian Railways

Sir Arnold Toynbee, the noted historian of the age, has rightly declared that the twentieth century will be remembered in history not for its wars and atom bombs but for having been the first stage, since the dawn of civilization, in which it became practicable to make the benefits of civilization available to the whole human race. The industrial Revolution heralded the modern age. The greatest contribution of Industrial revolution was the steam engine—the railways which has transformed the society, changed the face of the earth and dynamited the economy. Without railways renaissance would not have taken place in India. India would have remained as backward as Afghanistan, a country without railways.

The first public railways was opened between Stockton and Darlington in northern England in 1825 and railways became the fastest and most popular form of transport for both passengers and goods during the nineteenth century.

The growth of the railways was brought about by two interrelated factors. First, the stream engine was developed and applied not only to industry but also to transport. Secondly, the rapid rise of industry made it necessary to improve existing transport systems.

Indian Railways is the nation's lifeline and the principal mode of transport in the country. From a modest beginning in April 1853, when the first railway train steamed off from Mumbai to Thane, a stretch of 34 kilometre, the Indian Railways, with about a route 5 kilometrage of 65,000 has now grown into Asia's largest and the world's fourth largest railway system. It is also the biggest public undertaking in the country. The electrified route length has increased by more than 30 times since 1950-51. In other words, the story of Indian Railways is a story of continued success, advancement and achievement.

Railway travel is important in any country, but in a vast geographical landmass like India, it is a *sine qua non* of economic development. In such a vast country where distances and immobility can prove to be major deterrents to economic growth, such growth hinges on the national transport network.

Indian subcontinent is a vast landmass—it is aptly called an epitome of the world. Here people live with different religions, different languages and different cultures. But when we look at the cultural history of India, we find that in spite of multifarious differences, there is a basic unity in the thinking, feeling and living of Indians. Several times have the forces of disintegration threatened to shatter this unity but India's spirit of oneness has always reasserted itself and has blended opposing tendencies and movements into a new harmonious culture. To discover the spirit of India, one has to travel from north to south, from east to west. This is possible only by a journey by train.

The development of railways has had great effects on the mobility of people as well as goods. The availability of cheap transport greatly affects the mobility of labour. It allows far more people to work and trade in a town than actually live there. The development of railway transport has also been the basis for development of a completely new industry—tourism—which relies on the ability of people to move rapidly and easily from place to place. The development of railways has played a very important part in the diffusion of ideas.

More people are thus able to take advantage of advances of science and knowledge, learn about the ways of life and ideas of other people and gain a far greater understanding of India—their homeland-than was possible at any time in the past, which is applicable to tourist as well.

The political stability of India and its economy are greatly assisted by a good railway network. Brisk internal trade and links with overseas markets encourage the development of agriculture and industry. A well developed railway system and communication is vital to the establishment of political control, national unity and an efficient central administration.

India is a rich country inhabitated by the poor people. Poor people need cheap transport. Railways provides cheap transport. For long journeys, railways is still the best form of freight transport. Apart from its importance as freight carrier, railways play a very important role in passenger transport. It is by far the most efficient form of transport for commuters who have to come into large cities each day, because they do not contribute to traffic jams on the roads.

Underground trains (we already have such trains in Kolkata) too, are ideal for city transport because they take up little valuable space on the surface and can carry huge numbers of people from place to place at regular time intervals. Commuter trains are very important in Kolkata, Mumbai and Delhi. They carry thousands of people each day helping them to earn their livelihood.

The importance of railways also depends to a large extent on the availability of other forms of passenger transport. In India where roads are poor and proportion of people owning cars is small, rail transport is still vital for passenger transport. More people in our country travel by train than by any other means of transport.

Technology is a great agent of social change. Railways as an improved transport technology has brought revolutionary changes in Indian society. Every technological advance makes it possible for man to attain certain results with less efforts or at less costs; at the same time it provides new opportunities and established new conditions of life. As a modern technology, railways have changed the way of life of a large number of people.

Railways is an agent for urbanisation. Urbanisation is a process of transforming rural into urban areas. This process has a tremendous effect on the economic composition and to a proportionate rise in the urban population. It also develops new social attitudes and social institutions for the purposes of community living. The urban dweller supports itself mainly by manufacture and trade which flourish on specialisations. As a result, the city has brought together people of different castes, religions and languages from different parts of the country. Cities like Kolkata, Mumbai, Chennai and Delhi have attracted the ambitious and energetic elements of all caste groups.

The urban life is highly competitive in nature. Hence the role of city dweller in social life is not deeply fixed. In the big cities the so-called 'untouchables' are permitted to engage in occupation above their degree. The caste system is incompatible with the rationality, mobility, the educational system and the needs of a democratic society. Under the impact of railways and industrialisation, the caste system is weakening.

Urbanisation has also improved the social position of women. The city is becoming more and more a place of opportunity for women in outside activities. The changing functions of the family which the city encourages have been of a peculiar significance to women, in her role as mother, wife, housekeeper and economic producer. Her tasks have been limited and she has been greatly liberated from the exclusiveness of domesticity.

If one endeavours to discover the economic side of the railways one will be simply charmed by its impressive performance. Apart from the biggest employer in the country, railways provides the most important economic infrastructure of the national economy as it determines the qualitative character of economic development. Infrastructure does not produce economic goods for direct consumption but is essential for meaningful economic development.

Cheap and easy transport as provided by the railways is the most important condition of economic growth in a big country like India. In shuck a country where distances and mobility can prove to be major deterrents to economic growth, the rate of such growth hinges on the national transport network.

It is widely accepted that railways plays an important role in the smooth functioning of the economy. Without railways it would be virtually impossible for modern process of production and distribution to function.

Thus railway transport plays a crucial role in all developing economies, especially in a country like India, primarily for the extension of market, transportation of raw materials and finished goods, opening up of remote areas and bringing about the advantage of economic growth to the poor people of rural and other handicapped regions.

The role and significance of railway transport in the economy is exceedingly important on many considerations—historical, economic, environment, social and political. The network has always monitored the trend of development:

(*i*) Historically, because railways have provided the foundation for communications, trade and commerce and national defence;

(*ii*) Economically, as the network plays a major role in opening up the hinterland and widening the markets;

(*iii*) Environmentally, by being largely instrumental in the relative levels of ecological and environmental pollution;

(*iv*) Socially, by determining the trends of urbanization, population shifts the levels of employment; and

(*v*) Politically, as railways are vital to national defence and social security.

Railways have done away with the evils of casteism, untouchability and superstition. The destruction of casteism and other social evils have also influenced changes in values—changes in attitudes, beliefs, and habits. The getting together of people from different places and exchanging ideas would tone up the social makeup of the people. Cheap and quick railway transport is of great importance for a vast country like India with heterogeneous people, long frontiers and large coast lines. Railways helps people in their political integration. Even administrative homogeneity has become possible due to mobility of people made possible by transport facilities. Defending the country during war and keeping vigil on its frontiers in peace require all types of transport in general and railways in particular.

Railways help in bringing different regions of the economy 'close' to one another. This helps in the process of social integration of these regions as well as national integration. In the context of developing economies like that of India, this function of railways is very important.

It is railways which has helped us to discover that we, Indians, are all members of one growing human family and must stand and fall together.

As John Donne has put it, no man is an island, and the link between man and man has been established and isolation removed by the railways. Railways helps us discover our identity, our ancient history and culture, our unity, our very soul. The story of railways is really the story of modern India. The rails in India have no substitute. They are part and parcel of our existence.

## SEA TRANSPORT

Travel by ship was the only means to travel overseas till the middle of the twentieth century. We can broadly divide water borne transport into short sea ferry transport and ocean going cruises. Ferry transportation is the only option in the case of remote and small islands which have no airport. In Greece, there are only 15 airports to serve 95 islands.

Shipping made significant contribution to travel during the nineteenth century. Regular steamship services started playing on the North Atlantic from 1838. Opening of the Suez Canal in 1869 shortened the route between the East and the West and in turn stimulated better steamship service. The period just before the First World War can be considered the golden age for liner passenger service. By the 60s, passenger ships were losing ground to airlines till these vanished as passenger transport by the 70s. Some large ships have since been converted into luxury liners offering holidays to travellers who have money and time.

Water transport today plays two main roles in travel and tourism—ferrying and cruising.

The introduction of commercial airline led to the decline of the use of ships as a passenger transportation mode. Cruising has taken the place of scheduled liner services.

Modern vessels such as the wave-piercing catamaran, the hydrofoil and the hovercraft have been introduced on some short distance routes. There is a 40-minute hydrofoil service between Copenhagen (Denmark) and Malmo (Sweden). Hydrofoils have been introduced to connect some of the Hawaiians islands and also Hong Kong and Macau. The new fast jet foils cross 40 miles of sea between Hong Kong and Macau in 50 minutes. The speed of these new sea crafts is up to three times that of a conventional ferry, they can turn around quickly in port and need minimum dock facilities. In 1991 more than 3 million people took cruise holidays world wide.

### Indian Shipping

Overseas shipping has an extremely important role to play in India's international trade. The country has the largest merchant shipping fleet among developing countries and ranks seventeenth in the world in shipping tonnage. In 1995, the operative tonnage consisted 460 vessels totalling to 6.85 million GRT.

There were 71 shipping companies in the country in operation in 1995 including the Shipping Corporation of India, a public sector undertaking. Of these, 39 are engaged exclusively in coastal and overseas trade. Shipping Corporation of India which is the biggest shipping line of the country, has a merchant fleet of 124 vessels of 31 lakhs GRT and operates on almost all maritime routes. Shipping Corporation of India's tonnage accounts for about 49 per cent of the total Indian tonnage. We are trying our best to develop our shipping industry for greater national good.

## AIR TRAVEL

The aeroplane had a revolutionary impact on tourism from World War II onwards. The modern era can be termed the mass air travel era. The growth of air travel has been one of the most important socio-economic phenomena of the post-War period. Currently, some 400 million passengers are carried by scheduled international airlines and this figure is expected to double before the end of 2010.

Air travel is the most popular mode of tourist transport, for international travel. Air travel is attractive because of its speed and range and also because, for business visitors, it offers status as well as saves valuable work time when travelling on a long-haul basis. Air transport comprises both scheduled and chartered categories and in some parts of the world, air taxies.

In the development of international tourism, air transport has played the most important role. The multi billion dollar airlines industry has a very humble beginning. In Europe, in the sixteenth and seventeenth centuries one dare not think of flight because the Church considered it to be against the Laws of God.

The beginning of the jet travel in 1958 was the most dramatic event which gave a new dimension of speed, comfort and efficiency to air travel. The North Atlantic route—the golden route of tourist traffic—saw the introduction of excursion fares in 1948, family fares in 1955, economy class fares in 1967 affinity group fares in 1963; group inclusive tour fares in 1967, youth fares in 1972 and apex fares in 1975. Despite rising fuel costs, as a result of these innovations in air travel, fares actually declined.

International air travel is regulated by International Air Transport Association (IATA) with its head office in Montreal in Canada. It was established in 1945. IATA has 105 major airlines of the world as its members. IATA regulates the prices of air tickets in different areas of travel in the world. All international air fares are decided by the IATA but domestic fare are the concern of the respective governments. The air fares are determined on different considerations like the volume and traffic demand in an area, level of competition, etc. For example, the air fares between Europe and America are lower in terms of mileage compared to the same distance between London and Delhi. It is simply because the volume of traffic on the London-Delhi route is not as high as on the London-New York route.

There are two types of airlines—scheduled and chartered. Scheduled airlines are so called because they fly according to regular schedules. The non-scheduled airlines are called charter airlines. The charter flight operates only when there is a demand.

Airlines may be classified into two broad categories. Small careers that operate aircraft with fewer than 30 seats are defined as commuter airlines. Larger careers that fly direct routes between major cities are called major airlines.

To attract more passengers, airlines are offering cheaper promotional fares. Excursion fares and group fares are examples of such promotional fares.

Excursion fares are provided to the tourists on the basis of return journey and have conditions of minimum and maximum stay at the destination. The passenger must spend at least 10 days in the country where he is going. Restriction is applied to dissuade business executive who normally visits a country for three to four days but excursion fare involves a minimum stay of ten days, hence the businessman cannot avail the cheap excursion fare.

Group fares are applicable to groups and are discounted by 20 to 40 per cent. Hence again the restriction is that at least 10 persons must travel together on the same itinerary. Computerised Reservation System (CRS) is a development which has revolutionized airlines marketing.

The future of air travel is bright. It is highly probable that the number of air journeys made will increase substantially. Forecasts point to a market size before the end of the century, roughly double what it was in 1995 and that will double by 2005.

Secondly, it is likely that the industry will be less regulated, leading to more intense competition between airlines.

Thirdly, the consumer will become even more demanding both as a consequence of competition giving a greater choice and also from greater familiarity as the experience of air travel becomes steadily more widespread. The line diagram below shows the air traffic growth.

## CIVIL AVIATION IN INDIA

Civil aviation sector has two functional divisions—operational and infrastructural. On the operational side, Indian Airlines, Vayudoot and private air taxies provide domestic air services. Air India provides international air service. Pawan Hans provides helicopter services to ONGC in its share operations and to inaccessible areas and difficult terrains. Indian Airlines operations also extend to the neighbouring countries, South-East Asia and the Middle East.

Vayudoot Limited has merged with Indian Airlines. India is a member of International Civil Aviation Organisation (ICAO). There are, at present, six private scheduled airlines operating on the domestic network. Apart from this, fifteen air taxi operators are providing non-scheduled air services.

The charter flights bringing foreign tourists in the country are now allowed to operate to certain domestic airports cleared for tourist charter operations in addition to the international airports. The minimum payment to the Indian tour operator by the foreign charter operators 350 US dollars per person for a seven day package for the period from 1 October to 31 March and 300 US dollars for the period from 1 April to 30 September. However, for tourists from SAARC countries, the amount to be remitted is 50 per cent of the aforesaid amount.

Air taxi services can be operated as non-scheduled flights both on chartered and non-chartered basis to 93 airports in the country open to civil operations. The air taxi operators are free to charge any fare in their own commercial judgment.

The Airports Authority of India manages 92 civil airports and 28 civil air terminals as defence airfields in the country. It controls and manages the entire Indian airspace extending even beyond the territorial limits of the country, as accepted by the International Civil Aviation Organisation.

India has bilateral air services agreements with 74 countries. Air India Limited is the major international carrier of the country. It operates services to USA, Canada, Europe, Russian, Confederation, Middle East, East Asia, Far East, Africa, Australia. Air India owns a fleet of twenty six aircrafts consisting of nine B747-200, two B747-400, three A-300-B4 and eight A-310-300 aircrafts. During 1993-94, Air India carried 19,77,668 passengers.

Indian Airlines is the major domestic air carrier of the country. It also provides services to 11 countries, viz., Pakistan, Maldives, Nepal, Sri Lanka, Malaysia, Bangladesh, Thailand, Singapore, UAE, Oman and Kuwait. Its operations cover 66 destinations including 14 abroad. The Airlines owns a fleet of ten Airbus A-300, thirty Airbus A-320, an eighteen Boeing B-737 and two F-27. Presently six private scheduled airlines and fifteen air taxi operators are supplementing the air transport services provided by Indian Airlines on the domestic sector.

## QUESTIONS FOR ANSWER

1. *'Transport is the most vital element of tourism.' Discuss.*
2. *Discuss the role of railway transport in the development of tourism.*
3. *'Air travel has revolutionary impact on international tourism'. Discuss.*
4. *Write short notes on the following:*
   *(a)* *Role of road transport in tourism.*
   *(b)* *Role of sea transport in the development of tourism and international trade.*
   *(c)* *Civil Aviation in India.*

# 12

# The Role of Travel Agencies

## INTRODUCTION

Travel agencies are the basic ingredients of tourism industry, therefore, it is said that tourism revolves around travel agencies and tour operators. Travel agency is the private sector organisation which plays a vital and crucial role in the promotion of tourism, because in some countries 70 per cent international and 50 per cent domestic is organised by them. The important role of the travel agent in the present world is summarised in the *Principles of Professional Conduct and Ethics* of the American Society of Travel Agents (ASTA) as follows: "We live in a world in which travel has become both increasingly important and complex in its variety of modes and choices. Travellers are faced with a myriad of alternatives as to transportation, accommodation and other travel services. They must depend on travel agencies and others in the industry to guide them honestly and competently."

Travel agency business mostly functions in the private sector. The role of the private sector in organization of travel is therefore very crucial. In most countries, which are in any manner concerned with the tourist industry, the private sector plays a very important role. The private sector's role is not limited merely in selling the tourism product but often also in producing it as many individuals, companies and corporations are involved in promoting, developing and financing tourism. It is the travel agent who packages and processes all the various attraction of the country and sells these to the tourists. In addition, he also sells individual elements of the travel.

## BRIEF HISTORY OF TRAVEL AGENCIES

### Thomas Cook and the Organization of Travel

The organization and sale of travel, as it is known today, really began in July 1841. A book salesman-cum-Baptist preacher of

Derbyshire was on his way to a temperance meeting in Leicester when he was inspired with "the idea of engaging a special train to carry the friends of temperance from Leicester to Loughborough in England and back to attend a quarterly delegate meeting." He thought that it was a sounder proposition to persuade a railway company to carry a trainload of passengers at a very cheap fare than to run the train at 'Standard' fares, but possibly only a quarter full.

Thomas Cook's idea was put into operation with characteristic speed and efficiency. A few weeks later 570 travellers made the journey by the Midland Countries Railway at a specially reduced fare. This venture was soon followed by excursions to various other places, and in 1843, 3,000 school children were taken on a trip from Leicester to Derby in England.

Thomas Cook's real beginning as a 'mass excursionist' however was the Liverpool-Caernaryon trip of 1845. The tourists travelled by rail to Liverpool, from where they took a steamer to Caernaryon. The advertisement for the trip caused a sensation and the response was so overwhelming that a second trip had to be arranged. Cook thought of every detail. He made a preliminary survey of accommodation and facilities and produced a *Handbook of the Trip to Liverpool*. The excursionist's invasion of Scotland soon followed in 1846 and 1847.

From 1848 to 1863 Cook conducted circular tours of Scotland, with 5,000 tourists a season. With the citadels of the landed aristocracy falling before him it was no wonder that a man of Cook's humble origins saw ever and more enticing prospects opening before him: "I had become so thoroughly imbued with the Tourist spirit that I began to contemplate Foreign Trips, including the continent of Europe, the United States and the Eastern lands of the Bible."

### The Grand Circular Tour

By the mid-nineteenth century holidays away from home had become customary for a larger social group than ever before. Cook's initiative and organizing genius provided the final impetus. In the winter of 1850-51 Cook was offered the opportunity of conducting excursion trains to the Great Exhibition of 1851. Altogether, Cook conducted 1,65,000 people to and from the Crystal Place. In 1856 he succeeded in organizing his first 'grand circular tour of the continent.' The tour was so successful that it had to be repeated six weeks later.

Cook's conquest of Europe began in 1862 when he made arrangement with Brighton and South Coast Railway for passenger traffic to the continent. His Paris excursions are the first true 'package tours' in that all the details of transport and accommodation were pre-arranged. In 1863 Cook visited Switzerland where his ideas were greeted with enthusiasm by hoteliers and railway proprietors. His next stop was Italy. Cook first made a personal survey of Turin, Milan, Florence and Genoa, to familiarise himself with their touristic attractions and facilities.

### Hotel Coupons

The 1860s also saw the introduction of Cook's railway and hotel coupons. Cook personally examined the system by travelling through Italy to Vienna, down the Danube into Hungary and from there into Switzerland. By the 1890s, 1,200 hotels throughout the world accepted his coupons. Starting in 1868 Cook arranged regular circular tours of Switzerland and Northern Italy.

Thomas Cook and Son had established their first official London office in 1865. John Mason Cook now joined his father as a permanent partner and took charge of the London office. In the year 1880 John Mason Cook left for India and established offices in Bombay (Mumbai) and Calcutta (Kolkata) and formed the Eastern Princes Department. In 1887 this department arranged the visits of Indian princes to Queen Victoria's jubilee celebrations. By the end of the century, taking advantage of nineteenth-century advances in transport technology Thomas Cook and Son had effected a revolution in tourism and tourism was now an industry. Armed with Cook's hotel and rail coupons, the tourist could demand uniform prices and standards of service and accommodation. This new standardization had distinct advantages. It meant comfort and convenience and less need for decision making on the part of the individual tourist. The tourist was less likely to experience discomfort or embarrassment.

The management of the company passed on to John Mason Cook's three sons in 1898. At the time of John Cook's death, the Cooks business included three main aspects of travel—selling tours, banking and shipping. Soon after the Second World War, the British government acquired the principal interest in the company. In 1972, the British government sold the company to Midland Bank Consortium. Much has happened since that date. The business of the company has now expanded a great deal with about 1,000 offices around the world having about 14,000 employees.

**The American Express Company**

By an interesting coincidence, the two largest worldwide travel agents, Thomas Cook and Son and the American Express Company, may be said to have had their origins in the same year—1841. While Thomas Cook persuaded a railway company to carry a train load of passengers at very cheap fares in the year, Henry Wells started his freight business in the USA at the same time. Henry Wells commenced his business initially as a shipper who later began the well-known company of America known as Wells-Fargo.

The American Express Company, popularly known as Amex, is the World's largest travel agency. It was an offshoot of Wells-Fargo Company. Besides selling tours, the company deals in travellers' cheques. Amex is a major participant in international currency transactions, buying and selling huge amount in foreign currency on each working day. The company has also introduced American Express credit cards. These cards are very popular all over the world and the holder can pay his hotel bills, buy an international air ticket and many more things from places where these are accepted.

Above details deserve following observation:

It is a chance coincidence that the two large world-wide travel agents, Thomas Cook & Sons Ltd. and the American Express Company, have their origins in the same year 1841. Thomas Cook invented the hotel coupon in 1867 and the American Express invented the travellers' cheque in 1891.

The American Express Company, popularly Known as AMEXO, is the world's second largest travel agency after Thomas Cook & Sons. The AMEXO has introduced the credit card system. These cards are very popular all over the world and the holder of the card can buy anything against the card without having to pay cash.

The shops, hotels or airlines company accepting a credit card are immediately paid cash by the credit card company's local office after deducting 3 per cent commission. The company then raises a bill against the credit card holder which has to be paid in ninety days. Since the Indian rupee is not a convertible currency, or banks cannot issue international credit cards, but we too have rupee credit cards like the Diners Club card. Most Indian hotels and many shops dealing with foreign tourists accept international credit cards.

## INTRODUCTION OF AIR TRAVEL

However, it was the introduction of the air travel which boosted up the travel agency business. Holiday travel by air became cheaper than travel by sea. The introduction of 'economy class' on aeroplanes crossing the North Atlantic introduced a new age of travel agency and was responsible for its spectacular growth. In the early 50s, there were 3,000 travel agency offices all over the world, the number increased to 55,000 by 1991 and now it is nearing 70,000.

When the civil airlines evolved, the responsibility of selling tickets was taken by the retail travel agents. The retail travel agent must be distinguished from the tour operator. These two functions are often performed by the same company. A retail travel agent is one who acts on behalf of a principal *i.e.*, the original provider of tourist services, such as a hotel company, an airlines, a shipping company or a tour operator. The retail travel agent sells the principals' services and is rewarded by a commission on sale. But he undertakes no liability for the principals' services.

On the other hand, the tour operator buys the individual elements in the travel product on his own account and combines them in such a way that he is selling a package of travel, the tour, to his clients. He is remunerated by a mark-up on the prices he has period to the providers of the services which make up the package. The retail travel agent is just a retailer while the tour operator is a manufacturer of a particular travel product.

## FUNCTIONS OF A MODERN TRAVEL AGENCY

The functions of a modern travel agency have widened much after the introduction of air travel. The most important functions of a travel agency are described below:

### 1. Travel Information

A retail travel agency provides necessary travel information to the general public. The intending tourists come to the office of the travel agent and seek information regarding their proposed visit. The travel agent should be a very knowledgeable man and should supply upto date and concrete information relating to travel. He must have great communication skill and he should be thorough in the art of catching the potential customers. The knowledge of foreign language is a desirable qualification for those working in a travel agency.

### 2. Preparation of Itineraries

A tourist journey involves preparation of different types of itineraries. There are different means of transport with their respective advantages and disadvantages. A travel agent advises the potential tourist to choose the most convenient course.

### 3. Liaison with Providers of Service

A travel agent should maintain constant contact with the providers of various services like the transport companies, hotel managers and providers of surface transport like motor cars from airport to hotel and for sightseeing etc.

*Planning and Costing Tours*

The contracts and arrangements having been entered into, there comes the task of planning and costing tours, both for inclusive programmes and to meet individual requirements. This job is intensely interesting and at the same time challenging. This job calls for a great deal of initiative and drive. The job calls for travel to those places which are to be included in the itineraries.

This is essentially a job for a meticulously minded person and calls for considerable training and ability. Many agencies with the cooperation of airlines and other transportation companies take the opportunity of arranging educational tours for such staff to countries with which they deal.

Many agencies have people who are authorities on particular countries and, in addition to a general programme, many will issue separate programmes dealing with territories. Separate programmes dealing with holiday offers based on specific forms of transportation, *e.g.*, air, rail, road or sea, may also be prepared. Programmes also have to be issued to cover different seasons of the year.

Publicity is an important part of the programme. Having spent considerable time and money on preparing all that goes into the issue of a programme, publicity must feature considerably in the activities of a travel agency and more so if the agency happens to be a large one. The majority of large travel agencies have their own publicity departments under the management of a publicity expert.

### 4. Ticketing

Selling tickets to tourists for different modes of transport like air, rail and sea is a very important function of a travel agent. Ticketing is not an easy job as the range of international air fares is very complex. Computerised Reservation System (CRS) has revolutionised the reservation system both for air and train tickets and also a room in a hotel.

### 5. Provision of Foreign Currencies

Provision of foreign currency to an intending foreign tourist is an important function of a travel agent. The Government of India allows an Indian traveller going abroad 10,000 US $. The travel agent will arrange for the purchase of foreign exchange on behalf of his intending travellers. This facility will save a lot of time and harassment for the intending tourists.

### 6. Insurance

Insurance for personal accident risks and risk for loss of baggage is an important function of a travel agent.

The idea of buying a package of travel, accommodation and perhaps some ancillary services such as entertainment, became established in western Europe in the 1960s. By 1970, tour operation had become a full-fledged part of tourism. Its growth was spectacular. It succeeded in reducing the real price of travel abroad, in doing this, it brought holidays abroad to a segment of the market not reached by conventional methods of taking a holiday. Today in most countries which are generators of tourism, tour operation is the dominating feature of the holiday market.

An inclusive tour is a package of transport and accommodation and perhaps some other services which are sold as a single holiday for a single all-inclusive price. The popular term, 'package holiday' describes the nature of a tour more accurately than the term 'inclusive tour'. The original demand for inclusive arrangements came from the convenience of buying a single travel product.

## RETAIL TRAVEL AGENT

The retail travel agent provides a convenient location where the intending tourist may seek information about his travel plans and then a location where he may purchase the various travel products he needs. The retail travel agent also normally provides ancillary travel services such as obtaining travellers' cheques, foreign exchange, passport and visa.

The retail travel agent buys neither the seat nor the bed nor the tour from the principals until he has a customer standing at his counter. He relieves the principal of the need to open his own sales outlets over a wide area.

The functions of the travel agent are to provide information, to provide access to the principals stock via the reservation systems and to facilitate travel arrangements by providing various ancillary services.

Travel agents are not the only retailers of travel products. Airlines and tour operators possess a number of retail outlets too. Shipping companies have done likewise and the individual hotels of international hotel chains are acting as agents.

Only those agents who possess a principal's appointment or licence are eligible for commission on sales of the principal's tickets. Since 50 per cent of a travel agent's turnover arises from airlines ticket sales, the possession of an IATA licence is important.

A travel agent's sources of income are as follow:

1. Commission on the sales he makes of his principal's services.
2. Commission earned from ancillary services, such as travel insurance and charges made for such services as traveller's cheques.
3. Income earned from short-term investment of money received from his customers as deposits.

4. Profits from the sale of his own tours if he operates as a tour operator.

There are four main types of retail Travel agency:

1. *Business House Agency*: Catering mainly for the travel need of commercial and industrial firms. Such agencies incur high staff and office costs since they are located near their clients in city centres.
2. *City Centre Agents*: Located in or near to main shopping centres, they need a high turnover to justify city centre costs.
3. *Country Town Agencies*: This type is most profitable with a mix of business and holiday traffic.
4. *Suburban Agencies*: Selling principally tours with a markedly seasonal pattern of business.

The buying decisions of consumers are founded increasingly on the advertising campaigns and on the elaborate brochures of tour operators and other principals.

Many large industrial and commercial companies own retail travel agencies within their group. The sale of travel through large hotel chains or banks as in Australia seems a distinct possibility. In Germany, the main order selling of tours has proved successful.

## HOW DOES TRAVEL AGENCY ORGANIZE TRAVEL

There are various steps involved from the time a traveller visits a travel agent to buy a ticket until he returns back home after visiting a place of his choice. The various steps involved in organizing a travel are discussed in the following paragraphs.

Organized travel by a travel agency can be of two types: (*i*) single client (*ii*) group client. In order to effect the journey, the following main elements (in both types of travel) need to be considered: study of the journey, estimate of expenditure, execution of the journey and presentation of accounts.

### Individual or Ordinary Trips

The following steps are involved in organizing individual or ordinary trips:

(*i*) The client turns to the travel agent to organize for him a particular journey (cultural, natural, religious, etc.).

(*ii*) The agency from this angle will examine as to what will be involved, *e.g.*, scope of journey, when the journey is to take place, various services needed and the accessories required.

(*iii*) Based on the above evaluation and other elements in his possession, the travel agent will suggest the itinerary and will then communicate to the client the estimated maximum cost, for the client's approval.

(*iv*) Travel agent will then compile the definite estimates, a total of a series of various costs added up, *e.g.*, transport, accommodation, the services such as those of guides, operative costs (postage, telegrams, telephone, etc.).

(*v*) Next, the travel agent will present a document in duplicate to the customer of the amount of money to be paid. The client should return one of the debit copies signed for acceptance accompanied by a deposit (in anticipation). The deposit normally is about 25 per cent of the total cost.

(*vi*) Once the client's approval has been obtained, the travel agent's 'operation' department can now execute the journey.

(*vii*) The 'operation' department's task now is to book for the established dates the transport and various other services. After confirmations of booking have been received, the travel agent issues the vouchers.

(*viii*) The travel agent will now prepare the 'tourist itinerary' that will accompany the client through the entire journey. It will indicate the tickets to be used, the hotels and other services booked and will include vouchers, etc. Normally the itinerary is made in triplicate, one for the client, another for the agency and the third for the hotelier or those who will provide the required services paid by means of vouchers.

(*ix*) The last formality is the delivery to the client of the vouchers, confirmed tickets, the technical itinerary and of all the papers and the necessary guidance about the journey.

(*x*) On receiving the documents, the client will pay to the agency the remaining amount of money.

## Group or Organized Trips

The following steps are involved in organizing groups or organized trips:

(*i*) This type of travel is customarily arranged by the travel agent after establishing the estimated number of participants.

(*ii*) Groups travel can be a request from an enterprise (company) or a community and in this case the travel agent should be able to determine in advance the number of participants.

(*iii*) Even in a group travel, the implementation phases can be identified as (*a*) study of itinerary, (*b*) compiling of estimates, (*c*) execution of the journey, (*d*) documentation of accounts.

(*iv*) For the preparation of the itinerary it is necessary to know the type of locality to be visited, means of transport and type of hotel, etc., to be used. An important element regarding group travel is the itinerary planning.

(*v*) Group travel can also be arranged for certain events, *e.g.*, the Olympic Games, and in this case, there will be a need for launching a certain type of publicity campaign.

(*vi*) While compiling estimates, the travel agent needs to evaluate various services to be offered (accommodation, entertainment's, cost of messages, etc.).

(*vii*) For hotel bookings, the travel agent uses various means. During 'low season', he uses the allotment system: the hotelier pledges to hold at the disposition of the travel agent a certain number of beds that he will utilize and for which he need not pay a penalty if he is unable to fill them.

(*viii*) Once the consent has been received, the travel agent will send to the hotel or hotels a tentative rooming list giving names and various types of arrangements needed. Only at the time of group departure, the travel agent transmits a confirmed rooming list to the hotel with last-minute variations, if any.

(*ix*) When the group is particularly large, *e.g.*, for sports the travel agent needs to take extra care by way of informing public authorities for the purposes of security, etc.

The activities and range of services described above are very wide and comprehensive and are covered by the travel agents in a highly developed market. The role and the activities of the travel agents in any country depend on the extent of economic development of that country. The services of travel agents are increasingly utilized in developed countries. In some of the advanced countries like USA, Canada and Germany, a very large percentage of tourists use the services of a travel agent.

## INCLUSIVE TOURS BY CHARTER (ITC)

Although, at first, the term charter implied a single purchaser, in the present case of air travel organiser, its use does not necessarily preclude the air travel organizer selling the chartered capacity to the public. By doing so, he offers to the public a genuine alternative to a scheduled service. If he combines the transport and accommodation elements into a single package, he becomes an inclusive tour operator. The inclusive tour is sold to the public at a single price so that the prices of the component elements cannot be identified by the public.

This form of package, mainly for holiday purposes, has transformed tourism in Europe and the Mediterranean basin. By chartering aircraft and by making long-term contracts for accommodation with the resort hotels, the tour operator is able to price a package holiday at a lower level than could be achieved by any form of scheduled service.

## INCLUSIVE TOURISM ON SCHEDULED SERVICES (ITX)

The Scheduled airlines reached to the growth of chartered traffic by devising fares which were available only to travel agents for combination with accommodation into an inclusive tour, such tours using scheduled services being conveniently designated ITX. In operating scheduled services, load factors rarely exceeded 60 per cent and the incremental cost of carrying passengers beyond existing loads would be small. ITX operations could fill up seats which would otherwise be flown empty. This practice involves an element of discrimination for the businessman paying the full fare as against a holiday maker who has paid a fraction of the full fare.

In 1973, a new form of organised travel was introduced—the

Advance Booking Charter (ABC). This enabled the travel organizer to sell tickets for the chartered aircraft to the public.

## TRAVEL AGENCIES—ACTIVITIES IN BRIEF

Looking at the various activities mentioned above, it is clear that the travel agent's range of services in modern times has expanded a great deal. His field of expertise is quite large and is constantly growing with the fast-changing travel needs of the people. The job description of a modern travel agent was summed up in an American magazine in the following words:

(*i*) Preparation of individual, pre-planned itineraries, personally escorted tours and group tours and sale of prepared package tours.

(*ii*) Making arrangements for hotels, motels, resort accommodation, meals, car rentals, sightseeing, transfer of passengers and luggage between terminals and hotels, and special features such as music, festivals and theatre tickets.

(*iii*) Handing of and advising on the many details involved in modern-day travel, *e.g.*, travel and baggage insurance, language study material, travellers' cheques, foreign currency exchange, documentary requirements (visas and passport) and health requirements (immunization and inoculations).

(*iv*) Possession of professional knowledge and experience, as for instance, schedules of train connections, rates of hotels, their quality, whether rooms have baths, etc. All of this is the information on which the traveller, but for the travel agent, will spend days or weeks of phone calls, letters and personal visits.

(*v*) Arrangements of reservations for special interest activities such as religious pilgrimages, conventions and business meetings and sports events.

### Source of Income

The travel agency's source of income is the commission which it receives from various sources. He is also remunerated from certain other sources like; (*i*) commission on the sales he makes of his principal's service (the main principals include an airline, a hotel company, a shipping company and a tour operator); (*ii*) commission earned from ancillary services such as travel insurance and charges made for such services as travellers' cheques; (*iii*) income earned from the short-term investment of money received from his customers and deposits and advance payments; and (*iv*) profit from the sale of his own tours if he operators as a tour operator.

## TRAVEL ORGANIZATIONS

### The American Society of Travel Agents, Inc. (ASTA)

The American Society of Travel Agents (ASTA) is the leading professional society of travel agents in the industry. The world's largest professional travel trade association, ASTA was established in New York in 1931. Originally named the American Steamship and Tourist Agent's Association, its present name was adopted in 1944. The society was set up to foster programmes for the advancement of the travel agency industry, promote ethical practices and provide a public forum for travel agents. It has now over 25,000 members and is the only organization representing all segments of the travel industry. The membership consists of travel agents, carriers, hotels, etc.

#### *Purpose*

The purpose of ASTA is the promotion and advancement of the interests of the travel agency industry and the safeguarding of the travelling public against fraud, misrepresentation and other unethical practices. The society maintains legal representation and also a government affairs office in Washington, D.C. to provide direct contact with the federal government and the regulatory agencies in the travel and transportation field, and to protect the legitimate interests of travel agents.

ASTA's services to travel agents also benefit the general public. Such activities include sponsorship of frequent conferences on travel matters, involving airlines, steamship companies, agents, municipal and government officials, and other interested parties; discussions with airlines on fare structures and travel destinations; research studies into traveller preferences; close cooperation with various city, state and government agencies across the country in travel-oriented matters; and assistance to all agencies across the country in travel-oriented matters; and assistance to all levels of government consumerism departments in upgrading standards of service to travellers.

*World Travel Congress*

The year's foremost meeting place is the ASTA World Travel Congress. The Congress is the single most important meeting held annually in the travel industry and the programme includes workshops, seminars, business meetings, film presentations and social events. Members from throughout the world travel industry participate, give talks, lead discussion groups and conduct sessions.

The ASTA World Travel Congress has been the platform for launching many important and beneficial education programmes for agents. The Madrid Congress granted for Travel Hall of Fame awards, an honour given to those whose careers have made long-standing impacts on the development and expansion of the travel industry and tourism.

The Society consists of the following departments policy implementation and administration, industry relations, memberships relations and communications. The members of the Society derive various advantages which include education and training. ASTA has a comprehensive list of travel courses.

*Structure*

ASTA has 28 chapters in the United States of America and Canada and another 28 chapters overseas. Each chapter has elected officers and appointed committees. There is a National Board of Directors which establishes policies of the society. Every two years a new President and Chairman of the Board are elected by active members. Day-to-day activities of the society are looked after by a professional staff which works under the guidance of an executive Vice-President who, in fact, is the Chief Operating Officer of the Society. He makes recommendations on policy matters to the Board and Executive. He directs the headquarter staff in providing a broad programme of services and facilities to ASTA's membership and carrying on the day-to-day business of the society. ASTA world headquarters is located at 711 Fifth Avenue in New York city, USA.

## Universal Federation of Travel Agents Association (UFTAA)

Universal Federation of Travel Agents Association is an important organization of the travel agents on a worldwide basis. The federation was founded in Rome in November, 1966.

The aims of the federation are as follows:

(*i*) To act as the negotiating body with the various branches of tourism and travel industries on behalf of travel agents and in the interest of the public.

(*ii*) To ensure for all travel agents, through their national associations, the maximum degree of cohesion and understanding, prestige and public recognition, advancement of member's interest and protection from legislation and from other legal points of view.

(*iii*) To offer its members all the necessary material, professional and technical advice and assistance to enable them to take their proper place in the economy of world tourism.

The federation consists of the national travel agency association of over 84 countries which in turn represents more than 20,000 travel agencies from all over the world. The membership of the federation is split into nine regions each covering a group of countries. The UFTAA headquarters is located in Brussels, Belgium.

## IATA MEMBERSHIP (INTERNATIONAL AIR TRANSPORT ASSOCIATION)

An IATA appointed travel agency is reliable because it has the approval of international organization. The agencies which are not IATA members may not be reliable because they purchase tickets from the general sales agent of airlines and resell them to their clients sharing a part of the commission. Their margin of profit is so small that they cannot provide good service to the clients. If a travel agency is not approved by IATA, it cannot get commission directly from an international airlines. Most IATA approved travel agents in India are also members of a national organization called Travel Agents' Association of India (TAAI).

TAAI has its head office in Mumbai and it has seven branches in major cities of India. It has over 300 members. The objective of

TAAI is to protect the legitimate interests of the professional travel agency members. The National Committee on Tourism set up by the Government of India stresses the importance of travel agencies in marketing Indian tourism overseas. The Government of India has recognized the vital role played by the travel agencies in the development of tourism in the country.

SITA. The most important component of tourism industry is the travel agency. Students International Travel Association of (SITA) is a leading travel agency.

The SITA, a leader in conducted passage tours to all parts of the world had its genesis in a student's bicycle joint. In 1933, Jack Dangler formed the Students International Travel Association in New York. Under its auspices a group of nine students went for a European tour on bicycles. In 1936, a proper office was opened in New York. It was named SITA. Soon Dangler opened a travel bureau—SITA World Travels Inc.

After expansion in US the first overseas office was opened in London in 1955. Extensive training programme was mooted for personnel to manage SITA offices. Among these was Mr. Inder Sharma (present Chairman of SITA World Travel India Pvt. Ltd.) who returned to India and set up a small office in New Delhi in 1956.

Only three people manned the office and in the first year they handled 8 groups of American tourists. Soon branches were opened in Mumbai and Kolkata. In 1963, SITA was converted into an Indian Private Limited Company though Jack Dangler was still the Chairman and a major shareholder. The participating capital was provided by Mr. Inder Sharma. The same year SITA grew from a small tour operator into a full-fledged travel agency.

In 1970, Dangler sold his entire shareholding in the company to Indian shareholders. However, SITA continues having association with SITA offices world over enjoys their confidence. SITA India is a Member of the WATA (World Association of Travel Agencies). Over the years marketing offices were opened in Paris, Milan and Frankfurt. Besides, local representatives were appointed in London, Tokyo and Stockholm. Today SITA has a team 900 trained professionals with offices in 25 cities in India and 7 overseas offices.

## TRAVEL AGENCIES IN INDIA

As long back as in the year 1954, the Government of India was aware of the important role which the travel agents were to play in the development of tourism. It was recognised by the Government that tourists who visit a foreign country often prefer to secure the services of travel agents who assist them in order to make best use of time and money at their disposal. The government felt that many a time unauthorised persons offer themselves as agents and in return fail to render satisfactory services, and even exploit the ignorance of the tourists for their personal benefit. With a view to curb this the government evolved a system of granting recognition to travel agents. The rules for recognition were as follows:

(*i*) No firm shall be granted recognition unless it has been engaged actively in handling tourist traffic for at least one year before the date of the application.

(*ii*) Firms granted recognition shall be entitled to such right and privileges as may be granted by the government from time to time and shall abide by several terms and conditions of recognition.

(*iii*) Firms granted recognition shall undertake to maintain an office under the charge of full time members of their staff who should, apart from issuing rail tickets, be in a position to give upto date and accurate information regarding transport and accommodation facilities, currency and customs regulations and general information about travel, etc.

(*iv*) The recognition may be extended for the whole of the country or be limited to a particular region.

(*v*) Firms granted recognition shall undertake to employ only guides approved by the Ministry of Tourism.

(*vi*) All recognised firms shall furnish yearly statement of their activities and such other information in regard to the volume of tourist traffic actually handled and other relevant matters.

(*vii*) The decision of the government in the matter of recognition shall be final and it reserves the right to cancel or withdraw it at any time.

Subsequently, following clauses were also added:

(*i*) The recognition to be granted by Ministry of Tourism shall not automatically entitle the firm to be appointed agents for the sale of rail tickets by the Ministry of Railways (Railway Board). The agencies thus recognised shall apply separately to the Railway Board.

(*ii*) Firms seeking recognition as travel agents should have a minimum paid-up capital of rupees one hundred thousand.

(*iii*) Applications for grant of recognition by the Ministry of Tourism will be considered only if the firm:

(*a*) is approved by the IATA;

(*b*) has licence to book foreign passages issued by the Reserve Bank of India;

(*c*) has the approval of the Ministry of External Affairs to handle travel documents and to deal with passport offices; and

(*d*) is registered under the Local Shops and Establishment Act.

The recognition is now granted by the Ministry of Tourism in the Ministry of Tourism and Culture. The application for grant of recognition is to be made in the prescribed form and is to be addressed to the Director General, Ministry of Tourism who is the authority empowered to grant such recognition.

**Travel Agents Association of India (TAAI)**

The travel agents decided to form an association on all-India basis as long back as in the year 1952, when an All India Travel Agents Association was established. The main objective of the association is to safeguard and protect the interests of its members by way of having a constant dialogue with the concerned government agencies. The annual convention of the association is attended by a large number of representatives from travel trade both government as well as non-government. Important matters related with the promotion of product are discussed in these conventions. The Travel Agents Association of India has its registered office in Mumbai and regional offices in Kolkata, Delhi and Chennai. The association publishes a monthly magazine *Travel News* for its members.

The vital role played by the travel agents in the growth and development of tourism in the country and its promotion is recognised by all segments of the travel industry. The government works in close collaboration with them not only in India but abroad as well, encouraging them to plan and organize package tours for various destinations in India. In suitable cases, the Ministry of Tourism recommends the foreign exchange to travel agents to enable them to open their branch offices abroad. The ministry has also instituted a special tourism award which is given every year to the agency earning the maximum amount of foreign exchange.

## QUESTIONS FOR ANSWER

1. *Write short notes on the growth and development of travel agencies.*
   (*a*) *ASTA;*
   (*b*) *UFTAA;*
   (*c*) *TAAI.*
2. *Discuss the role of travel agents in the growth of tourism.*
3. *Explain the functions of a modern travel agency.*
4. *What is retail travel agent? What are the different types of retail travel agents?*
5. *Write Notes on (i) Inclusive Tours by Charter, (ii) Inclusive tourism on scheduled services.*
6. *Write a note on the functions of modern travel agency.*
7. *Discuss how the travel agency organizes various types of travel tours.*
8. *Write short notes on the following:*
   (*a*) *International Air Transport Association.*
   (*b*) *Planning and costing of tours.*
   (*c*) *Sources of income of travel agencies.*
   (*d*) *Hotel coupons and American Express Travel Cards.*

# 13

# Communications: The Tourism Promoters

## INTRODUCTION

Tourism promotion is one of the elements of the marketing mix and an important tool for marketing. The term promotion is interpreted and defined in many ways. Basically, the purpose of promotion is to inform, to persuade, to encourage or, more specifically, to influence the potential customers or trade intermediates (travel agents, tour operators, reservation services, hotel and charter brokers), through communications, to think and to act in a certain manner.

Successful marketing in tourism cannot rely only on a product of the right kind, on a market-related pricing policy and on a reliable and effective distribution network. Systematic communication with actual and potential customers and with the trade intermediaries, bridging the gap between producer on the one hand and the consumer on the other, is also needed.

The basic function of all tourist promotion activities is to have an effective communication with the consumer. The consumer must be aware of the existence of a tourist product. How is this awareness to be brought about in the minds of the consumers in the market areas? Some of the easily identifiable methods are advertising, sales support and public relations. These are the three major marketing tools which every organization uses to inform the actual as well as the potential customer about the product.

## ADVERTISEMENT

In today's changing and competitive international marketplace, advertising is important. Advertising is an activity designed to spread information with a view to promoting the sales of marketable goods and services. As such, it operates in two ways: first, by spreading information amongst consumers about the possibilities of consumption, and second, by seeking to influence their judgment in favour of the particular goods which are the subject of the advertisement.

Any organization which uses this promotional instrument has to use certain print and non-print media space which is paid for. In other words, we can also define advertisement as "paid public message designed to describe or praise a product." This product in tourism is any destination area which is visited by a tourist.

## ADVANTAGES

Advertising has several inherent advantages in this method. The biggest advantage is its wide coverage. Advertising is especially appropriate for communication with a large number of prospective purchasers of a commodity or a service. A uniform sales message is directed towards all prospective purchasers. An advertisement can be placed before a large number of prospective customers as compared with the efforts of a salesman. Frequency is another advantage. It can make its appeal more frequently, whereas the calls of salesman are usually not so frequent.

Another advantage is its *accessibility*. It may reach prospects whom salesman would find difficult to interview, owing to lack of interest, or inaccessibility to salesman. Advertisement may reach such prospects through many types of media and under a variety of circumstances, and may thus attract their attention and arouse their interest. *Lower cost* is another major advantage. Large numbers can be reached economically, *i.e.*, at a lower cost per contact than in any other technique available.

### Planning the Advertising

While planning the advertising, the agency must give careful consideration to the actual make-up of the advertisement. This headline copy, illustrations, colour scheme, size, layout, and method of printing or reproducing the advertisement must be planned very carefully. This is necessary in order to gain attention of the customer, maintain his interest in the message, and secure the action desired by the seller.

How frequently to advertise? For instance, is it better to use a full-page advertisement once a month or a quarter-page weekly? A frequently presented thought is likely to force itself into our consciousness. People are inclined to believe statements they hear or see repeatedly and hence the logic of frequent repetition of advertisements. This is desirable because consumers forget rapidly at first and much more slowly later on. After the facts are retained by the prospects, the advertisements can be presented at much longer intervals.

## Media Selection

The advertiser should give careful attention in planning to the selection of the medium or media especially adopted to his needs. The selection will depend upon the factors like the area to be covered, the type of audience to be reached, the appeals to be used.

The important factors which influence the media selection are: (*i*) media habits of the target audience; (*ii*) product characteristics (for example, TV may be the appropriate medium for those products which may require a demonstration of their operation for effective impact on the target audience); and (*iii*) cost of the media.

## Message Selection

The message selected for use in the advertisement should be such that it retains the interest in the minds of the customers about the product. The important characteristics of an effective message are:

(*i*) *Information*: It should be adequate for a decision;

(*ii*) *Interest*: It should be able to catch the attention of the target audience;

(*iii*) *Authenticity*: It should avoid exaggerated claims;

(*iv*) *Persuasion*: It should be capable of creating a favourable conviction in the target audience; and

(*v*) *Memory value*: It should have something in it which can help the target audience to remember it.

## Cost of Advertising

The agency must relate the estimated cost of the objectives planned and the contribution expected from advertising. Can the advertiser carry on a campaign large enough to make it effective? Are the funds available or will they become available through the sale of the product at the earliest. The advertisement must be cost effective and appealing.

In today's world, advertisement through any medium has become extremely expensive. Hence, it is important for the agency to ensure that the money spent on it does bring returns by way of increased sales. This could be done by way of evaluating or testing the effectiveness of advertising. Testing methods may be used to evaluate the results of an advertising campaign.

In tourism, advertising is used extensively for promotion of various tourist products. This is a far cry from the era when colourful folders and posters were the only apparent form of travel promotion. In the field of tourism, advertising is mainly used to create initial awareness and interest in the tourist service or destination to be promoted and motivates potential tourists to decide to make further enquiries about costs, bookings, facilities, etc. It implies indirect communication with selected target groups.

There can be two principal forms of advertising: (*i*) consumer advertising and (*ii*) trade advertising. To reach a wide number of consumers, such media as newspaper advertisements, radio spots, TV prime-time advertising are used.

A large number of people today travel in groups. A tourist for various reasons chooses to travel as a member of a group, as opposed to travelling individually. The result, therefore, has been that a number of large tour operators puts together inclusive tour packages, the tourist merely pays one package price for all services and is assured of a holiday. Such packages are then sold in retail by numerous smaller travel agents located in various market areas, and the result is that a group is formed.

Tourism organizations all over the world resort to advertisements as a tool to achieve desired results. This is done as a campaign having following six stages:

1. Defining the product—the tourist attractions and facilities.
2. Defining the marketing segments, which includes, consumer information, distribution information, sales information attitude segments.
3. Interpreting the marketing objective.
4. Further planning the advertising campaign—opting media for the purpose.

5. Creating media mix for various promotional objectives.
6. Assessing the impact and value of a campaign, which include awareness, attitude-purchase and repurchase of the product together with sale support techniques.

## PUBLIC RELATIONS

Public relations is an important promotional technique. It involves measures designed to improve the image of a service, to create a more favourable climate for its advertising and sales support activities. It covers such a wide range of activities and is used for so many different aims that it is not easy to define it. Public relations is the "art and science of planning and implementing communication and understanding between a company and the many different groups with which it is concerned in the course of its operation."

Public relations may also be defined as the continuous and consistent representation of an organizations' policies to the public at large and to sections of the public who have a special interest in the organization's activities, *e.g.*, to various strata of employees, shareholders, actual and potential customers as well as its local and national government. A positive attitude to public relations in an organization's activities is evidence that it recognises a duty to keep the public aware of those activities, and of their impact upon society and its environments.

From the definitions of public relations, it is evident that its main function is to inform public about the activities of an organization. In other words it is a part of a firm's or an organization's total communication effort. Its purpose is to create best possible reputation for the firm or the organization by way of presenting facts. In a climate of favourable public opinion, an organization's or a firm's goals can be achieved more effectively.

In the field of travel and tourism, the need for making information and facts available to both potential and actual tourists assumes special significance. It involves measures designed to create and improve the image of the tourist product, create a more favourable climate for its advertising and sales support activities, especially in regard to travel trade intermediaries and news media. Favourable acceptance of any tourist destination by the public is of utmost importance.

In fact, no business is more concerned with human relations than the business of tourism. Public relations in tourism used to create and maintain a positive image for a country, a tourist destination in the minds of people who are in a position to influence public opinion (journalists, editors, travel writers, etc.), or in the minds of sales intermediaries (travel agents, tour operators, etc.). It is oriented towards creating and maintaining an atmosphere whereby travelling public at large is convinced of the advantages of visiting the country concerned.

Public relations is one of the important functions of the official tourist organization. In fact, tourist organizations primarily are public relations organizations. The objectives of public relations in the field of tourism may be divided in two parts: the dissemination of information and the creation of a favourable image for the tourist product.

### Public Relations Techniques

Public relations consists of a number of interrelated activities oriented towards creating and maintaining a favourable positive image for the tourist product. The main techniques of public relations in the tourist promotion are as follows:

(*i*) Organizing familiarization tours for travel writers, editors, travel agents, photographers and other key personnel from different parts of the world as guests to visit the country and to get first-hand knowledge about it. These persons then write about the country visited in well-known travel and other general interest magazines.

(*ii*) Organizing television and radio contests featuring the destination country.

(*iii*) Organizing press releases and arranging press conferences with key personnel connected with tourism field with a view to disseminate information about the destination.

(*iv*) Arranging seminars and workshops in the place where the tourist promotion office is located.

(*v*) Organizing cultural programmes, musical and folk shows, TV interviews, exhibitions and national friendship weeks in the country where the national tourist office is located.

(*vi*) Organizing various types of contests about the country.

## TOURISM PUBLICITY—MODERN TRENDS

Tourist publicity in the beginning developed in an empirical way under the pressure of the growth of international travel, and to the extent that information had to be supplied to an ever-increasing number of tourists. Thus, at its outset, it was simply informational publicity. With the growth in volume of commercial tourist publicity, particularly in the sphere of transport, and great increase in the number of tourists, various countries realized the importance of tourism in the national life. They recognised it especially in economic terms—earning of foreign exchange. This necessitated the countries to organize their institutional tourist publicity with a new approach and employ experienced commercial publicity technicians to draw up a long-term publicity strategy.

For a successful tourist publicity, one important factor is to be placed at the top of all considerations. In the field of tourism, motive forces and effects lie on different planes. The motive forces of tourism lie mainly on a plane which is outside the scope of economic factors, while the results of tourism are represented in a series of economic processes.

### Methods of Tourist Publicity

The methods of tourist publicity in their evolution have lagged behind in comparison with the developments of the publicity methods of other branches of economy which utilize applied psychology and sociology. They are still mainly based on experience, instinct, routine and technique. Publicity still proceeds from the object with a more or less arbitrary combination of rational and emotional appeals and perhaps in consideration of the results obtained by research in publicity media, but in utter disregard of the person to whom the publicity is addressed.

It is not yet clear at all how tourism, whose fluctuating character was proverbial, has now grown into a phenomenon almost impervious to crises, why the tourist need has undergone a re-classification to other needs in order of importance, as also why, despite the fundamental universality of the tourist need, different human groups have different conceptions about its composition and the urge for experience.

Professor Krapf was the first to undertake a close examination of the tourist consumption. It is of particular importance for tourist publicity when he states that all considerations of tourism must now free themselves from objective facts and institutions and cover the emotional world of man and the conduct of his life. This should be followed up by an examination of tourist behaviour.

## Coordination of Measures

Rising demand and expanding supply characterize the present day situation of the travel market with its publicity competition. In this competition, two methods stand out which are quite suitably designated as the methods of the advanced tourist countries and those of the developing tourist countries. The advanced tourist countries show a constantly increasing tendency towards a graded publicity beginning with the publicity of the individual travel trade firms, of resorts, areas, provinces and finally countries, while the developing tourist countries, begin with the country's publicity to which regional and travel trade publicity is added. As yet the differentiation between tourist institutions is too limited for them to enter into competition with each other.

However, in the well-known tourist countries this competition takes place inside the country and finally between corresponding tourist resorts and enterprises. This carries in itself the danger of a frittering away of the forces and since the percentage of the ineffective residual part of local publicity is relatively large, it is necessary to undertake campaigns in a manner which is more than proportionate. This has special relevance to publicity abroad, where the desire for the most extensive possible coverage of the demand is somewhat restricted by the available financial means. This reason alone points to the necessity of concentration and coordination of all tourist publicity measures.

## The Brand Concepts

Each country is a travel mosaic composed of a variety of distinctive features. These features however spread uniformly over the whole country but are very frequently regional or even characteristic of a place. Thus every land has regions which through their distinctive climatic, physical, morphological, cultural or other kind of features, constitute the tourist attractions or can be developed to that end.

It is very rightly mentioned in the *General Theory of Tourism* of Hunziker-Krapf that "the organizational forms of publicity abroad may differ in detail, but there must be a single goal to put national tourism to the fore and the regional and local features on the second plane. A tourist publicity programme for a country may be conceived in the following way:

(*i*) The creation of concepts of satisfaction which, taken together, could form the tourist brand of the country;

(*ii*) A coordination of all publicity measures of the economic, cultural and tourist institutions of a country in conjunction with a coupling of the brands; and

(*iii*) Constant analysis of satisfactions, market observations and research, as well as publicity effectiveness.

## Motivation Publicity

The motivating factors of tourism originate in their preponderant majority from the emotional sphere. Consequently, tourism stands out prominently in the world of experience-seeking ideas and conceptions and it can be said that the holidaymaker lives between imagination and reality and the relationship between the two determines his judgement on the land visited. This will be positive in proportion to the extent that reality corresponds to the world of imagination.

It may be inferred from this how very important it is for publicity to steer the formation of imagination towards facts as they really exist. This is easiest in the field of comparable satisfactions whereby guiding information on trends may be obtained through a planned investigation of judgements and criticism—in other words, public opinion research. This publicity based on motivation forces and influencing the imaginative world of the tourists can be referred to as motivation publicity or the irrational approach.

Within the framework of this method a relatively larger importance is conceded to landscape publicity for relaxation and pleasure travel. In this connection the importance of this subject, insofar as it does not relate to a particularly beautiful landscape or one especially suited for the practice of certain sports, is too much exaggerated.

Each region of the global has a landscape to offer and every one of these landscapes has a particular charm, especially for those whom its special features make it seem strange and therefore worth the experience. To the primary motivations of holiday and pleasure travel, the pressure of the rhythm of our life has added other factors like the escape from the everyday life, freedom from ties and commitments, the urge to adventure, etc.

The second method of tourist publicity is the "reason why" publicity or the rational approach. It extols in the first place the merits or the arguments in favour of visiting the country on behalf of which the publicity has been undertaken and acts in accordance with the principle of suggestion. The form of expression it assumes is the slogan. It is appreciably more strongly competitive which makes it easily liable to fall into the blunder of superlative forms which we come across constantly in tourist publicity.

## Tourist Publicity Media

The publicity itself is carried out through media whose scope is that there are constantly new possibilities. This is of particular relevance in respect of tourist publicity whose new forms and scientifically based planning in publicity media seem to be constructed as a result of the fact that in general their publicity effect is limited to the visual and auditive senses. Illustration, copy and the spoken word are therefore the primary publicity media for tourism. They are multiplied through the media compounded out of them.

The greatest importance appertains to *illustration*, for it can achieve emotional effects in the reproduction of a landscape and its atmosphere and is also universally understood. Even if one is inclined to accept the psychological argument that every human being only projects his own personality in every consideration, the illustration retains from this standpoint also considerable publicity effectiveness because it is viewed and perceived differently by different persons.

Given the differences of individual tastes, the illustration motivation plays a decisive role, for the illustration should be bearer of the emotional contents which it should radiate on the viewer. Consequently the best illustration is just good enough for tourist publicity.

With *copy* as a publicity factor, the urgent necessity for originality with the object of giving expression to the publicity idea also arises. The purpose of every publicity media is to arouse and sustain attention. Illustration and copy must therefore create desires. In tourist publicity the tendency towards schematisation is extremely strong and counteracts the necessity for publicity originality. The similarity of the printed publicity material of hotels, travel agencies, tourist resorts, areas and even countries furnishes proof of this.

The *spoken word* is of decisive importance in the case of personal publicity. The proper use of the spoken word is difficult but effective. "Words are not only conveyors of thoughts and ideas, but also of emotional contents and consequently they reach not only the intellect but also the psychism of the recipient and are expressed to this end."

The three primary publicity media mentioned—illustration, copy and the spoken word—form the basis of the composite publicity media which can suitably be arranged in the following groups:

(*i*) Printed publicity material,
(*ii*) Advertising publicity,
(*iii*) Projected publicity,
(*iv*) Structural forms and publicity,
(*v*) Personal publicity.

*Printed Publicity Material*

Printed publicity material in the field of tourist publicity is mainly composed of the publicity leaflet, folder, brochure and poster. The publicity leaflet is used among others as inset and enclosure in the case of conveying an information or communicating to the knowledge of the largest possible number of persons. The folder is the most commonly used and the most important medium for tourist publicity.

*The brochure* is different from the folder in size as well as in content and detail. The importance of the brochure in tourist publicity has not been adequately appreciated and, on account of financial reasons, it has been insufficiently utilized. The brochure offers greater possibilities than the folder to combine with each other publicity and service, suggestion and information.

The *poster* is another important publicity medium of tourism. The difficulties in respect of the production of the general folder occur especially in the case of the poster. The tourist poster should combine its effectiveness based on psychological factors with the task of expressing the impersonation of a country as a tourist destination working on the limited means at its disposal.

*The publicity journal* which is utilized at present by almost every national tourist publicity organization is more representative than all other forms of printed material. As such, it is expensive and therefore limited in its circulation. For the sake of comprehensive coverage, mention may also be made of the printed publicity material which really belongs to the sphere of customer service, like maps, guide books, directories, inserts, etc.

*Advertising Publicity*

Discussed earlier in this chapter

*Projected Publicity*

Projected publicity media comprise film and slide publicity. Of particular importance is the film which is an outstanding publicity medium, not only on account of its representational potentialities, but also because of its suggestive power. The colour film is assuming increasing significance within the framework of tourist publicity. The central idea of the film should be expressible in terms of motion and this accounts for the cardinal rule of all publicity films: short text but plenty of action which should captivate the attention of the spectators and also aim at influencing memory through emotional factors.

Publicity effectiveness is a characteristic not only of the purely publicity film, but also of the feature film as well as the instructional or didactic film. In the United States of America and Western Europe the travel film with a commentary known as the "travelogue" has won extensive popularity. Television is a suitable medium to spread the interest in foreign countries and thus serves tourist publicity.

*Structural Publicity*

Structural publicity comprise all publicity measures which manifest themselves in constructions and structures, as for example, in the establishment and equipment of a tourist publicity office abroad, in participation in fairs and exhibitions, in the preparation of showcases and window displays, etc. There is also the possibility of publicity combinations whereby tourist publicity can be undertaken in conjunction with business publicity. For example, shops selling sports goods, fashion articles, travel accessories, etc., are willing to have such combinations in their show-windows. Similarly at fairs the joint stands of a country procure publicity advantages for tourism because the exhibition as a whole shows tourism in relation to the country and succeeds in creating lasting impressions.

### *Personal Publicity*

Personal publicity in tourism has various forms of application ranging from the informational and sales talk to publicity travel, which serves the need of maintaining contact with the travel industry and to support it in its sales efforts, and includes the publicity lecture. In all these spheres the personal effort holds away. Also to this category belong interviews, radio broadcasts, television interviews, receptions, etc.

## QUESTIONS FOR ANSWER

1. *'Promotion of tourism largely depends upon proper utilization of media communications'. Justify this statement.*
2. *Write a note on the concept of advertisement for promotion of tourism. Include various aspects concerning this concept.*
3. *Discuss the nature and concept of 'Public Relations' as promoter of tourism.*
4. *Write a note on 'Modern Trends' in tourism publicity.*
5. *Discuss various methods of tourist publicity.*

# 14

# Significance of Marketing in Tourism

Marketing is the key of all benefits in each and every industry, since tourism is an industry of vital national importance as it is the single highest net foreign exchange earning industry in India, but since we have better environment and various types of tourist attraction we have great potential to develop this industry if we are able to market it properly. Hereunder, we will discuss various aspects of tourism marketing:

## INTRODUCTION

Marketing helps to match the organisation's human, financial and physical resources with the wants of customers along with maximum economy and efficiency.

Customers do not always run to a producer and demand supplies, however useful and valuable the product may be. They will not make the effort to buy, if the effort is not commensurate with the perceived value. It must be available when needed, at places that are convenient and at prices that seem reasonable. They have to know what is available, where and at what price. Often they have to be persuaded that the purchase is beneficial to them.

Services are bought by customers and they produce satisfaction. The producing organization creates a capacity through human, financial and physical resources for rendering the services. Most effective utilisation of these resources is possible through the application of marketing concepts. You must remember that tourism is a service oriented industry.

## TOURISM MARKETING—THE NEED

It is now accepted fact that tourism is a catalyst for stimulating economic, social and cultural activities and as an engine of economic development. It is to be noted that money spent by tourists tends to percolate through many levels and has a multiplier effect. Similarly, the development of a tourist circuit results in the development of the hinterland too from which the entire community is benefited.

Thus, tourism acts as a positive force in stimulating economic development, to foster national integration, and to bring people and culture of different nations closer. Significantly, marketing India abroad will require effective marketing and management of tourism needs a change in orientation and implementation of a better defined, better targeted market driven strategy.

Tourism is a service industry. Investments are made in and around a tourist destination in the hope that increasing numbers of tourists will visit it. A product (the attractions and facilities at the destination) is designed and offered to the consumers (tourists) in the hope that they will buy (visit the destination) and derive satisfaction therefrom. Only then will the investment be worthwhile. Tourists have to be persuaded to buy the product. But there is competition as other destinations are also trying to persuade them. The "wooing" of the tourist is becoming more intense. And here the marketing concepts provide techniques to do the "wooing" effectively.

## CONCEPT OF TOURISM MARKETING

Krippendrof has defined marketing in tourism as follows: Marketing in tourism is to be understood as the systematic and the coordinated execution of business policy by tourist undertakings whether private or state owned at local, regional, national or international level to achieve the optimal satisfaction of the needs of identifiable consumer groups and in doing so to achieve an appropriate return.

The tourist product may be seen as a composite product, as an amalgam of attractions, transport, accommodation and entertainment. Each of these components is supplied by the individual hotel company, airlines or other supplies and is offered directly to the tourist by them. The tourist product can be sold as a package or assembled by the tourist himself. The tourist product an be analysed in terms of its attractions, its facilities and its accessibility.

Attractions may be defined as those elements in the tourist product which determine the choice of the tourist to visit one destination rather than another. They are the factors which generate a flow of tourist to particular location. Attractions may be either site attractions or event attractions.

Site attractions are those where the place itself is the major inducement to the tourists to visit it, for example, Kashmir or Niagara Falls. Event attractions are those where the event staged is a greater factor in the tourist's choice than the site, *e.g.*, the Olympic Games, World Book Fair, etc. Often the site and the event together form the major factor in the tourist's choice.

Tourist facilities are those elements in the tourist product which do not normally themselves generate tourist flow but whose absence might deter the tourist from seeking the attractions. Accessibility is another component in the tourist product. It includes transportation to the attraction.

A tourist market may be identified corresponding to each tourist product. In this sense market means buyers and potential buyers of each tourist product. The identification of a segment of the total market is very important.

## BASIS OF TOURISM MARKETING

The concept of tourism marketing is based on the marketing concept in that it is the process of : (*i*) identifying and anticipating consumer demand (and desire) for tourism products and services; (*ii*) developing a means of providing products and services to fulfil these needs; (*iii*) communicating this to the consumer, thereby motivating sales, consequently satisfying both the consumer, and the organisation's objective.

Significantly, through marketing planning, segmentation, and marketing research a tourism marketing mix can be developed to achieve the tourism organization's goals through strategic marketing.

Tourist market may be identified and segmented on the following basis for proper marketing and planning of activities of tourism industry in India.

- Place or origin of tourists.
- Destinations.
- Purposes of tour like holidays, pilgrimage, sightseeing, shopping, etc.
- Economic status and spending tendencies.
- Demographic characteristics like age, sex, occupation and attitudes.
- Preference for staying like camping, luxury hotels, caravans, etc.
- Preferences of travel like air, sea, road or rail.

Each segment of the market differs in terms of needs and expectations. No one organisation can cater to the needs of all the segments. Each organisation has to decide on the particular segment or segments it would cater to. The segment so identified is called the target segment. The identification has to be made on the basis of what the organisation identifies as its objectives and its capabilities.

Having identified the target market all activities will have to be planned and executed keeping this target market in mind. The service being offered, the messages in communication, the media used for communication, the pricing policies, the arrangements to access the service, all have to be consistent with the preferences and behaviour patterns of the target market. For example, if the hotel is targeting on the domestic tourists in the circuit of religious places, there would be little point in advertising in business magazines or providing foreign cuisine in the restaurant. Simple vegetarian *thali* food would be more satisfying to its patrons.

## DIFFERENCE BETWEEN TOURISM INDUSTRY AND OTHER SERVICE INDUSTRIES

There are four main characteristics which distinguish the tourism industry from other service providers.

1. *Inflexibility*: The tourism industry is highly inflexible in terms of capacity. The number of beds in hotels, or seats on an aeroplane is fixed so it is not possible to meet sudden upsurges in demand. Similarly, restaurant tables, hotel beds and aeroplane seats remain empty and unused in period of low demand.

2. *Perishability*: Tourism service products are highly perishable. An unused hotel bed or an empty airplane seat represents an immediate loss of that service as a means of earning profit. This has an impact on overall industry profitability.
3. *Fixed Location*: Tourism destinations are fixed locations so effort must be concentrated in communicating the facility to potential consumer. A consumer can conveniently watch a Hollywood movie at the local cinema but has to be persuaded to travel to India to see the Taj Mahal.
4. *Relatively Large Financial Investment*: Every modern tourist establishment and facility requires large investment, frequently over a long time scale. This means that the level of risk and the rate of return are critically important to tourism management.

## ANALYSIS OF TOURIST MARKET ENVIRONMENT

Kotlar and Fox have stated that analysis of the market environment consists of three major tasks. These are:

1. *Market Measurement and Forecasting*: Determining the current and future size of the available market for the region and assisting the tourism business units in this regard.
2. *Market Segmentation*: Determining the main groups making up a market in order to choose the best target groups to be served and again assisting the respective tourism business units in this regard.
3. *Consumer Analysis*: Determining the characteristics of tourists—specifically their needs, perceptions, preferences and behaviours in order to adapt the offering of the region to these tourist characteristics.

## GOAL AND STRATEGY FORMULATION

The environment and resource analysis component of strategic marketing planning is intended to provide the necessary background and stimulates for the regional tourism organisation's thinking about the tourism goals and objectives for a region. While reviewing the pertinent literature we find that there are different interpretations of the terms mission, goals and objectives. Kotlar and Fox (1985) have viewed as follows.

**Mission**

The purpose of the regional tourism organisation *i.e.*, what it is trying to accomplish with regard to tourism development in the region. Emphasis is placed on what should be aimed at in the light of long term opportunity.

**Goal**

A major factor that the regional tourism organisation will emphasise for long range purpose, such as regional image development, increase in market share, and new product development. Goals are not usually quantified or limited to a specific time period.

**Objective**

A measurable goal that is made specific with respect to magnitude, time and responsibility. It is, furthermore, judged to be attainable at some specific future date through planned actions.

An analysis of various sources indicates that the development of a mission statement for a region will have to take into account a number of key aspects:

1. The past experiences in the region with regard to tourism must be considered, including the salient characteristics and history of the region, the regional tourism organisation, and the tourism business units.
2. The regional tourism organisation must be prepared to adapt the region's mission in response to the characteristics of the regional tourism environment.
3. The region's tourism resources make certain missions possible.
4. The preferences of the region's major tourism policies, such as regional tourism organisations, tourism business units, local government, and community organisations, must be considered.

   A successful mission statement will attempt to incorporate the priorities and expectations of the major publics in the region.

5. The mission must be based on the region's distinctive competencies. A concerted effort must be made to concentrate on the region's strengths.

A mission should be feasible, motivating and distinctive. Similarly, Getz (1986) has suggested that following issues should be covered when developing required tourism goals: (*i*) community development; (*ii*) heritage and environmental conservation; (*iii*) enhancement of cultural identity; (*iv*) provision of leisure opportunities; (*v*) population and demographic change; (*vi*) social welfare, and (*vii*) the provision and maintenance of living amenities.

Following the goal formulation process, regional strategy formulation can be undertaken in which a broad strategy is determined to reach the region's goals. A first step in regional strategy formulation can be to undertake an analysis of the regions current product portfolio. This portfolio analysis can assist in determining which of the region's major tourism products should be built, maintained, harvested, or even terminated. The second major step in strategy formulation is the development of a growth strategy where use can be made of product market expansion matrix.

## TARGET MARKETING

After analysis of tourist market environment and formulation of goal and objectives of tourism as well as identification of segmented tourist markets the strategy should aim at target marketing as discussed hereunder:

Tourist market targeting is the process of aiming a company's or public authority's marketing efforts to identified groups of potential tourists who are accessible to the company or authority in terms both of promotional media and of product design. It is founded on the twin recognition that tourists travel for diversity of reasons ranging from communing with nature, visiting attractions, enjoying heritage, participating in spans, participating in other entertainments, relaxation, health, shopping, and business activities; and that this diversity should be reflected in the marketing mixes of companies, of which promotion is part.

Market targeting should be an integrated part of producing the marketing part of a company's business plan, namely the identification of what sales and marketing position the company currently holds, what is believe it can achieve, the steps to be taken to achieve its aims, and where the company considers it will be placed in the future market.

The company's effectiveness depends in this area on both its ability to define markets and on its skill in producing products or services which the identified groups of tourists see as providing sufficient added benefit to buy. In this sense, target marketing applies both to situations which are market led and to those which are product led.

### Consumer Behaviour

Marketing scholars and practitioners, in tourism as elsewhere, set out to investigate consumer needs, and attitudes, thus preparing to take measures to influence consumers. Consumer research has developed as a discipline recommending which explanatory variables should be monitored in order to understand consumer decision-making process.

As consumer behaviour deals with multiple causes and compound variables, the measurement techniques are of special importance. The widespread use of multivariate methods means that the marketing manager today can rely on efficient data reduction and comfortable visualization of the research output.

A consumer's decision process reaches its crucial stage when the evaluation of alternatives takes place. Depending on the character of evaluative criteria employed, the outcome may be portrayed by a theoretical construct such as image, attitude, perceived risk, and cognitive dissonance.

## MANAGING THE MARKETING MIX

The concept of the overall tourism product is central to understand the meaning and practice of marketing management in all sectors of the travel and tourism industry. It has important implications for the marketing of commercial organisations and national and regional tourist offices; it is also highly relevant for planning and development, both in its community aspects and as a focus of feasibility studies for commercial organisations.

Products are defined as anything that can be offered to a market for attention, acquisition, use or consumption that might satisfy a want a need. It includes physical objects, services, persons, places, organisations, and ideas. As such, product decisions in any industry, not only tourism, are the forced point of all marketing activity, around which the other aspects of the marketing mix (pricing, promotion, and distribution) are organised.

Many variable make up the regional marketing mix. These can be grouped into the four P's: product, price, place and promotion. However, the characteristics of tourism are somewhat different to many of the products that have been the traditional. The product is not transported to the consumer, rather the tourist travel to the destination area where the product is experienced.

The cost of transporting products to markets are an important for most producers but, in the case of tourism and for some market segments, the journey may be a positive part of the trip and there may be an incentive to travel an additional distance to acquire an unaccustomed or unusual experience.

Tourism's product not only includes the salient attributes of the regional tourism offering, but also management of the regional tourism products over their life cycles, managing the development of new tourism products, and developing appropriate product strategies. Place is concerned with distribution. The appropriate channels and institutions should be used to give the tourism the most effective access to the regional tourism product.

Promotion communicates the benefits of the regional tourism offering to the potential tourists and includes not only advertising, but also sales promotion, public relations and personal selling. The right and appropriate regional promotion mix must be developed where each of these promotional techniques are used as needed.

Price is a critical variable in the regional marketing mix. The right price must both satisfy tourists and meet the profit objectives of tourism business in the region.

Package tour products will be broken down into different types to suit the identified needs of consumers. Typically, these will fall into the categories of escorted and unescorted tours, and group tour bookings.

Significantly, branding plays a very important role in tourism marketing, car rental firms, hotel chains and airlines in particular employ tremendous efforts to ensure that their name is widely recognised and synonymous with quality, value or some other characteristic. Travel agents and tour operators depend on reputation to a large extent, and so it is imperative that they have a strong, recognisable identity.

The promotional mix in the tourism context fall into three main categories: (*a*) to inform, (*b*) to remind, and (*c*) to persuade. It will always be necessary to inform potential consumers about new products, and services and other related issues may need to communicate to tourists; new uses, prices changes, information to build consumer confidence and to reduce fears, full descriptions of service offerings, image building etc. are a few examples.

Similarly, consumers may need to be reminded about all these types of issues, especially in the off peak season. Promotional designs will help in persuasion of prospective consumers (tourists).

Pricing in tourism is a fairly complex issue because the price eventually said by the consumer may be made up from the prices changed by various independent service providers in the case of a package tour. Therefore, pricing policy decisions should be distincted by strategic objectives.

Distribution management is concerned with two things (*a*) availability; and (*b*) accessibility. If tourism marketing management is to be certain that their products and services are both available and accessible to the target market, they must design a channel strategy that will be effective.

## MARKETING TOOLS

There are several activities which are commonly used in the conduct of a marketing campaign, *e.g.*, advertising, development of a sales force and the use of public relations.

Market research refers to the systematic collection of information relating to the supply of and demand for a product. Market research provides management with information. In tourism much of the basic information about markets is available from published materials. Special investigations in consumer markets can be made by sample survey.

With sufficient information available from market research and market information, it is possible to identify the key market segments. The criteria for distinguishing between segments of the total market will be demographic and socio-economic. The product must then be formulated and given a unique identity to match the segment of the market for which it is intended. Much of the physical character of the destination, its attractions and nature are given and could be changed slowly and perhaps expensively.

In the marketing of consumer goods, the efforts of the sales force are directed towards ensuring that the retailers carry stock of the product. Without adequate stockholding the retailers, the final consumer will not find the product. But in the case of tourist product, the retailer does not buy the stock but only orders from the supplies when he has a customers at the counter.

The salesman's role as directed towards the retail travel agent is largely one of educating the travel agent's staff about the nature of the product and of training the agent's staff accordingly. He should be able to explain the merits of his firm's products, the locations and nature of the individual hotels in a group, the extent of the airline's network and its relations with other forms of transport. He should be able to train the travel agent's staff in his firm's reservation procedure and to assist in selling the firm's product by installing window displays and in the display of brochures.

## Advertising and Sales Promotion

Advertising refers to those methods which are available for communicating with the consumer when his identity is unknown and when the advertiser is not in direct touch with him. It thus embraces most forms of media advertising, TV advertising, press advertising and so on. Sales promotion describes those methods of communication where the identity of the consumer is known, as when the advertiser is reaching his retailer by a letter or when he is in touch with conference organizers of club secretaries or other intermediates. Both advertising and sales promotion are methods of communication with the consumer or with his intermediary.

The role of advertising is to impel the consumer towards the point of sale where the product is accessible. The object of advertising is to persuade the consumer that he needs the product and in particular the advertiser's brand of it.

Advertising must not be fraudulent or misleading. The advertiser is an advocate for his product, the rational consumer is the judge.

In most cases, advertising is entrusted to an advertising agency who undertakes the planning of the campaign and its detailed realization. Advertising agencies are professional firms staffed by a variety of experts in various areas of advertising and marketing.

The effectiveness of an advertising campaign depends chiefly upon the credibility oı the message converted by the advertisement and on the extent to which the message is seen by that segment of the market to which it is addressed, *i.e.*, the coverage achieved by the campaign. Coverage depends on the frequency with which the advertisements are seen.

The broad features of the most common advertising media must be noted. The press means newspapers and magazines of all kinds. The advertiser should advertise in a newspaper or magazine which is read by that segment of the market he wishes to reach. By contrast, television advertising is very much a mass market medium and thus indiscriminate.

### Tourist Literature

Printed matter, such as brochures, prospectuses are not usually classed among advertising media but they play a prominent part in the marketing of tourism. Because the product in tourism is intangible, there is a need to describe fully the product and this can be done by producing an elaborate brochure. The advertising policy considers the prime objective to get the brochure into the hands of the final consumer and then relies on the brochure to impel him to buy the product. Brochure is given the widest possible distribution even wastefully so, for it forms the main marketing tool in many tourist campaigns.

Other minor media are commercial radio, outdoor poster advertising, direct mailing and cinema film.

### Public Relations in Tourism

Public relations may be defined as the continuous and consistent representation of an organization's policies to the public at large and to sections of the public who have a special interest in the organization's activities as well as to its actual and potential customers.

In tourism the main concern of tourism organizations is the creation and maintenance of an attractive image of the destination. This is often promoted by giving facilities to journalists visit to the country.

Tourism is particularly prone to natural as well as man-made disaster. Snowfields give rise to avalanches, many of the world's resort areas are in hurricane belts or in earthquake zones. Hotels catch fire, aircraft crash. Tourist authorities who are caught up in a disaster have a special public relations need which can be met by advance planning for the possibility of disaster.

The tour operator is the manufacturer of a true tourist product, he buys the components of the package, the inclusive tour (transport, accommodation etc.). The inclusive tour is the fastest growing mode of tourism in Western Europe and it has been created with deliberate marketing policies.

## GUIDELINES FOR TOURISM MARKETING

In order to harness the available potential, the areas that need immediate and sustained attention are discussed below:

1. Formulation of a strategic marketing plan with a focus on a select number of tourism generating sources as out thrust centres.
2. Exploration and development of new tourist generating markets with integrated and aggressive marketing in foreign countries.
3. Tourism as a product requires continued updating and modernization.
4. Advance preparation and integrated planning is needed before visit India years are announced.
5. Domestic tourism must be seriously promoted for proper utilization of the infrastructure required for tourism.
6. Infrastructural bottlenecks pose serious challenge for tourism promotion.
7. Transport and communication facilities are further promoted, strengthened and modernized.
8. User and eco-friendly infrastructure including transport, accommodation, courteous services etc. are to be strengthened and further promoted.
9. Greater role of private and a non-government sector is required to develop tourism.
10. Streamlining of visa policy, facilitation at airports, manning of immigrations and customers with suitably qualified personnel and change in their attitudes towards

making the tourist comfortable will earn us a lot of goodwill.

11. Functional distributional and promotional marketing mix should be further promoted and strengthened.

It may be concluded that effective marketing and management of tourism needs a change in orientation and implementation of a better, defined targeted market drives strategy. Coordinated and well designed marketing strategy should be developed by State Government as well as Central Government.

## QUESTIONS FOR ANSWER

1. *What do you mean by marketing in tourism? What are the tools that are commonly used for conducting a marketing campaign.*
2. *Write a note on the need of tourism marketing and the concept of tourism marketing.*
3. *Write short notes on the following:*
   (*a*) *Segmentation and target market.*
   (*b*) *Difference between tourism industry and other service industries.*
   (*c*) *Advertising in Tourism.*
   (*d*) *Public Relations in Tourism.*
4. *Discuss the concept of formulation of goals, objectives and strategies in tourism.*
5. *Write short notes on the following:*
   (*a*) *Target Marketing.*
   (*b*) *Managing the Marketing Mix.*
   (*c*) *Guidelines for tourism marketing.*

15

# Political Determinants of Tourism

Basically travel and tourism is related to human urge to know more about the concept or area of his choice for his benefit and to enjoy the environment for his better way of life, thus tourism is an activity of academic as well as socio-economic nature but these tourist destinations are in various parts of the world under the control of various types of political philosophies, therefore, politics is a major determinent of tourism in particular nations. Hereunder we will discuss how politics determines tourism industry in various parts of the world.

The flows of tourism between two nations can be used as a sign of the level of salience between the two nations and their people.

Most nations have several policies towards foreign tourists that are based not only on anticipated length of stay but also on the degree of international cooperation existing between the two countries. For example, Canada requires no passport or visa from citizens of USA or Commonwealth countries but may require such documents from other nationals. Similarly, India requires no passport or visa from citizens of Nepal or Bhutan.

Tourism is the largest industry in the world and is expected to maintain that distinction until at least the middle of the twenty-first century. Over 125 nations consider tourism a major industry and one-third of those countries it is a leading industry, a top-earner of foreign exchange and a critical source of employment. In USA tourism is the second largest industry, the largest tradeable services export, one of the top three sources of revenue for 39 of the 50 states and as the employer of approximately 6 million Americans, the country's second largest employer.

The United States has sought to use international tourism as a political weapon against the Soviet Union. American efforts to mobilise a boycott of the Moscow Olympic games as an international rebuke to the soviets for the invention of Afghanistan were intended to deny the USSR global prestige.

On several occasions the USA used tourism as a political weapon. The USA demonstrated opposition to the People's Republic of China and Cuba by forbidding travel to those countries for several years. As a result of change in political relationship the USA has lifted the travel ban to China and allowed some travel to Cuba.

Chinese tourism policy was negative in nature—the fewer outside the better. This attitude was due to the fact that major tourist generating countries were hostile to the communist regime. Travel to China was forbidden by the USA and many other western governments. China reciprocated by denying entry to most foreigners. In 1954, China International Travel Service was established to shepherd groups of "foreign friends" to a few sites.

It was in the early 1960s that China was eager to increase tourism. But only formal exchange visits, a few sympathetic writers and some business people on specific assignments were allowed to visit China before 1977.

Tourism as an industry began in China in 1978. China now recognised that tourism not only promotes mutual understanding and friendship but accumulates funds for modernization. In 1978 1,24,000 foreign tourists visited China. Between 1977 and 1980 tourist arrivals doubled each year and this process is growing in China.

Tourism in Thailand is unique because it ranges from cultural pilgrimages to the most degraded and dangerous sex odysseys. Private sector giants such as the Oriental Hotel of Bangkok and Grace Hotel operates brothel. Over 3.2 million tourists visited Bangkok. Tourism industry is criticized because of its reliance on sex tours and general prostitution has become more pronounced. As the nation has had a history of concubinage and prostitutes in its traditional culture, opposition failed to recognise social decay implied by sex tourism.

The Government of Thailand recognises tourism's central place in the economy of Thailand. In 1982, tourism surpassed rice as the leading earner of foreign exchange. Tourism earned a billion dollars in 1981 from more than 2 million international tourists.

The Tourism Organisation of Thailand began in 1960 and was

entrusted with the task of promoting Thailand as a tourist destination. At that time, Thailand was receiving less than 100,000 tourists. That changed soon as the Vietnam war escalated and Thailand became a rest and recreation (R & R) base for war-weary soldiers. Prostitution as an occupation grew dramatically from its Thai-based, more or less stable clientele to an increasingly large and fleeting dependence on foreigners.

By 1975, when Vietnam War ceased, Thailand's tourist base was no longer dependent on soldiers. Today it is based primarily on group tours and business travel. However, sex continues to be a major motivation for travel for Thailand for each of these groups. It is women who are focused in tourism promotion. Thailand has become infamous as Thighland. In Bangkok there are 400,000 more female than male residents, yet 89 per cent of all tourists are male.

The primary objective of tourism development has always been to earn foreign exchange that will ease the balance of payments problem and so it did. A study in 1982 showed that of the entire trade deficit, 40 per cent was reduced by tourism revenues.

Those who are attracted by sex tours are not limited to any particular geographical area. In that sense there is someone for everyone. Chiangmai in the north has its share of brothels, mainly catering to westerners; Bangkok is international in its attractions.

Sex tours and prostitution in general has been a major feature of Thai tourism. It is necessary to know the background regarding prostitution in Thailand. Courtesans, concubines and prostitutes have been commonplace throughout the country's history. Courtesans operated in monarchical circles, the number of concubines was a measure of aristocratic power and commoners patronised the local brothels.

Women are divided into wives and whores. Prostitution is so widespread in Thailand that many have looked for ways to explain its domination of the tourist industry. Some see it as a reflection of Thai culture. They argue that Thailand has always had prostitution and that the new depravity is merely a response to a global demand. Some women who are not attached to brothels or "sex shows" refer to their jobs as "working with foreigners."

Prostitution in Thailand for the tourist industry has proved a real drawing card for a certain stratum of clientele. Not only sex but sex shows are part of the attraction. The Government attempted to crack down on prostitution and the infamous blue shows in 1981, but attempting an outright abolition of what is already theoretically illegal has been difficult to do. Today Thailand is losing some sex tourists because fear of disease or police crack downs.

Political objectives have made tourism an attractive policy area for Israel. The new country with a troubled history wants to attract young and enthusiastic immigrants. Such policy has been apparently successful because during the 1970s, over 10 per cent of all tourists visiting Israel opted to migrate there.

Tourism is also important as a means of initiating or enlarging the scope of cooperative alliances with other nations through such bodies as the ASEAN and the UNESCO. For example, ASEAN has set up a permanent committee on tourism, which is exploring the idea of an ASEAN passport, eased interregional currency exchange and special fares as well as the development of region-wide policy on tourism promotion.

The politics of Indian tourism policy is just the opposite of China. India encouraged tourism since the days of Alexander the Great. "There is no happiness for him who does not travel." India has used tourism for national development. Indian tourism policy, like its politics in general, is shaped by India's geopolitical setting as the dominant country on the South Asian subcontinent. Despite long tradition and richness and diversity of its cultures and scenic attractions, the levels of international tourism are not very high.

Domestic tourism in South Asia has developed along two lines. The old pattern centres round the traditions of festivals and religious pilgrimages to the numerous Hindu, Buddhist, Sikh and Muslim holy places. A second pattern of domestic tourism was the retreat to the hills during the hot season. Dozens of hill stations such as Darjeeling, Simla, Moussorie and Ooti became the destinations of choice of the English and upper class Indians.

Colonial rule contributed to tourism development in many ways. Railways provided an infrastructure for inexpensive surface travel. For India, size and diversity are additional factors that help to encourage domestic tourism.

'War, politics, public opinion and civil unrest can be the greatest enemy of tourism'. War and civil unrest are definitely detrimental to tourism. Expansion of tourism has suffered from unrest such as wars with Pakistan in 1965 and 1971 and quarrels with Sri Lanka over the later's treatment of Tamils of Indian descent.

Violence in Delhi, Punjab and Assam and religious riots in Hyderabad have adversely affected domestic as well as international tourism. Following the assassination of Indira Gandhi on October 31, 1984, 70 per cent of all tour bookings for November were cancelled, an immediate US 1.00 million dollar loss to this industry.

Indian tourism continues to be the victim of the political problems of other countries in the region, factors that interrupt air travel, make overland travel impossible, or lead to the cancellation of multi-country tours of the region. Iraq and Iran conflict led to the cancellation of Pan Am's round-the-world service, which had a stopover in Delhi. Martial law in Pakistan and Bangladesh discouraged travel to those nations. Since July, 1983, sporadic communal violence in Sri Lanka has discouraged travel there.

There are five main policy phases in Indian tourism development. From 1949 to 1966 tourism gradually grew with limited involvement from the Government. Most states were not active and since tourism is primarily a state, the Centre had only a minor role. In 1958, a separate Tourism Department was created within the Ministry of Transport.

The Second policy phase marked the beginning of major changes in both the administrative and operational development of tourism. In 1966, the Indian Tourism Development Corporation was created and it has become a model for tourism promotion throughout South Asia.

Tourism policy in India is a combination of both national and state policies. Tourism organisation very clearly reflects the federal character of the country. As a concurrent subject in the Indian Constitution, tourism is the responsibility of both the Union and the States.

Phase three was marked by the defeat of Indira Gandhi's Government. The ascendancy of Morarji Desai's much more puritanical Janata Party had a major impact on the direction of tourism policy between 1977 and 1979. In early 1978, the Janata Party Minister for Tourism announced that the Indian Government would no longer assist in the construction of four-star or five-star hotels. The limited resources available for tourism would be used entirely for the creation of facilities for domestic and foreign tourists in the middle and low income groups. The Janata concept never has much chance to get off the ground as the Party was defeated in 1979.

The fourth policy phase was ushered in with the return of Indira Gandhi's Government in 1980. Tourism industry was in bad shape during this period.

The fifth phase in tourism policy began in 1984 with the tragic assassination of Indira Gandhi and the assumption of Prime Minister by Rajiv Gandhi. The Bhopal gas tragedy, Indira Gandhi's death and the subsequent tour cancellations put the industry in desperate shape.

Rajiv Gandhi had unprecedented commitments to tourism. The Planning Commission has tripled its previous commitment to tourism spending and the National Development Council has accorded tourism official status as an industry.

After its stagnation in the early 80s tourist growth became significant. In 1986, for the first time, over one million international tourists visited earning India about Rs. 18 billion. By 1990s, 2.5 million arrivals have been estimated. The fifth phase growth is a reflection of several factors.

Political stability has been established but major tourist-generating markets have been stimulated by exposing India's numerous attractions through several outstanding films and exhibits. *Gandhi, A Passage to India*, the *Jewel in the Crown* and the *Far Pavilions* have exposed tens of millions to the lure of India. In addition, the Festival of India has attracted widespread attention to India. Private sector is encouraged to build one to three-star hotels. Immigration procedures and health checks are being simplified, and training centres for hotel industry staff are being planned.

Last five years of Atal Bihari Vajpayee as Prime Minister of India have proved to the most rewarding for the tourism industry, as national income from this source have gone up more than 100 per cent as compared to any other period of five years in the history of India's tourism industry, and we hope that this process will continue for long if peace process to normalize Indo-Pak relation started by him, bear fruits.

There are countries that do not use tourism for development because they do not want tourists and so do not issue tourist visas, for example, Saudi Arabia. But Pakistan has failed to succeed in using tourism for development though Pakistan's tourism potential is enormous.

The ethnic diversity of its 100 million people, the archaeological importance of Mohen-Jodaro, Harappa, Taxila and lesser-known sites throughout the country; the religious shrines, the wide variety of terrain and the dramatic scenic beauty make it globe's most popular destination. Despite all this, growth in tourism has not been very impressive. In 1980, 292,000 tourists visited Pakistan and since then there has been a gradual growth.

'Pakistan is not known to the outside world as a tourist destination mainly because the foreign tourist is not aware of the attractions that the country has to offer and does not know what specific places to visit in case he does arrive in Pakistan.'

Tourist fit well with Bhutto's design to reorient Pakistan westward following the 1971 war, without East Pakistan, the nation looked to the Middle East for trade and the cultural identity. Pakistan became a recreational oasis for Middle Eastern elites. Bhutto accordingly promoted plans to build a casino in Karachi and other facilities to attract tourists. Middle Eastern rulers responded by vacationing in Pakistan and giving sizable grants.

Bhutto also saw in tourism development a way to make the society more modern and less parochial in its politics and social views. Traditional barriers to the emancipation of women might erode if a large number of tourists arrive. Bhutto's political and social vision of tourism was not given time to be tested.

The July 1977 coup replaced Bhutto with Zia-ul-Haq. Zia is more fundamentalist in his religious and social views that any of his predecessors, with deleterious consequences for tourism; Islamic injunctions against social mixing of the mixing of the sexes, consumption of alcohol and gambling adversely affected arrival of European and American tourists.

For Muslims, the most important travel is to Mecca, a trip meaning tremendous foreign exchange leakage from Pakistan. In fact, Haj has been given high priority in the tourism planning of the Government. Other forms of travel by Pakistani tourists involve summer trips to the hills.

Islamization or Nizami-i-Mustafa (Rule of the Prophet) of President Zia is not conductive to domestic or international tourism. One month during Ramjan, all restaurants and all catering facilities closed between dawn and dusk. Even after dusk facilities for tourists are spartan. All night clubs have been closed, strict prohibition is enforced. Folk dances as well as belly-dancing have been axed. Muzak has gone.

Sri Lanka, 'the Pearl of the Orient' is often referred to as the 'Resplendent Isle.' Sri Lanka has a 15 million population and is a 'tourist Paradise'. Sir Lanka with a good infrastructural base of railroads, guest houses and administrative experience upon which it build its tourism programme. In 1967, 19,000 tourists visited Sri Lanka and spent US $ 1.3 million. In 1982, 407,230 tourists visited Sri Lanka and tourism has become the fifth largest source of foreign exchange. Tourism has been the major casualty of ethnic violence in Sri Lanka.

The Maldives with a population of 150,000 has been discovered as a tourist spot in 1970. The country at the south west coasts of India and Sri Lanka consist of 1,187 tiny islands most of which are uninhabited. In fact, the Maldives have not even bothered to build jails. Most offenders are put under house arrest and more serious crimes are punished by banishment to a remote atoll. By 1984, more than 40 resorts had opened in the Maldives.

The Government has taken an active interest in tourism development. The Government has offered some concessions to build hotels to the Taj Group from India.

"People Power, the Unarmed Forces of the Philippines" mean a new era in the Philippines. Expelling Ferdinand Marcos, Corazon Aquino like Marcos felt that tourism policy would be a useful political weapon. The Philippines had the reputation of a lively democracy in the midst of the authoritarian nations of South-east Asia. It was President Marcos who in 1972 demonstrated that tourism could be developed to convey and create regime legitimacy in ways not attempted before Marcos had to prove the legitimacy of his military law so that it might not jeopardize the flow of foreign capital investment into the country.

The imposition of martial law was a legitimate response of an emergency situation created by communist subversion. Tourism which had fallen off dramatically in the period immediately before martial law was quickly seized upon as a means to refurbish the Marco's image. Tourism now became a priority industry eligible for a variety of tax incentives and customs concessions. The regime had set up its first Department of Tourism (DoT) in May, 1973.

For sometime Mrs. Marcos had nurtured expansive and

expensive ambitions to see Philippines and particularly Manila, blossom into an international oasis for the luxury traveller.

It was the IMF—World Bank Conference in October, 1976 that stimulated the most politically motivated use of tourism.

Selective acts of terrorism against tourists had been increasing as the Marcos family became identified as the prime beneficiaries of the Government's expensive tourism development programme. In 1970s there were kidnappings of two Japanese tourists on the southern island of Mindanoo. This event had severe repercussions. A strong military police and stiff sentences for crimes against tourists were the Government's attempt to keep lawlessness to a minimum in Manila's tourist belt.

Tourism policy under Aquino had attempted to diffuse benefits more broadly than was true under Marcos.

Under Martial Law tourist brochures promised, "a tanned peach on every beach, sex tours including those for pedophiles" flourished and the Lady Marcos's own notorious motels and massage parlours were exempted from the martial law curfew. Re-emergence of democracy was a tourist attraction in Philippines.

## QUESTIONS FOR ANSWER

1. *How politics has a direct impact on tourism? Explain by giving examples.*
2. *Civil unrest and war not only effect the tourism in the effected nation but also in the near by nations. Discuss.*
3. *Explain the five main policy phases in Indian tourism development.*
4. *Political objectives and tourism in Pakistan.*
5. *Write short notes on politics and tourism in following nations:*
   (*a*) *Thailand.*
   (*b*) *USA.*
   (*c*) *India.*
   (*d*) *China.*

## 16

# Tourism: The Psychological Dimensions

The impact of psychological elements such as human will, desire, aptitude, inclination, dedication, determination etc. on human and institutional or organization is a well established principle because institutions are managed by the human beings. Since tourist is a human being and persons managing travel activities are also human beings, therefore, psychological factors play a vital role in tourism industry. Hereunder, we will discuss various aspects of this impact in brief:

## TOURISM AND HUMAN BEHAVIOUR

In attempting to account both for consistency of and change in behaviour, psychologists have found it useful to use certain concepts. We have been able to understand behaviour by determining (*a*) the motives, drives, or concerns which are being satisfied by the action, and (*b*) the attitudes and information that the person uses to decide what response he should make in a given situation. A motive can be defined as a person's basic predisposition to reach for or to strive toward a general class of goals.

Attitude is a more circumscribed concept. It can generally be conceived of as an inner factor predisposing one to react positively or negatively towards particular objects, acts, or institutions. As person's disposition or attitude towards an object is likely to depend upon (*a*) the basic motive with which the object is associated; and (*b*) the degree to which the object is received as instrumental for satisfying or blocking these motives.

In any account of the behaviours of people we start our

description with reference to some kind of active driving force: "the individual seeks", "the individual wants", "the individual fears", and so on. In addition, we specify an object or condition towards which that force is directed: "he seeks wealth", "he wants peace," "he fears something".

The study of the relationships between these two variables, the driving force and the object or condition towards which that driving force is directed, is the study of the dynamics of behaviour or motivation. The basic principles or dynamics accounting for the behaviour of going to a temple, joining a particular association, choosing a mate, etc., are the same no matter how simple or how complex the activity.

Such principles, if they are to be helpful in making accurate predictions of individual behaviour and in increasing our understanding of social phenomenon, must answer questions such as: What induces these driving forces of wanting, seeking, fearing in the individuals? What determines, for different individuals the specific nature of the objects or conditions towards which these driving forces are directed.

The question of motivation is the question of "why". Why do some people travel and others not? Why in a particular country do more people engage in tourism than in another? Or for that matter why one member in a family undertakes travel and others do not? The answers to all these questions have been given in the preceding paragraphs. Various studies of tourism psychology and motivation show that individuals normally travel for more than one reason, and for many, perhaps the majority, tourism is the outcome of a combination of motivations.

## PSYCHOLOGY OF EARLY TRAVELLERS

Prior to the emergence of mass tourism the growth of tourism was the result of certain sets of influences. As a result of the Industrial Revolution in the nineteenth century, there emerged a large and prosperous group in the Western society, since there was a general increase in the material wealth as industrialization grew and trade and commerce developed. This gave rise to new settlements and towns and cities were built to accommodate the increasing number of workforce which was engaged in industries, trade and commerce. Population came to be increasingly concentrated in towns and cities. The introduction of the railway system resulted in cheap and quick means of inland travel. The steamship met the need for international travel, therefore, travel organizations emerged, which made travel very easy because travel agencies fulfilled all the needs of tourists.

The three major developments—increase in the wealth of the industrial society, development of the means of transport and the organization of travel—were first witnessed in England and America. However, their influence soon spread across into other countries in Europe and elsewhere. The basic motives to engage in tourism, which had been apparent even much before the middle of the nineteenth century, can be said to be curiosity, seeking material gains by engaging in trade and commerce and education and health.

As no scientific studies were made in that period to determine the motive for travel, it can be safely said that there could have been many more motives besides the basic motives of curiosity, trade and commerce, education and health and recreation. Motivation also includes secondary needs such as success, prestige, achievement, recognition and socialization.

## PURPOSES OR MOTIVATORS OF MODERN TOURISM

We will discuss motivational factors in tourism, in detail in the next chapter, therefore, hereunder we will outline only one aspect, very briefly:

Travel motivators are those factors that create a person's desire to travel. They are the internal psychological influences affecting individual choices. Motivations for travel incorporate a broad range of human experience and behaviours. A brief list of travel motivations might include rest and relaxation, recreation, excitement, social interactions with friends and relations, status, adventure, physical challenges, status and escape from routine work and stress. With the advent of mass tourism, especially after the Second World War, various studies have been made to find out the reasons as to why people wish to travel and become tourists.

McIntosh has stated that basic travel motivators may be grouped into the following four categories.

(*i*) *Physical motivators*, which are related to physical relaxation and rest, sporting activities and specific medical treatment. All are connected with the individual's bodily healthy and well being.

(*ii*) *Cultural motivators*, which are connected with the individual's desire to travel in order to learn about other countries and their people and their cultural heritage expressed in art, music, literature, folklore, etc.

(*iii*) *Interpersonal motivators*, which are related to a desire to visit relatives, friends, or to escape from one's family, workmates or neighbours, or to meet new people and forge new friendships, or simply to escape from the routine of everyday life.

(*iv*) *Status and prestige motivators*, which are identified with the needs of personal esteem and personal development. These are related to travel for business or professional interests, for the purpose of education and the pursuit of hobbies.

The above-mentioned categories of motivators can be broken down and elaborated as under:

(*i*) *Pleasure*: Getting away from all that routine of everyday life is perhaps the most importance motive of all in recent times. The individual's desire and need for pure pleasure is very strong indeed. An individual likes to have fun, excitement and good time whenever possible. The significance of the pleasure factor is widely utilized by travel agents and tour operators who are astute psychologists when it comes to selling the tours. Various brochures and folders particularly emphasise the pleasure aspects of the holidays and travel.

(*ii*) *Relaxation, Rest and Recreation*: Industrialization and urbanization has created great pressures on modern living. The stress and strain of modern city life has made it still more necessary than ever before for people to get away from all this and relax in an atmosphere which is more peaceful and healthy. Relaxation is very essential to keep the body and mind healthy. There may be various forms of relaxation and rest. Whatever form the holiday takes, relaxation is always sought in a certain measure by the holidaymaker.

(*iii*) *Health*: The benefits to be gained from fresh air and sunshine have long been recognised. The development of spas during the Roman Empire was the result of people's desire to seek good health. The subsequent establishment of many sanatoria is Switzerland was the result of awareness on the part of the people of the various benefits of good health. These sanatoria laid the foundations for future resort developments. Many travel to spas and clinics for curative baths and medical treatment. In some countries like Italy, Austria and Germany, great importance is given to spa treatment. In Russia along the Black Sea coast and in the foothills of the Caucasus Mountains, there are many world-famous sanatoria where millions of Russians and international tourists throng every year.

(*iv*) *Participation in Sports*: There has been an increasing participation in a wide variety of sporting activities such as mountaineering, walking, skiing, sailing, fishing, sunbathing, trekking, boating, surf-riding, etc. The visitors go to places primarily to indulge in a sporting activity to which all their energies are directed.

(*v*) *Curiosity and Culture*: An increasing number of people are visiting different lands, especially places having important historical or cultural associations with the ancient past or places holding special art festivals, music festivals, theatre and other cultural events of importance. Curiosity has been one of the major reasons for tourism. There has always been curiosity in man about foreign lands, people and places. In the present-day world technological developments in the area of mass media have made it possible for people to read, see and hear about different places. The increasing interest shown by many in architecture, art, music, literature, folklore, dance, paintings and sports, of other people's culture or in archaeological and historical remains and monuments is but another aspect of man's curiosity to seek more knowledge. This curiosity has been stimulated by more education. International events like the Olympic Games, Asian Games, national celebrations, exhibitions, special festivals, etc., attract thousands of tourists.

(*vi*) *Ethnic and Family*: This includes visiting one's relatives and friends, meeting new people and seeking new friendships. A large number of people travel for interpersonal reasons. There is considerable travel by people wanting to visit friends and relatives. Every year thousands of people visit India for ethnic reasons. Many friendships have been made as a result of holiday acquaintances.

(*vii*) *Spiritual and Religious*: Travel for spiritual reasons has been taking place since a long time. Visiting religious places has been one of the earliest motivators of travel. A large number of people have been making pilgrimages to sacred religious places or holy places. This practice is widespread in many parts of the world. In the Christian world, for instance, a visit to Jerusalem or the Vatican is considered auspicious. In the Arab-Muslim world, a pilgrimage to Mecca is considered a great act of faith. In India there are many pilgrimage centres and holy places belonging to all the major religions of the world. A large number of pilgrims from all over the world come to India every year.

(*viii*) *Status and Prestige*: This concerns the ego needs and personal development. Many people undertake travel with a view to talk about it to their relatives and friends. They like to impress them by relating their experiences in the various places visited. They also travel because they think it is fashionable to do so and, perhaps, show that they can afford to do it. Foreign tour is a magic word and people like to mention it to their friends and other acquaintances.

(*ix*) *Professional or Business*: Attending conventions and conferences related to the profession, industry or commerce or to some organization to which the individual belongs has become very popular. Convention travel has made great strides in recent times. In order to attract more tourists many countries have established grand convention complexes where all kinds of modern facilities are provided for business meetings and seminars. Hotels also provide facilities for conventions as a large number of people travel for business and professional reasons. Conventions and conferences associated with education, commerce, industry, politics and various professions are increasingly being held in various parts of the world. Although some people travel strictly for business purposes, the majority link business travel with pleasure.

Motivations can also be classified as (*i*) destination related and (*ii*) non-destination related.

Destination-related travel motivators are those that allow a tourist to select any area/attraction where he/she would like to go. Tourists are not restricted to a specific destination or an area within a destination. A cost comparison can always be made before making a decision. The determining factor in this travel is the cause rather than the destination itself. This would include travel for business, education, visiting friends and relations (VFR travel), health and pilgrimage.

In his summary to the history of tourism, Professor Krapf cites a series of motivations which he considers as the determining impulses of tourism in the past and present. As the first motivating factor, Krapf mentions the exploration of the close and distant neighbourhood. If we proceed from the fact that foreign lands and people were originally looked upon as dangerous and even hostile, it is obvious that considerable personal courage was required to visit or confront them. Only a strong man with initiative could dare to forsake the security of the family or the clan and travel to nearby or distant places.

The second motivation advanced by Krapf is divine service. Originally, this also implied an exceptional social position, for it was a prerogative reserved for priests to visit places considered as abodes of the deities, and it was only gradually that the worldly high-ranking persons were able to approach them.

The same held true for the third motivation, which is participation in events of religious or secular authority. Such participation was again reserved for the selected few, *i.e.,* those of higher social positions.

The utilisation of natural medical cures or journey to watering-places, as the fourth motivating factor, is again characterized by being restricted to particular social classes, at first the nobility and later the well-to-do bourgeoisie. Here the restrictions followed from the fact of long distances and the related high costs of travel and sojourn.

The final motive force mentioned by Krapf is the enjoyment of nature which must, however, be regarded as of relatively late validity at a time when man began to take a pleasure in nature and did not look upon it as something self-evidence to be taken for granted or even to some extent dangerous. It was the intellectual call for a "return to Nature" which first exercised the spell and made trips into what was now considered as "magnificent Nature" a favourite social practice. But here again the high costs resulted in this practice being restricted to the well off, that is the higher social classes.

Some of the motivations cited in respect of modern tourism can be enumerated as follows:

(*i*) The exploration of the close and distant neighbourhood has become travel aimed at knowing other countries, regions or people, and also travel for studies and cultural ends.

(*ii*) Divine service as a travel-motivating force subsists in journeys to sacred religious places and in pilgrimages.

(*iii*) Participation in events of religious or secular authority manifests itself today in the form of travel to political meetings and ceremonies.

(*iv*) The utilisation of natural medical cures comprises in the widest sense all travel undertaken with the object of rest and relaxation, medical care or treatment of diseases.

(*v*) Travel for the enjoyment of the beauties of the landscape has undergone modifications both in the conception of what is beautiful and in the expression of sentiment.

(*vi*) A further motive of tourism is constituted by sports travel. This includes travel for the sake of travelling, the joy felt in motion. In fact, this is only one sports activity projected on the travel screen in addition to the numerous other motive forces connected with sports for which landscape and nature provide the setting for the best possible practice and exercise of sports.

Various reasons as to why people wish to become tourists have been considered. In considering the reasons we are thus dealing with the motivations. After examining the motivations, two broad distinguishable groups of travellers emerge. The first group consists of those who have to visit a particular place and includes businessmen and those who may be described as common-interest travellers, such as those visiting relatives and friends. The second group consists of tourists in the pure sense who have a freedom of choice. This group decides for themselves whether they should apply a part of their leisure time to participate in tourism. They also decide for themselves where and when to go. The demand for travel for this group as compared to the demand for the former group is highly price-elastic, that is susceptible to price inducements.

It may be stated that the prime motivation to engage in tourism is to be elsewhere and to escape, however temporarily from the routine of everyday life. From this basic motivation, two principal and distinct motivations may be stipulated as dominant. These have been described by Professor Gray as (*i*) wanderlust and (*ii*) sunlust. *Wanderlust* describes the desire to exchange the known for the unknown or familiar with the unfamiliar, to leave things familiar and to go and see different places, people and cultures or architecture of the past in places famous for their historical monuments and also past associations.

*Sunlust*, on the other hand, generates a type of travel which depends on the existence elsewhere of better amenities and facilities for a specific purpose than are available in the home country of the traveller. It is commonly associated with such activities as sports and search for sunshine.

## QUESTIONS FOR ANSWER

1. *Write a note on the motivators of modern mass tourism.*
2. *Write short notes on the following:*
   (*a*) *Psychology of Early Travellers.*
   (*b*) *Tourism and Human Behaviour.*
   (*c*) *Wanderlust and Sunlust tourism.*
   (*d*) *Destination related motivators of tourism.*

# 17

# Tourism: The Motivational Factor

The nature of travel and the destination of tourism in the product of the motive of tourist. In American parlance the four 's' formula—Sun, sea, sound and sex motivates a tourist, but this is one aspect only. There are many more reasons of tourism, known as motives or motivational aspect of tourism.

Dann has pointed out that there are seven elements of motivation in tourism.

1. *Travel is a response to what is lacking yet deserved.* This approach suggests that tourists are motivated by the desire to experience phenomena which are different from those available in their home environment.
2. *Destination pull in response to motivational push.* This approach analyses the motivation of the individual tourist in terms of the level of desire (push) and the pull of the destination.
3. *Motivation as fantasy.* This approach suggests that tourists travel in order to undertake behaviour which may not be culturally sanctioned in their home setting.
4. *Motivation as classified purpose.* This approach analyses the main purpose of a trip as a motivator for travel. Purpose may include visiting friends and relatives, enjoying leisure activities, etc.
5. *Motivational typologies.* This approach divides the tourist's behaviour into sunlust and wanderlust.
6. *Motivation and tourist experiences.* This approach is characterized by the authenticity of tourist experiences.
7. *Motivation as auto-definition and meaning.* This suggests that the way in which tourists define their situations will provide a greater understanding of tourist motivation than simply describing their behaviour.

McIntosh and Goeldner mentioned four categories of motivation.

1. *Physical Motivations*: These are related to refreshment of body and mind, health purposes, sport and pleasure. This group of motivations, are seen to be linked to those activities which reduce tension.
2. *Cultural Motivations*: These are identified by the desire to see and know more about other cultures, to find out about the natives of a country, their lifestyle, music, art, folklore, dance, etc.
3. *Interpersonal Motivations*: These include a desire to meet new people, visit friends or relatives, seek new experiences. Travel is an escape from routine relationship with friends or neighbours and the home environment or it is used for spiritual reasons.
4. *Status and Prestige Motivations*: These include a desire for the continuation of hobbies and education and are also seen to be concerned with the desire for recognition and attention from others, in order to boost the personal ego.

There are two broad groups of travellers. The first group comprises those who have to visit a particular place and those visiting friends and relatives. The decision to travel—where to go and when to go—is to a great extent outside their control. They are not much influenced by price or distance.

The second group—holiday tourists or pleasure travellers—have a freedom of choice. They decide for themselves whether they should spend a part of their income and leisure time for tourism. Their demand for travel is highly price elastic.

The prime motivation in tourism is the desire to be elsewhere and to escape the routine, constraints and stress of everyday life. From this basic motivation two distinct motivations may be seen which have been described by Prof. Gray as wanderlust and sunlust.

Wanderlust indicates the desire to exchange the known for the unknown and to go and see different places, people, cultures or relics of the past in places of historical importance.

On the other hand, sunlust indicates a type of travel which depends on the existence elsewhere of better amenities for a specific purpose than are available locally. It is prominent with particular activities such as sports and with the search for the sun. A hunt for the sun is typified by tourist flow to the Mediterranean, Caribbean or South Pacific. Wanderlust might be thought of as a push factor whereas sunlust is largely a response to 'pull' factors elsewhere.

The essence of 'break from routine' is, in most cases, either locating in a different place or changing the dominant social context from the work milieu.

Crompton has identified seven socio-cultural motives as follows:

1. Escape from a perceived mundane environment,
2. Exploration and evaluation of self,
3. Relaxation,
4. Prestige,
5. Regression (less constrained behaviour),
6. Enhancement of kinship relationships,
7. Facilitation of social interaction,
8. Novelty and education.

Grinstein explained the regressive element as: lying on the warm sand, being buried in the sand, being in the nude, are all examples of pleasures which represent manifestations of partial regression.

Tourism enhances leisure opportunities for rest and relaxation. Leipet distinguishes between recreational leisure and creative leisure which produces something new. He sees three functions of recreation as:

1. Rest, which provides recovery from physical or mental fatigue;
2. Relaxation, *i.e.*, recovery from tension; and
3. Entertainment, *i.e.*, recovery from boredom.

Iso-Ahola has proposed a theoretical motivational model in which the escaping element is compounded by a seeking component. One set of motivational forces are obtained from an individual desire to escape his personal environment (personal problems) and/or the interpersonal environment (co-workers, family members and friends). Another set of forces result from the desire to obtain certain psychological rewards by travelling to a different environment.

## TOURISM—THE LAW OF DEMAND

Like any other product, tourism is a product and is subjected to the law of demand. The demand for tourism is determined by a number of economic, social and psychological factors.

### Economic Determinants of Demand

*(a) Income*

The demand for tourism can be expressed as follows.

$$D_t = f(P_t P_i \dots P_n, Y, T)$$

where $D_t$ = Demand for tourism
$P_t$ = Price of tourism,
$P_i = P_n$ are prices of all other goods,
$Y$ = Income, and
$T$ = Taste

It simply means that as income increases the demand for tourism is likely to increase. However, empirical studies indicate that in the developed countries the demand for tourism has actually increased faster than the growth of national income. In the West when a person's income rises by one unit they spend 1.5 units on tourism. This indicates a high propensity to travel. The emergence of two-income families has encouraged tourism. Total family income has risen steadily as more wives have entered the labour market.

Tourism is an expensive activity that demands a certain threshold of income before participation is possible. The most useful measure of the ability to participate in tourism is discretionary income *i.e.*, the income left over when tax, housing and the basics of life have been accounted for.

*(b) Price of Holiday*

The second economic determinant of demand for tourism is the price of the holiday. The price that the tourist pays the holiday covers three components.

- Cost of travel,
- Cost of accommodation, and
- The cost of the activities undertaken by the tourist at the destination area.

The components of the cost of travel are as follows:

$$C_t = f(F.O) + f(R)$$

where $C_t$ = Cost of Transport
$F$ = Cost of fuel
$O$ = Other travel costs, and
$R$ = Profitability of airlines,

In the case of holiday costs, approximately forty per cent of the price of a package holiday arises from the flight costs. Of the flight costs, an important variable is the fuel cost. Fuel costs are subjected to wide fluctuations.

Cost of accommodation is determined by the hotel costs, *i.e.*,

$$C_a = f(H)$$

where, $C_a$ = Cost of accommodation
$H$ = Hoteliers' costs.

The growth of tourism demand has been stimulated by a combination of growth in income and increase in leisure time permitted by increases in paid holiday time and free weekends. In addition, the introduction of flexible working patterns permits people to plan and take extended weekend breaks more easily than in the past. Thus the tourism/work ratio has moved towards tourism as the number of hours of holidays have increased and the number of hours of work have decreased.

## PSYCHOLOGICAL FACTOR—THE DETERMINANT OF DEMAND

Last but not the least, holiday meets a series of deep psychological needs. Tourism is a product which represents either an escape from daily reality or a means of self-fulfilment.

The following psychological needs have been identified.

(*a*) *The Escape Motivation*: This is essentially a wish to get away from a perceived mundane environment.
(*b*) *Relaxation*: This is a wish for recuperation.
(*c*) *Play*: This is a wish to indulge in activities associated with childhood. Play on holiday is culturally approved. Adults indulge in games not otherwise permitted. There is a regression into the carefree state of childhood.

(*d*) *Strengthening Family Bond*: In the common situation where both partners work full time, the holiday represents a time when both can renew their relationship.

(*e*) *Prestige*: Status and social enhancement can be temporarily gained on the basis of the destination chosen for the holiday. Certain destinations are fashionable and prestigious, such as, for an Indian a visit to Kashmir or Goa is considered prestigious.

(*f*) *Social Interaction*: The holidays provides an opportunity for social interaction with the people of the host society. In many cases the rationale for the holiday is simply an opportunity for sexual activity which we find in the sex tourism of the Far East in Thailand or the Philippines.

(*g*) *Educational Opportunity*: Tourism provides a chance to see new and strange sights, to learn about other places of the world and talk with people of other cultures. Also there is a chance to see the sites of history and the original great works of art.

Level of educational attainment is an important determinant of travel properly as education laroadens horizons and stimulates the desire to travel.

(*h*) *Self-Fulfilment*: The voyage of discovery may not be simply a discovery of new places and people but also an opportunity for self-discovery. The search for self-discovery might change life or perspective.

(*i*) *Wish Fulfilment*: For some the holiday is an answer to a dream. The popularity of theme parks is an escape into a fantasy.

(*j*) *Shopping*: Shopping is not only one of the most common tourist activities but it can also be the motivating factor for travel away from home and indeed for international travel.

The following types of activities represent tourism demand:

(*a*) *Communing with Nature*: Demand for parks, open areas, commons, walking, rambling, etc.

(*b*) *Attractions*: Visiting zoos, safari parks, theme parks etc.

(*c*) *Heritage*: Visiting castles, museums, religious sites, ancient monuments, battle fields etc.

(*d*) *Sport Activity*: Taking part in or watching various forms of indoor or outdoor sports.

(*e*) *Entertainment*: Apart from sports, these include visits to the cinema, theatre, discos, casino, etc.
(*f*) *Relaxation*: Sunbath, resting, reading, etc.
(*g*) *Health*: Massage, change of air.
(*h*) *Shopping*: Antique hunting, new equipment, etc.
(*i*) *Business Activities*: Meetings, conferences, exhibitions, etc.

## DEVELOPMENT OF TOURIST ENVIRONMENT

Tourist environment are extremely dynamic. They are influenced by the changing tastes of holiday makers. The notion of life cycle change in tourist destination is helpful in explaining changes in tourists environments. Butler popularised the idea of a resort life cycle to explain the growth and decline of resorts. He suggested a six-stage cycle of the evolution of tourist destination areas expressed in terms of changes in the numbers of visitors over time.

1. *Exploration*: Small number of visitors are attracted by natural beauty or cultural characteristics-number are limited and practically no tourist facilities exist.
2. *Involvement*: Limited involvement by local residents to provide some facilities to tourists is present and markets begin to emerge.
3. *Development*: Large numbers of tourists arrive, control passes on to external organisations and there is increasing tension between locals and tourists.
4. *Consolidation*: Tourism becomes a major part of the local economy although rates of visitor growth start to fall.
5. *Stagnation*: Peak number of tourists is reached but the resort is no longer considered attractive.
6. *Decline*: Attractiveness continues to decline, visitors are lost to other resorts and the resort depends more on day visitors than longer time visitors.

A great deal of leisure consumption is about myths and fantasies. The creation of unreal images is essential for many tourists seeking to escape the dullness of their home and work routines. Early tourist sought such differences in the romantic authenticity of the Grand Tour through an examination of ancient cultures.

The present day equivalents of the groups still search for

holiday experiences that bring them into contact with original cultures and societies untouched by the modern world. In contrast, we can also represent a very different set of tourist environments which have been deliberately set out to attract visitors by falsifying both place and time. Theme park is a case in point. Walt Disney is credited with the original notion of the theme park, with the creation of Disneyland in California in 1955.

## YOUTH TOURISM—A NEW DIMENSION

A recent origin of urban tourism in the West is the Youth tourism. Young people with suitcases in hand are found in all important cities of Europe, America and India. They form the clientele for cheap hotels and Youth hostels and sometimes in the summer they sleep in the parks. In Helsinki, during summer, the Dooms Acadenica turns into a hostel for young tourists. In the summer time, the vondelpark in Amsterdam virtually turns into a dormitory for young tourists.

Some countries try to restrict this youth tourism as it brings very little money and at the same time creates problems, *e.g.*, drug use, theft, snatching etc. But there are other countries which accept these tourist and to attract them offer cheap airfares, cheap railroad passes. Special guide books are written for young tourists with information for cheap eating places, lodges, night life, how to meet the opposite sex, etc.

Artificially created attractions for tourists are not less important. Disneyland in California, Disney World in Florida, Tivoli in Copenhagen, Vauxhall Gardens in London, Skansen in Stockholm or Sentosa in Singapore are such examples.

The establishments in frontier areas devoted to gambling, drinking, prostitution or the sale of goods unobtainable or more expensive in the hometown attract tourists. The gambling casinos of Las Vegas and Nevada are such examples. On the international level, red light areas of Tijuana, Juarez and others near the Mexican borders are said to be bringing sixty per cent of Mexico's tourist revenue.

The phenomenon of "frontier prostitution" exists also along the Belgian side of Belgian-Dutch border where a number of red-light cafes cater to the Dutch from the towns of the Southern Netherlands.

An innocuous form of border tourist is the shopper who wishes to take advantage of cheaper price in a foreign country. An example is Calexico, California which attracts shoppers from Mexicali in Mexico. Everyday more than 50,000 Mexicans cross the border to buy egg, meat and other goods for their better quality and lower price.

## QUESTIONS FOR ANSWER

1. *What elements motivate a person to undertake a tour? Explain.*
2. *Explain the factors that determine the demand for tourism.*
3. *What are the psychological needs that are satisfied by tourism? Explain.*
4. *What is a resort life cycle? Explain the growth and decline of resorts.*
5. *Write a note on youth tourism as a new dimension of tourism.*

# 18

# Tourism: The Socio-Economic Impact

Tourism is the world's largest export industry and its growth is very fast, it has grown from opulent class to mass movement of the people with an urge to discover the unknown, to explore new and strange places, to seek changes in environment and undergo new experiences, therefore it is a source of mass contact between persons of different socio-economic, socio-cultural, socio-political and ecological conditions, hence tourism has its impact on all these areas, which we will discuss hereunder:

## SOCIO-ECONOMIC IMPACT

During the past few decades many economies have experienced growth in their service sectors, even when the more traditional agricultural and manufacturing sectors have been subject to stagnation or decline. Tourism is a service-based industry and as such, has been partly responsible for this service-based growth. In developing countries, the service-sector is responsible for 40 per cent of the GDP while in developed economies it is responsible for more than 65 per cent GDP.

The provision of tourist service generates employment. It must be remembered that much tourist activity is seasonal and numbers employed vary a great deal from one time of the year to another time.

In India, tourism has created direct employment for 7 million people. In UK, total tourism-related employment is about 7 per cent of total employment in that country.

Tourism as a source of employment is particularly important for areas with limited alternative sources of employment, *i.e.*, non-industrial areas deficient in natural resources.

According to one estimate an investment of one million rupees creates 89 jobs in the hotel and restaurant sector, a key component of the tourism industry, as against 44.7 jobs in agriculture and 12.6 in manufacturing industries. This ratio obviously increases if one takes into account ancillary services associated with hotels and restaurants.

Who benefits from tourism? The simple answer is the tourist industry—that part of the economy which caters for the tourist, those firms and establishments which have a common function supplying tourist needs. Some of them, such as holiday camps, many restaurants and many souvenir are mainly dependent on tourism for their business.

In addition to being a source of income and employment, tourism is frequently a source of amenities for the resident population of the tourist destination. Because of visitor traffic, residents may enjoy a higher standard of public transport, shopping and entertainment facilities than they would be able to support otherwise. The provision of incomes, jobs and amenities for the resident population may therefore be regarded as the three beneficial effects of tourism to tourists destination.

In some locations tourism may provide an infrastructure which in turn forms the base and the stimulus for the diversification of the economy and for the development of other industries. Thus tourism expenditure may be said to stimulate an economy beyond the sector concerned with tourism.

In both developed and developing countries, government authorities have identified tourism as a means of generating employment and income. Third World countries such as Gambia in West Africa have placed tourism as a major component of their economic policy.

The economic significance of tourism varies from country to country. In a developing country, the economic significance of tourism may be measured in terms of its ability to generate an inflow of foreign exchange. On the other hand, in a developed country, its significance may be measured in terms of its ability to assist diversification and combat regional unbalances.

Economic impact of tourism can be measured in terms of the multiplier process. The concept of multiplier was developed by Kahn and Keynes. Keynes argued that economic growth was determined by two groups of flows of activity—leakages from the economic systems and injections into that system. The injections comprise investment, exports and government expenditure. Investment is important because it creates jobs and income. Exports means the selling of goods overseas and thus earning money from overseas residents. Government expenditure is a means of financing investment. Exports and Government expenditure are injections that add to economic growth. From the standpoint of tourism, the building of the tourist attraction is investment; it helps to attract overseas visitors and thus it is a form of export.

The leakages in the system are savings, taxation and imports. The act of saving withdraws money from the economy and diminishes the level of demand for goods and hence employment. By raising taxation, the government withdraws money from the economic system and so diminishes the level of demand. Imports are a leakage in the sense that jobs associated with the production of these goods are also to be found overseas.

When both the injections and leakages are in equilibrium, then the economy is also in equilibrium. Economic growth is generated by the injections being greater than the leakages. There is another important economic flow—consumer expenditure and this is placed in both sides of the equation. Consumer spending is an injections in that it is the spending that simulates the demand for goods and services and thus creates employment and income. On the other hand, if the recipient of the consumer expenditure does nothing with the revenue, the money flows out of the economic system.

The economic impact of tourism has a disproportionate effect on the host community because of the multiplier effect which spreads the benefits for beyond the resort. The economic impact can be divided into three stages. First, there is a direct expenditure by tourists on good and services provided by hotels and restaurants. Second is the indirect expenditure due to the resultant business transactions arising from the first stage. Finally, there is the induced expenditure due to the responding of income by local nationals employed in or benefiting from the tourism expenditure in their regions.

Tourism has economic effects by—

1. Creating employment and income,
2. Contributing to the balance of payments.

The term tourist multiplier refers to the ratio of two changes—the changes in one of the key economic variables such as output (income, employment of government revenue) to the change in tourist expenditure.

There are different types of multiplier as follows:

(*a*) *Sales Multiplier*: This measures the amount of additional business revenue created in an economic as a result of increase in tourist expenditure.

(*b*) *Output Multiplier*: This measures the amount of additional output generated in an economy as a result of an increase in tourist expenditure.

(*c*) *Income Multiplier*: This measures the additional income (wages, rent, interest and profits) created in the economy as a result of increase in tourist expenditure.

(*d*) *Employment Multiplier*: This is a measurement of the total amount of employment generated beyond additional unit of tourist expenditure. Employment multipliers provide a useful source of information about the secondary effects of tourism.

(*e*) *Government Revenue Multiplier*: This measures the impact on Government revenue from all sources associated with an increase of tourist expenditure.

The basic formulation of Tourism Multiplier is thus,

$$\text{Tourist Multiplier} = A\left(\frac{1}{1-BC}\right)$$

where $A$ = proportion of tourist expenditure remaining in the area after first round leakages,

$B$ = proportion of income that local people spend on local goods and services—propensity to spend locally,

$C$ = proportion of expenditure of local people which accrues as local income.

Tourism multipliers have been found to be weak for the following reasons:

1. Comparatively low levels of pay,
2. Costs as well as income are generated,
3. Nature of the tourist regions.

Tourism multipliers measure the present economic performance of the tourism industry and the short-run economic effects of a change in the level or pattern of tourism expenditure. They are particularly suitable for studying the impact of tourist expenditure on business turnover, incomes, employment, government revenue and the balance of payments.

One of the means of assessing the impact of tourist expenditure on other areas of the economic system is the use of input-output analysis. This technique attempts to show the flow of economic transactions through the economy within a given time span, usually a year. It is a refinement of the basic multiplier process in that it seeks to show the inter-relationship between different sectors of the economic system.

Last but not the least, the impact of tourism on the balance of payments may be significant. In the case of developing countries one reason for tourism is that it is a means of earning foreign currencies.

## SOCIO-CULTURAL IMPACT

### Positive Nature of Impact

There are many examples of the way in which tourism has benefited a particular place, buildings or cultural activity. In Britain many great buildings of the past would have been lost had it not been possible to convert them into living museums for the tourists. Whole inner cities and dockland areas have been restored and developed to make them attractive as tourist cities. Even a city like London would be a poorer place without the tourist; 40 per cent of West End Theatre tickets are bought by tourists. In rural areas and small seaside resorts, many of the smaller shops could not be economically viable without the summer tourists. This is applicable to Taj in India.

The rapid growth of tourism in the twentieth century has produced problems as well as opportunities in a vast scale for both developed and developing countries. The governments of these countries have realised that unplanned tourist development can easily aggravate these problems to a point where tourists will no longer wish to visit the destination. In other words, without proper planning tourists may destroy what they have come to see. This problem is compounded, as long-haul travel to previously unaffected destination increases.

Now, such remote areas of the globe as the Antarctic continent are appearing on the tourist trial—a 100 room hotel was recently—opened in Antarctica by the Chilean armed forces to cater to tourists who are looking for diversion such as snow-mobile riding and above 10,000 tourists are now visiting the continent each year. One unexpected result of this influx has been that among the huge colonies of penguins inhabiting the area, a number are falling prey to chicken disease, thought to be the result of food carelessly discarded by tourists paying visits to the colonies. Geologically sensitive region such as the Galapagos Islands, Costa Rica are now controlling tourism development and introducing the concept of sustainable tourism to ensure that the environment are not destroyed by mass tourism.

**Negative Nature of Impact**

Tourism is a curious modern disease. The people of Corfu were blessed with a magnificent island of staggering beauty, probably one of the most beautiful islands in the whole of the Mediterranean. What they have done with it is vandalism beyond belief. Tourism damages not only the landscape but also the indigenous way of life, culture and sets of values.

It is not without reason that local people hate tourists. In the 1960s, hostility towards tourists in Europe was seen in "Yankee go home" posters. The European press termed the foreign tourists as New Barbarians or New Invaders. Herman Kahn described the rapidly growing tourism as next only to atomic power in its potential for environmental destruction.

More than 300 mountaineering expeditions since 1949 have caused widespread deforestation, pasture destruction and serious accumulation of litter on the slopes of Mt. Everest and other peaks in the Himalayas. The Dal Lake in Srinagar is now half of what it was fifty years ago and if current pollution continues, it may turn into a pond in the next fifty years. Tourism damages the culture and peace of the people of the host country.

In some developing nations, premature exposure to western ideas and technologies has created a variety of social problems. The introduction of tourism to a new region inevitably altered people's daily lives. In some cases, too, rapid tourism development contributed to high crime rates and introduced gambling, drinking and prostitution, materialism and greed. Unpleasant experiences with nude travellers has brought about open resentment towards tourists.

Tourism is often seen as an intruder by the farmer and the forester in particular who have been sole users of the land before.

The problem is much wider than that. Tourist traffic in route and where it concentrates in particular locations affects the rural environment, cars and buses create congestion on the roads as well as noise and other forms of pollution. Aircraft noise distrubs the residents and causes damage to wild life. Tourists damage crops and flora and leave litter behind. Without tourism the rural environment would have a better chance of being preserved.

It is alleged that tourism generates crime. Many researches have perceived a positive correlation between tourism and crime. Through the generation of friction between the host population and tourists many criminal activities have generated. Tourism creates situations where gains from crime may be high and the likelihood of detection small.

Other evil effects of tourism should not be lost sight of. For example, tourism in Ladakh has seriously affected the agriculturists, in Kerala, it has affected the rights of fisherman and in Goa it has replaced traditional occupations. In most modern tourist projects there has always been a conflict of land use and environmental damage through hotel construction and waste disposal.

In certain cases the curio trade has encouraged the vandalisation of our architectural heritage and art objects. Even trade in banned items like Rhino horns and tiger claws and ivory have encouraged the continuation of poaching. There is also the practice of illegal trade in hard currency. Such activities turn a section of the local population into pimps, touts and black marketeers. Sometimes tourists may provide the market for such activities.

## SEX TOURISM

Sex has for long been the fourth—S, the others being sun, sea and sand has often utilised in the selling of the holiday product.

Tourism associated with prostitution or what is called sex-tourism has assumed alarming proportion in many South-East Asian Countries. Sex tourism, drug peddling and bride buying have become interlinked particularly in the Third World countries with some form of tourists. Thailand, Nepal, Sri Lanka, Vietnam, Hong Kong and Bali have clearly seen the negative impact of such tourists.

The essential reasons for the girls entering into prostitution are not different from that of their European counterparts. The main reason is poverty. With no social welfare benefit system and if the girls possess no marketable skills for use in industry and commerce, prostitution may seem to be the only means of supporting themselves.

Prostitution resulting from the tourism industry has reached crisis levels at destinations such as Thailand, Philippines, Bali, Vietnam, the Caribbean Island and parts of East Africa. Sex tourism has taken the shape of an organised industry. Governments in many countries are encouraging sex-tourism as an easy means of securing foreign exchange.

Investigations show that an increasing number of Asian children forced into sexual relations with paedophiles from the West. A global campaign to end child prostitution in Asian tourism has succeeded in highlighting this ghastly reality internationally.

In South-East Asia, the historical origins of sex tourism lie in the R & R (rest and recreation) centres. These emerged during the Vietnam war where US Army soldiers were provided with a paid holiday from trauma of combat. Bars, brothels and sex was the standard formulae for R & R. With the end of the war and the departure of troops, hundreds of bar girls have been left in the lurch. Some segments of the tourism industry, quick to cash in on a profitable opportunity, readily jumped into the breach.

By the 1970s brothels catering to tourists flourished in South-East Asia under a variety of guises. Massage parlours, sexshows, yoga bars, health clubs, cocktail lounges—all existed with the sole purpose of meeting the sexual needs of male (and sometimes of female) visitors.

The promotion of sex-tourism increased in the early eighties when sexual services of young Asian women were openly sold, as part of a package tour by travel agents in Germany, Netherlands and elsewhere in Europe.

The phenomenon of mail order brides, a system by which clients in Europe could purchase a woman of their choice. This they could do just by going through a brochure which gave photographs and other details of women. The mail-order traders also threw in a bargain, they offered a sample tours during which a client would spend a few days with the intended bride and reject her if she could not satisfy his sexual expectations. While some of the marriage is just a way of getting the women to enter a foreign country, where they are soon forced into prostitution. Another way in which women are sold into international sexual trafficking trade is that of direct recruitment for work in bars; discos and so-called dancers and entertainers as in Bangkok, Philippines and Vietnam.

The 'predatory tourist' seeking sexual pleasures is not always male. The largest group of African in Sweden by mature Swedish women who befriended them on a holiday.

Sex-tourism is not a major factor in tourism in India. Yet, unfortunately symptoms have started emerging. In Darjeeling, Goa and Kashmir there are agents who secure; 'good girlfriends' or 'call-girls' for foreign tourists at a very high price. It appears that AIDS menace might act as a deterrent, but for this also awareness has to be created.

While the external reality of sex-tourism is appalling enough, it is associated by a far more distressing story; that of capture, slavery, brutalisation, violence, fear and despair. Many women and children who cater to sex tourism have been sold into prostitution by their families out of economic desperation, with scant knowledge of the fate that awaits them.

From an initial euphoria about tourism, Third World communities exhibit xenophobia in tourism for its association with prostituting; gambling, drug peddling.

Asian Women United, a Christian group has researched tourism in South-Asia and has arrived at high estimates of the number of women working in prostitution and related activities such as masseuses and bar hostesses. One report estimates that the number of prostitutes in South Korea may be between 600,000 and 10,00,000 in a country of 41 million and another report estimates that in 1985, there were approximately 500,000 prostitutes in Thailand. There were as many as 100,000 'hospitality' girls in Manila. These estimates would need to be tampered by impact of AIDS but still sex-tourism is significant in tourism in some of the

Far-East countries. In Bangkok 50 per cent of the prostitutes are child under the age of 13.

In other parts of the world, prostitution can be found in tourist areas. Amsterdam's redlight district is itself a tourist sight, whilst the legalised brothels of Nevada are widely advertised in tourist areas such as Las Vegas. Tourism has created an environment which attracts prostitutes and their clients. Las Vegas is known as the 'Entertainment Capital' of the world. Entertainment in the western sense is impossible without gambling and flesh trade.

Unchecked prostitution is commonly associated with an expansion of tourism. Sex-tours to Korea, Thailand, the Philippines, Vietnam have drawn strong criticism from religious, feminist and other writers. However, Joses in his study of prostitution in Bali, concluded that it is not caused by tourist demand.

In areas like Tahiti, Philippines and Bermuda, some studies reveal that high birth rate of illegitimate children was attributed to the carnival atmosphere generated by international tourism. Sex-tourism is associated with prostitution but gay travel is not so.

Amsterdam has a reputation for being a free and open city. It has great cultural diversity and considerable tolerance has been extended to different ways of life. It has an image as an entertainment and fun place. Possession of drugs is illegal but personal consumption of marijuana is tolerated in designated coffee shops. This all makes it an attractive place to live and to visit, especially for young people. The city is second only to San Francisco in its social acceptance of homosexuality.

## TOURISM—IMPACT ON ENVIRONMENTAL POLLUTION

The technological complexity of twentieth century living has led to various forms of pollution which are both initiated and compounded by tourism development. Large scale tourist movement requires the use of mass transportation and the fuel burn from aircraft adds to air pollution; civilian aircraft account for the emission of 3 per cent of all carbondioxide created by man and a similar amount of nitrous oxide. The introduction of quieter, more fuel-efficient and cleaner jet engines unfortunating has the side-effect of increasing the emission of nitrous oxide. Emissions from the exhausts of cars and boats used in tourism compound the problem. All three forms of travel can also contribute unacceptable levels of noise, which must be considered a form of pollution. Waterborne vessels, by dumping fuel or waste overboard also contribute to water pollution which, in turn, affects the wildlife on the rivers. Beaches give particular cause for concern in that polluted waters can lead to serious illness among bathers.

The environment, whether it is natural or man-made, is the most fundamental ingredient of the tourism product. As soon as tourism activity takes place, the environment is inevitably changed or modified to facilitate tourism.

It is not difficult to argue that tourism is damaging the environment. Tourism has its impact on the wildlife of Africa, on the pollution of water in the Mediterranean and on the coastal areas and mountains.

The environmental impacts associated with tourism development can also be considered in terms of their direct and indirect effects. The impacts can be positive or negative. It is not possible to develop tourism without incurring environmental impacts but it is possible, with correct planning, to manage tourism development in order to minimize the negative impacts while encouraging the positive impacts.

In the Himalayas, a trek to Everest has to well established a tourist path that in 1989 a special expedition was undertaken to clean up the litter that lay around base camps. To obtain hot water to meet the needs of tourist for a wash after the day's trek, wood is cut down. The trekking tourist burns about 14 lbs of wood per day resulting in further deforestation. This results in damage to the water drainage pattern. The Nepalese government should develop schemas of afforestation.

The World Tourism Organisation has mentioned five situations where tourism might harm the environment:

1. Alternation of the ecological situation of regions where the environment was previously in good condition both from the natural, cultural and human viewpoints;
2. Speculative pressures leading to destruction of landscape and natural habitat;
3. The occupation of space and creation of activities producing irreconcilable land-use conflicts;

4. Damage to traditional values in the zones concerned and a lowering of standards on the human scale in existing developments; and
5. Progressive over capacity which drains the environmental quality of the area concerned.

To counteract the problems posed by tourism development some writers have sought to promote the concept of Green Tourism. Green Tourism should be consistent with its environment and arise naturally from the activities that are natural to the area. As an example, in the Swiss Cantons host communities have sought to impose regulations that limit tourism within the carrying capacities of the area. It is increasingly recognised that tourism needs to be developed in harmony with natural resources. Tourism should be managed in such a way as to minimize its adverse impacts.

Noise pollution is a problem of twentieth century, living especially in towns but tourism has also made a significant contribution to the problem. In the resorts of the Mediterranean, the peace of the night is destroyed by the late night discos and bars, catering to tourists. Noisy motorboats disturb the tranquillity of yachts people on the waterways, while aircraft taking off and landing at busy airports severely disturb local residents, especially if there are no restrictions on flying.

Authorities have recognised the problem of air traffic noise and some have taken action to reduce it. For example, aircraft are categories under three classes known as chapters, according to the noise level they emit. In USA, under government regulations, the most recently introduced chapter 3 aircrafts, such as Airbus, are 85 per cent less noisy than were chapter 1 aircraft and are consequently allowed greater freedom to operate.

Visual pollution can be ascribed to insensitivity in the design of buildings for tourism. Lake of planning control is very often to blame, as developers prefer to built more cheaply, leading to high-rise concrete hotels lacking character and out of keeping with surrounding architecture. Today, the skyscraper hotel is ubiquitous, from Wiakiki in Hawaii to Benidorm in Spain, with a conformity of architecture which owes nothing to the traditions of the country in which it is built.

Some authorities insist that hotels must conform to vernacular styles of architecture. Others require buildings not to exceed a certain height—for example, Tunicea requires that new hotel developments in tourist resorts should be no higher than the normal height of trees which will surround them. Mauritius has imposed constraints on both the architectural style and the materials employed in hotel buildings.

*Congestion and Erosion*: Mass tourism has led to a new problem in the recent time that of congestion.

Some idea of the effect of erosion can be gained from a report in the Guardian which revealed that 400 tons of sand are removed from the beach of Benidorm each year on the sole of holiday-makers' feet.

## PROBLEMS OF TOURISM

This aspect has been discussed in the chapter captioned 'Problems Faced by Tourists and Tourism Industry', therefore, hereunder, we discuss this problem very briefly:

Tourist is a newcomer and is often seen as an intruder by the farmer and forester, in particular, who have been, sole users of the land before and unaccustomed to share their domain. The concern is wider than that. Tourist traffic en route and where it concentrates in particular locations affects the rural environment. Cars and buses create congestion on the roads and at sites as well as noise and other forms of pollution. Aircraft noise disturbs the residents and causes damage to wild life. Tourists damage crops and flora and leave litter behind. Without tourism the rural environment would have a better chance of being preserved. Some tourist countries are already seriously affected by pollution. Almost two-thirds of the beaches of Italy have been polluted by sewage and garbage. Israel and Lebanon also polluted by sewage and garbage. Israel and Lebanon also report that pollution is becoming a major problem facing the future development of their tourist industry.

Lastly, tourism is, to a considerable extent, a seasonal activity. Most of the facilities of the town are used for a few months. This leads to a wasteful use of resources and may result in seasonal unemployment.

## BALANCING ECOLOGICAL ENVIRONMENT AND ECONOMIC DEVELOPMENT THROUGH TOURISM

According to the Worldwide Fund for Natural-India (WZF),

eco-tourism is an alternative tourism and it respects social and cultural traditions. It is decentralised in nature and seeks to integrate rural development. Eco-tourism would ideally generate revenue for conversation of natural and cultural wealth and afford cultural exchange among rural and urban population. But its most avowed objective would be to attain a balance between natural and human beings and ensure the co-existence of both.

Till its opening in 1992, the high altitude desert zones of the western Himalayas remained a peaceful wonderland occupied by god-fearing Buddhists who needed to see very little beyond their prayer leads. Free from diseases and other civilization-borne vices, they survived happily in close communities at heights higher than 1,300 fit above the sea level where the scarce vegetation was enough for the sustenance of a population with a density of 2 per sq. km.

With the opening of the valley to uncontrolled tourism, pressures on the limited resources of the fragile ecosystem have been extreme, calling for subsidised supply of firewood from places as far as Chandigarh. With the removal of grass and junipers, the wild herbivores and all the available endangered species are forced to remain in the higher reaches even during the winter months.

The conflict of ecology and economy is a general one. When a tourist visits a place he goes there with three primary expectations—that it will be a nice place to see, there will be activities to participate in and there will be nice memories to bring back home. And he disobeys all laws that prevent him from achieving his objectives. The government policy should be whenever there is a clash between tourism and the ecology, the decision should always go in favour of the ecology.

Eco-tourism is largely a participatory process. In Lachung in Sikkim two young locals have taken the entire responsibility of guiding and educating the tourists. Being natives of the land, they feel for it in a way that no outsider would ever be able to.

Eco-tourism today is a concept that has just begun to catch on. At present only 2 per cent of the market share of world tourism can be attributed to such specialised tourism. But with time, the figures should change.

## CONCLUSION

In part, the difficulty of quantifying the environmental and social impacts of tourism has delayed the development of impact methodologies. But the rising tide of environmentalism has caught up with tourism and has lent support to the view that in some cases the economic benefits of tourism are more than outweighed by the environmental and social costs of tourism. Concept such as 'sustainable' tourism development and the responsible consumption of tourism are seen as the answer, along with the enhanced planning and management of tourism.

However, the issue of management is closely related to the notion of carrying capacity as a destination can be managed to take any number of visitors. Large volumes can be accommodated without an unacceptable decline in the environment or the experience. The question must therefore be asked, management for whom? In pluralistic societies the conflicts and tensions between the stakeholders in tourism—tourists developers, planners, environmentalists—will in the end determine levels of tourist development.

After all, tourism takes place within political and social contexts. It is, however, heartening that current pressure for sustainable responsible tourism will give a different emphasis continuing debate amongst the various groups in society, and may change the perceived balance of the positive and negative effects of tourism in the feature.

## QUESTIONS FOR ANSWER

1. *Explain the economic impact of tourism.*
2. *What is sex-tourism? Explain the causes of its emergence in South-East Asian countries.*
3. *Explain the relationship between tourism and environmental pollution.*
4. *Write a note on eco-tourism.*

# 19

# Impact of Tourist Behaviour

Indian culture considers visitor equal to God. First the visitor is a tourist, he becomes a guest and eventually a friend, but if the guest by his behaviour does not become friend then he feels eased on being ceased to be a tourist, likewise the locals also feel happy when such unsocial tourist leave the destination, thus we see that the impact of tourist behaviour both negative and positive. Hereunder we will consider these aspects:

The tourist behaviour may be determined by a set of antecedent conditions. He arrives with a set of expectations and motivations and his knowledge and perception of that area.

During the first few days of tours, a process of comparison takes place, a comparison between the expectation shaped by him and the immediate environment. Expectations may be met, surpassed or disappointed.

A tourist is a guest, but an impersonal guest. The result is that he may be victimised as being a stranger ignorant of local laws and customs. Patterns of tourist behaviour have an important impact on the relationship that tourists have with the local population.

Having arrived at the scene of their dreams many tourists behave in much the same way as they do at home. It has also been found that for many tourists' aggressive or abnormal behaviour becomes normal while on holiday. Holiday makers become totally self-oriented having little regard for the host population.

Tourist behaviour focuses on the following activities:

1. Sightseeing;
2. Strolling in the countryside;
3. Going to the beach;
4. Shopping;

5. Visiting historic buildings/museums/art galleries;
6. Visiting restaurants/cinema/theatres.

Tourists bring with them positive and negative impacts but the negative impacts dominate host-guest relations. Such views are most extreme when tourists come in contact with sensitive cultures. It is because developing nations have few alternatives to tourism with which to earn much needed foreign exchange. The analogies with prostitution come at a psychological level as developing nations are forced into a servile role in order to secure foreign exchange.

Doxey's index of irritation is used for describing the effects of tourists on a host society. This shows the changing attitudes of the host population to tourism in terms of a linear sequence of increasing irritation as the number of tourists grows. In this perspective host societies in tourist destinations pass through stages of euphoria, apathy, irritation and antagonism in the face of tourism development.

The 'demonstration effect' of the tourists on the life style of local residents is critical. Local people, especially young people, try to imitate the behaviour and consumption patterns of the tourists. It may have some benefits if local people are encouraged to get better education in order to improve their living standards. But disadvantages are generally greater then benefits as local residents adopt the marks of affluence paraded by tourists and live beyond their means.

The adoption of foreign values also leads to a premature departure to modernisation producing rapid and disruptive changes in the host society. As a result, social tension develops as the hosts become divided into two classes—those adopting new values (usually young people) and those retaining a traditional way of life.

The moral changes brought about by tourists are very significant. The rise in crime, gambling, prostitution and more recently the spread of AIDS through sex tourism. A positive correlation between tourism and crime has been found in Mexico and Maimi. In developing countries large differences between the income of locals and guests lead to increased frustration in the local community which sometimes spills over as crimes against tourists.

However, not all crimes are directed to the tourists; local

people are increasingly the victims. In many circumstances the tourists themselves behave in extremely antisocial and criminal ways. To show bare-breasted African female dancers in Muslim areas of Africa or the peep show in London or Paris is a reflection of the tourists' cultures, not those of the host countries.

In tourism and prostitution Mathieson and Wall suggested four main hypotheses. The first is locational, is that tourism development often creates environments which attract prostitutes. Second is related to the breaking of normal bonds of behaviour by tourists when away from home—circumstances conducive to the expansion of prostitution. Third, prostitution offers employment opportunities to women to upgrade their economic status. Finally, tourism may be mere scapegoat for a general decline in moral standards.

Sex-tourism is largely focused in parts of South-East Asia, especially in Thailand, the Philippines, South Korea, Vietnam and Indonesia. The motive behind such development seems to be economic since young female prostitutes can earn at least twice as much as in other employment.

There are other explanations why there is a high level of prostitution in Thailand. There is employment discrimination against females in most formal sectors of employment, there is economic crises facing many rural areas from where most prostitutes are drawn and there is breakdown of many marriages which leaves women cut off from traditional society. In Thailand, since 1987, there has been a decrease in single male tourists and an increase in family tourism due to the fear of contracting AIDS.

## SPENDING TIME

The amount of time available determines the mode and destination of travel. Time is spent in one of the following three ways:

Much time is spent on maintenance activities. Maintenance activities are necessary to maintain life. Eating, sleeping, marketing, repairing house are such activities. Time is also spent at work. Generally, eight hours a day are spent at work. The time remaining after work and maintenance is leisure time.

If total time is broken down into the above three categories, there is a relationship between all the three. Since time is fixed twenty-four hours in a day and seven days in a week—any change in one of the three parts will automatically affect the others. With given time for maintenance, as the work week declines, more time will be available for leisure activities.

More important than the absolute amount of leisure time available is the way in which it is spent. Leisure time may be thought of as being divided into following three categories:

Leisure is available on weekdays, weekends and vacations.

The concepts of works, leisure and money are interrelated as far as tourism is concerned. A man needs both leisure and money to travel. In other words, a consumer has both a time budget and a money budget and he has to take a rational decision between the two.

## QUESTIONS FOR ANSWER

1. *Discuss the conditions that determine tourist behaviour.*
2. *Explain the levels of host irritation to the tourist.*
3. *Write an essay on guest-host relationship.*

# 20

# Tourist Accommodation: The Growth of Hospitality Industry

Accommodation is the basic component of tourism. The concept of travel accommodation has transformed itself as Hospitality Industry on account of its utility in tourism and life away from home. Tourism is to a great extent dependent on the range and type of accommodation available at the destination. Accommodation is a core area of the tourist industry and plays a distinctive role in the development of this ever-expanding industry.

The United Nations Conference on International Travel and Tourism held in Rome in 1963 considered, in particular, issues relating to means of accommodation. The conference acknowledged the importance of means of accommodation, both traditional (hotels, motels) and supplementary (camp, youth hostels, etc.), as incentives to international tourism.

The conference recommended that governments should consider the possibility of including tourism projects, and particularly those relating to accommodation, in the list of projects eligible for loans from their industrial or other corporations, and that, where required, they should establish special financial corporations for tourism. It also recommended that governments should give sympathetic consideration to the possibility of granting special facilities and incentives for accommodation projects.

Many countries have recognised the importance of accommodation industry in relation to tourism and their governments have coordinated their activities with the industry by providing big incentives and concessions to hoteliers, which have resulted in the building up of a large number of hotels and other type of accommodations. For example, availability of hotel sites on liberal repayment terms, special concessions in the form of long-term loans, liberal import licenses and taxation reliefs, contributions to the equity capital, cash grants for construction and renovation of building, and similar other concessions are provided to the industry.

## BRIEF HISTORY

Historically, accommodation for travellers may be conveniently viewed in two ways. The traveller who left his home on a journey which cannot be completed in a single day required accommodation at his destination. Inns were perhaps the first such accommodation units which catered to the needs of travellers in early times. In ancient times and during the Roman Empire many such inns were established which provided food, drink and also entertainment to weary travellers. However, with the decline of the Roman Empire by about A.D. 500, the institution of innkeeping lost its importance and for many years there was not much development.

Travel subsequently grew for religion pilgrimage purposes. Travellers in the thousands visited religious centres. Many monasteries and cathedrals welcomed the traveller and made their stay a comfortable experience. The accommodation provided at these places was free. By the fifteenth century, inns had developed in several countries of Europe, especially in England and France.

During the seventeenth and the eighteenth centuries, the facilities provided in the inns were expanded. Some of the inns had as many as 30 or more rooms. English common law declared the inn to be a public house and imposed social responsibility on the innkeeper for the well-being of the traveller. Even today large number of old inns still operate in England as hotels. Some of these were built about four hundred years ago.

In the Untied States another type of accommodation unit known as the tavern was opened in 1634 by a man called Samuel Coles. Coles had come to the New World in search of a fortune in 1630 by a ship. By 1780, taverns were popular meeting places where people used to come for eating, drinking and entertainment.

Many important events were associated with taverns. In 1783, General George Washington bid farewell to his top-ranking officers at the Frances Tavern in New York city. The famous Boston Tea Party was planned in a tavern called Green Dragon.

With the growth of travel in the eighteenth century there appeared in London the prototype of the modern hotel with the opening by one David Low in 1774. The next fifty years saw a gradual increase in the recognizable ancestors of the modern hotel in London and in resorts such as Brighton and Buxton and also certain other places. In the United States of America, hotels emerged from taverns by the simple expedient of a change of name.

By about 1800, the terms tavern and hotel were used to describe the same thing. By the year 1820, hotel became the accepted term to describe a place where people stayed for the night and took their meals on payment. In the 1820s the first tourist hotel appeared in Switzerland.

Until about the middle of the nineteenth century the bulk of the journeys were undertaken for business and vocational reasons, by road and within the boundaries of the individual countries. The volume of travel was relatively small and was confined to a fraction of the rich segments of the population in any country.

Inns and similar establishments along the main highways and in the principal towns grew to become the hallmark of the accommodation for the travellers. The traveller could reasonably expect at most inns a clean and comfortable accommodation when he wished to eat or spend the night. It provided the bulk of accommodation en route. This trend continued until the end of the nineteenth century, as most of those who did travel did so by coach.

## EVOLUTION OF HOTEL INDUSTRY

Although the earliest hotels date to the eighteenth century, their growth on any scale occurred only in the following century when the railways created sufficiently large markets to help make large hotels possible. During this period a large number of hotels grew up at important designations. The hotels were developed along the main railways and highway routes in major towns.

Substantial development of the hotels thus awaited the volume and the type of traffic only the railways could bring. With the development of railways systems in many other countries within and outside Europe, the number of hotels also increased. These hotels catered to the increasing volume of traffic. The 1860s also saw the introduction of Thomas Cook's railway and hotel coupons.

Starting in 1868, Cook arranged regular circular tours of Switzerland and northern Italy from England. By the 1890s, 1,200 hotels throughout the world accepted hotel coupons.

Thus, we find that railways greatly influenced the development of hotels during the early twentieth century. The demand for accommodation of tourists was thus met by a variety of facilities ranging from inns, taverns, private houses and hotels.

The main changes in the demand for tourist accommodation have come about from changes in tourist transportation and in the popularity of different forms of holidays. After the introduction of the motor car and the aircraft, a large number of hotels sprang up at various tourist areas and destinations. The growth of hotels continued until the 1950s. Hotels as a unit of accommodation dominated the scene all over the world.

## DEFINITION OF HOTEL

Hotels provide accommodation, meals and refreshments for irregular periods of time for those who may reserve their accommodation either in advance or on the premises. In broad terms, hotels provide facilities to meet the needs of the modern traveller. The dictionaries define hotel in several ways: 'a place which supplies board and lodging', 'a place for the entertainment of the travellers', 'large city house of distinction', and 'a public building'.

The common law states that a hotel is "a place where all who conduct themselves properly, and who, being able and ready to pay for their entertainment, are received, if there be accommodation for them, and who without any stipulated engagement as to the duration of their stay or as to the rate of compensation, are, while there, supplied at a reasonable cost with their meals, lodging, and such services and attention as are necessarily incident to the use of the house as a temporary home."

A definition of the hotel as a business entity was presented by hotel operators during the consideration of the hotel business to authorities of the National Recovery Administration, in Washington in 1933. This definition, as formulated by Stuart McNamara, was as follows:

Primarily, and fundamentally an hotel is an establishment which supplies board and lodging, not engaged in interstate commerce; or in any interstate commerce, competitive with or affecting, interstate commerce (or so related thereto that the regulation of the one involves the control of the other), but is a quasi domestic institution retaining from its ancient origin certain traditional, and acquiring, in its modern development, certain statutory rights and obligations to the public, where all persons, not disqualified by condition or conduct, prepared to pay for their accommodation, are to be received and furnished with a room or place to sleep or occupy if such accommodations are available, and with such services and attention as are incident to their use of the hotel as a home, and/or with food, at stipulated prices, and with or without contract as to duration of visit, and which conducts, within the confines of its physical locations, this business of supplying personal services of individuals for profit. Incidental to such fundamental and principal business, the hotel may furnish quarters and facilities for the assemblage of people for social, business or entertainment purposes, and may engage in renting portions of its premises for shops and business whose contiguity is deemed appropriate to an hotel.

## CLASSIFICATION OF HOTELS

Over the years the concept and the format of hotels have changed a great deal. There are various types of hotels catering to the increasing demands of tourists. The size, the facade, architectural features and the facilities and amenities provided differ from one establishment to another.

### International Hotels

International hotels are the modern Western style hotels seen in almost all metropolitan and other large cities as well as principal tourist centres. These hotels are luxury hotels and are classified on the basis of internationally accepted system of classification. The hotels are placed in various star categories. There are five such categories ranging from five star to one star depending upon the facilities and services provided. These hotels provide, in addition to accommodation, all the other facilities which make the stay a very comfortable and interesting experience. Various facilities provided include well-appointed reception and information counter, banquet halls, conference facilities, etc.

There are also shops, travel agency, moneychanger and safe-deposit facilities. Restaurant facilities, bars and banquets are an integral part of the business of a hotel. The various services provided in these hotels include international and local cuisine, food and beverage service and restaurant service. These hotels also provide entertainment for the guests in the form of various dance and music programmes, sports and games.

A number of these hotels belong to the luxury category. There are some international chains which own a large number of such luxury hotels. Hotels belonging to international chains are mostly owned by public companies and controlled by a board of directors. These hotels have various departments which are managed by persons qualified and experienced in the field of hoteliering.

The chief of the hotel, designated as general manager, is responsible for the overall management and operation of the hotel through his departmental heads. International hotels are suitable for metropolitan cities and for other large business and commercial towns and principal tourist centres. The potential of these hotels is therefore limited to theses areas. A number of hotels of this type have conference/convention facilities and are suitable for holding meetings, conventions and conference.

## Resort Hotels

Resort hotels cater to the needs of the holiday-maker, the tourist and those who by reasons of health desire a change of atmosphere. Resort hotels are located near the sea, mountain and other areas abounding in natural beauty. Rest, relaxation and entertainment are the key factors around which resorts are built. The primary motive of a person visiting resort hotels is rest and relaxation which he is looking far away from his routine busy work life. Resort hotels are built with a view to provide special services to the visitors and are marked by an atmosphere of informality.

The type of services and amenities available in resort property include recreation facilities such as swimming pool, golf course, tennis courts, skiis, boating, surf-riding and various other indoor sports. Other important amenities include coffee shops, restaurants, conference rooms, lounge, shopping arcade and entertainment. The emphasis of resort hotels, however, is on recreational facilities. The clientele of resort hotels is mostly persons with considerable income looking for relaxation and recreation. Resort hotels rarely attract commercial patronage.

Resorts can be of various types and can be classified on the basis of climate and topography. Broadly they fall in the following categories: (*i*) summer resorts, (*ii*) winter resorts, (*iii*) hill resorts, (*iv*) all-season resorts, and (*v*) health resorts. A majority of the resort hotels are seasonal establishments which work to capacity during the high tourist season. Generally the high tourist season is the period when there are holidays at educational institutions.

However, in recent years many of the resort hotels with a view to extend the season provide certain special facilities and offer various concessions to the guests. The concessions provided include reduced tariffs, free entertainment, sightseeing, gifts, etc.

### Commercial Hotels

Commercial hotels direct their appeal primarily to the individual traveller as compared to international or resort hotel where the focus is on group travel. Most of the commercial hotels receive guests who are on business although some have permanent guests.

As the hotel caters primarily to people who are visiting a place for commerce or business, these are located in important commercial and industrial centres of large towns and cities. These hotels are generally run by the owners and their success depends on their efficient running and the comforts and facilities they provide. In some of the large industrial towns, fully licensed commercial hotels exist complete with restaurants, grill room, functional accommodation and a garage for those travelling by automobile.

### Residential Hotels

Residential hotels can be described as apartment houses complete with hotel service. These are often referred to as apartment hotels. The tariff of rooms in these hotels is charged on monthly, half-yearly or yearly basis and is charged for either furnished or unfurnished accommodation. These hotels which are located mostly in big cities operate exclusively under the European plan where no meals are provided to the guests.

These hotels were developed in the United States of America where people discovered that permanent living in hotels offers many advantages. Service and amenities provided in these hotels are comparable to those of an average well-regulated home. These are very popular in the United States and western Europe where these are also known popularly as *pensions*.

### Floating Hotels

As the name suggests, floating hotels are located on the surface of the water. It may be on sea water, river water or on a lake. All the facilities and services of a hotel are provided in these hotels. These hotels are very popular in many countries. In some countries old luxury ships have been converted into floating hotels and are proving very popular among tourists. The atmosphere they provide is exclusive and exotic. In India, floating hotels in the form of houseboats are very popular with tourists.

### Heritage Hotels

Heritage hotels have unique architectural features used in different periods of time which blend with the culture and tradition of the area. The main idea is to convert those properties which are not being used any more for residential purposes into hotel in order to preserve their uniqueness. Heritage hotels are operating in palaces castles/forts/hunting lodges/*havelis*/residence built several decades ago. The façade, architectural features and the general construction is of distinctive character. The properties are to maintain general features conforming to the overall concept of heritage with distinctiveness. The properties so converted have all the facilities of a modern hotel.

## SUPPLEMENTARY ACCOMMODATIONS

Supplementary accommodation plays a very important role in the total available tourist accommodation in a country. This type of accommodation can cater to both international as well as domestic tourist traffic. In fact, in some countries more tourists utilize this type of accommodation than hotels. In France and Italy, as also in some other countries in Europe and elsewhere, there are more campers than hotel clients. Some of the principal forms of supplementary accommodation are: (*i*) motel, (*ii*) youth hostel, (*iii*) camping sites, (*iv*) pension, (*v*) bed and breakfast establishments (*vi*) tourist holiday villages, and (*vii*) time-share and resort condominiums.

### Motels

The concept of motel and motel-hotel originated in the United States of America. Motel was meant for local motorists and foreign tourists travelling by road. Primarily designed to serve the needs of motorists, motels almost exclusively meet the demand for transit accommodation. They serve the function of a transit hotel except that they are geared to accommodate motor-travelling guests, for overnight stay.

The services provided by motels include parking, garage facilities, accommodation, restaurant facilities, public catering and recreational facilities. With a view to provide the above services to the motorists, all the motels are equipped with filling stations, repair services, accessories, garages, parking space, elevator service to the automobile entrance, restaurants, etc. There is also equipment and tools available which the guest can use himself if he wishes to repair his vehicle. The price charged for accommodation and meals/refreshments is much cheaper as compared to that in hotels. Motels are mostly located outside the city limits in the countryside along with the main highway and preferably at an important road junction.

**Youth Hostels**

In the form of a movement, youth hostels made their first appearance in Germany in about 1900. The movement which spread rapidly all over the world was based on the educational principles emphasising the need by youth of large cities to travel on foot throughout the country. In order to provide some sort of accommodation and services, the dormitories in the inns were equipped with cots, mattresses, sheets and blankets. Large rooms in inns were used as dining and living areas providing full board at low cost to the guests. There was also provision of additional kitchen where travellers could themselves prepare their own meals.

Since the movement was started with a view to encouraging youth to travel in order to learn and know more about the country and also to socialize, it had an educational value. As such, no service was provided in the inns. The persons staying were themselves required to look after the unit. Subsequently, exclusive youth hostel buildings were constructed to accommodate young travellers.

Youth hostel can be defined as a building which offers clean, moderate and inexpensive shelter to young people exploring their own country or other countries and travelling independently or in groups on holiday or for educational purposes. It is a place where young people of different social backgrounds and nationalities meet together and come to know each other. The objective of youth hostel is therefore not merely to provide accommodation and board, but also to serve as centers which offer opportunity to young people coming from different parts of the country as also young travellers from abroad to know and understand each other.

### *Caravan* and Camping Sites

*Caravan* and camping sites constitute a significant accommodation category in many holiday areas. These are very popular in some European countries as also in the United States. These are also known as open air hostels, tourist camps or camping grounds. Camping, originally practised by hikers on foot, is increasingly giving way to car camping. The sites are usually located within the large cities in open spaces.

Equipped to receive mobile accommodation in the form of caravans, the camping sites provide facilities for parking, tent-pitching, water, electricity, toilet, etc. Tough the services provided generally include restaurants, recreational rooms, toilets and at certain places a grocer's shop, the type of services often vary from place to place. Some countries have enacted legislation establishing the minimum facilities that must be provided which include health and sanitation standards and prices to be charged for providing various services.

### *Pension*

*Pensions* are very popular in certain European countries, particularly in Italy, Austria, Germany and Switzerland. These establishments are used extensively by the tourists. A pension is also described as a private hotel, a guesthouse or a boarding house. Catering facilities are optional and are usually restricted to the residents. Many of them stay for a longer period than a week or a fortnight. The reservation for accommodation is made in advance. Mostly managed by a family, pension accommodation is much cheaper than hotel accommodation.

### Bed and Breakfast Establishments

Also known in some countries as apartment hotels and *hotel garnis*, they represent a growing form of accommodation units catering for holiday as well as business travellers. These establishments provide only accommodation and breakfast and not the principal meals. These are usually located in large towns and cities along commercial and holiday routes and also resort areas and are used by en-route travellers. Some of these establishments are very popular with holidaymakers.

**Tourist Holiday Villages**

Tourist villages were established in some European countries after World War II. These villages are situated at warm seasides and in the regions which offer certain facilities for the tourists. In some countries like Italy and Spain, tourist villages are located in the regions which are economically not developed thereby helping the region economically. The villages are mostly promoted by important clubs, social organizations and also by tourist organizations.

The village complex is a centre of accommodation providing extensive sports and recreation facilities, riding, swimming, tennis, volleyball, football, sauna, mini-golf, badminton, table tennis and yoga. These provide both board and lodging. The atmosphere in these villages is kept as informal as possible. Telephones, radios, newspapers and TV are banned unless there is an emergency. Wallets and other valuables are locked away at the beginning of one's stay. Instead of money, one uses colourful beads which can be worn anywhere as bracelets, necklaces, etc.

The staff are educated young people who live on an equal basis with the holiday makers. The accommodation provided is usually in multiple units and may provide for self-catering. The furnishing provided in the rooms is minimal. The easy mixing of guests is encouraged by the banning of advance booking of tables in the village restaurants so one rarely finds oneself sitting with the same group twice.

The holiday villages are usually based on family units, each providing a convertible living room, bath/shower and sometimes a kitchen. The villages are self-sufficient providing almost all necessities required by the residents. There is also a small shopping complex where one can buy articles of daily need. The services of a doctor are also available in the village. The accommodation is sold for a week or a fortnight at an all-inclusive price. In Spain and Italy, these are classified into three categories according to the service and amenities provided.

### Time-share and Resort Condominiums

Time-share and condominiums provide a unique range of accommodation to a tourist. This type of accommodation provides on-site fun, flexibility and affordability to a large number of tourists around the world. In the case of condominium, a tourist owns a room or a suite within a condominium or hotel complex and uses the same as required. The same accommodation unit can also be rented our to her tourists. Normally, the owned condominiums are located within a complex of rooms or suites that are rented out as regular hotel or resort rooms.

Time-share holiday, on the other hand, represents a very unique example of both international and domestic accommodation. It is a modification of condominium-ownership concept. In the past, in western Europe the tradition has been for prosperous individuals to buy or build second homes. However, as these properties are often empty for large parts of the year, these are costly to maintain.

Resort Condominiums International (RCI) in the world's premier and largest exchange company in the field of time-share resorts. Established in 1974, RCI is widely recognised as a catalyst for the growth of the global time-share industry. RCI is credited with having invented and pioneered the time-share holiday concept worldwide. Today, RCI is the largest time-share exchange company with over 3,300 resorts in 90 countries with more than 2.4 million time-share-owning households.

Many hotel properties around the world have benefited from this concept. This concept enables them to tide over low occupancy rates during lean or low seasons. Several hotel chains worldwide have opted for the mixed use concept whereby a certain number of hotel rooms are put into time-share. This enables them to tide over the problem of low occupancy during lean seasons.

Many time-share properties are affiliated with a time-share exchange programme that permit members to trade their weeks for time at another property with which it has an affiliation agreement. RCI exchange programme works like this. When a member asks to make an exchange request, his/her weeks are deposited into the SPACEBANK Pool for someone else to take. The computer searches through its data bank to find a suitable holiday match to the member's request. If a match is found immediately then the member will receive confirmation in writing within 21 days. If a close match is found, the same will be offered to the member. If the member accepts, then the confirmation is made immediately and member's holiday booked.

## GRADING SYSTEM OF HOTELS

An individual operator needs to bring information about his accommodation to the tourist before he sets off on his journey and also when he reaches his destination. Similarly, the tourist, on the other hand, needs to know in detail what accommodation is available at what price in particular destination from which he can make a choice about what and where to stay. Schemes of classification, registration and grading of the tourist accommodation are intended to meet these requirements.

The United Nations Conference on International Travel and Tourism held in Rome in 1963 also emphasised the need for some sort of regulation of the accommodation with a view to safeguard interests of the users. Considering that special attention should be given to relations between the public authorities and the operators of tourist accommodation facilities, the conference advocated the adoption of a hotel trade charter codifying the regulations applicable to the hotel industry and, in particular, giving official tourist organizations powers enabling them to perform the activities devolving on the state in that field.

The conference observed that many states classify tourist hotels or are considering doing so. Acting upon the recommendations put forward by IUOTO and the International Chamber of Commerce, the conference advocated the standardization of methods of classification, and in particular, the subdivision of hotels into five categories, each identified by a conventional sign (stars) in conformity with sets of standards appropriate to different climatic conditions. The conference also considered the question of classifying supplementary means of accommodation such as tourist bungalows and camps.

### Classification

Classification separates accommodation into different classes or categories on the basis of certain criteria, for example, by type of accommodation such as hotels, holiday camps and caravan sites. A scheme of classification seeks to present information about tourist accommodation in a form which will enable the user to find information he requires easily and quickly and to be able to compare it with similar types. Apart from having the information classified by location, a tourist needs to know the availability of accommodation which meets his requirements as to type, price and other criteria.

### Registration

The aim of registration is to provide a complete list of register of tourist accommodation within a particular definition. A registration scheme results in an inventory of accommodation which can be kept upto date. In order to be comprehensive, it normally has to have statutory legal authority and is administered by a government authority or a statutory body. Because of the wide range of accommodation used by the tourists, a scheme of registration should normally cover all forms of accommodation used by them.

### Gradation

Grading separates accommodation into different categories or grades on the basis of judgments on the amenities and facilities of a particular accommodation unit in a form which enables the user to choose the quality of accommodation he requires. This may refer to the physical facilities, food and other services of the establishment, various amenities provided, etc. The establishments are graded individually or collectively by way of giving them numbers, letters or symbols.

The schemes of classification, registration and grading in operation differs in various countries. Some countries incorporate only registration, some others classification and some grading. The standards adopted also differ from country to country.

## CHANGING PROFILE

The probable future developments in the accommodation sector according to a study undertaken by WTO are as follows:

(*a*) A significant growth in accommodation supply will continue to be contributed by chain operators, including airlines. This expansion will result mainly from the further development of management contracts and franchise agreements.

(*b*) There will be a continuing move towards the further diversification of accommodation. The development of budget accommodation, covering budget hotels, and also supplementary means of accommodation, is likely to continue as mass tourism stimulates new demands for competitively priced accommodation.

(*c*) The standard of accommodation will continue to rise. Demand for recreational and sporting facilities will increase in both business and leisure accommodation.

(*d*) Rising building and operating costs, growing environment and conservation pressures, as well as the need to keep staffing levels at a minimum, will influence design and construction of accommodation units.

(*e*) Advances in technology will both influence the traditional construction methods; for example, more frequent use of prefabricated building techniques as well as traditional methods of hotel operations.

## QUESTIONS FOR ANSWER

1. *'Accommodation is the basic component of tourism'. Justify.*
2. *Write a note on the growth of Hospitality Industry.*
3. *Define Hotel and write a note on its classification types.*
4. *How does Commercial Hotels differ from Resort Hotels? Discuss.*
5. *Write short notes on the following:*
   (*a*) *Supplementary Accommodation.*
   (*b*) *Tourist Holiday Village.*
   (*c*) *Time-share and Resort Condominiums.*
   (*d*) *Floating Hotels.*
   (*e*) *Heritage Hotels.*
   (*f*) *Youth Hotel.*

# 21

# Hospitality Industry in India: Evolution and Development

## INTRODUCTION

Accommodation facilities constitute most important part of tourist supply, therefore, it has developed into an industry—termed as hospitality industry, which offers a home away from home to the tourist. Alike Indian civilization, the history of hospitality industry is oldest in the world, hereunder, we will consider various aspects of Indian hospitality industry:

## BRIEF HISTORY

In India the concept of shelter for travellers is not new. In fact, it is as old as its recorded history. The historical records are replete with mention of *viharas, dharamshalas, sarais, musafirkhanas,* etc. These establishments provided a home to all wayfarers, be they pilgrims, scholars, adventurers or merchants. The shelter under various names have always been a part of India's culture as a valuable institution providing a vital service.

The ancient Buddhist monks were probably the first to institutionalise the concept of a shelter in India. The cave temples scattered all over the south-western region of India have both a *chaitya* (sanctuary) for worship and prayer and a *vihara* (monastery). These monks, although living in their quiet retreats, away from towns and villages, were nevertheless mindful of the needs of travellers and pilgrims who found shelter and food at these monasteries.

It is interesting to note that these monasteries are located on the ancient trade routes between important deities of the region.

It is gathered from some inscriptions that merchants gave liberal donations for the construction and maintenance of these establishments. Mere charity was obviously not the motivation in these displays of generosity. The trader travelled with their merchandise and money on these routes and the *viharas* were their hotels.

In the medieval period this ancient institution gradually assumed a more secular character. Although religious centres invariably had *dharamshalas* and *musafirkhanas* attached to them, the caravanserai appeared as an exclusive traveller's lodge with a *nanbai* or cook attached with it.

Sher Shah Suri, the Afghan Emperor and the builder of the Grand Trunk Road, is credited with having built caravanserais at regular intervals all along this highway creating favourable conditions for commerce and travel. However, he was not alone in this venture. The Mughals built such facilities all over their empire.

Later kings, rajas, navabs, rich businessmen and philanthropists built *sarais* making travel less arduous. At approximately the same time, the inn was the Western counterpart of India's *sarais.* With the expansion of commerce, travelling became profitable and with it emerged the business of providing comfortable shelter and good food to the growing number of travellers.

The *sarais* in India like inns in Europe or the stagecoach stations in the USA of the eighteenth and nineteenth centuries stood all along the well-travelled routes. They provided food and shelter to the travellers and fodder to their horses. The amenities these early hotels offered would seem to us to be primitive but they conformed to the lifestyle of that age.

With the passage of time the age-old institution of the *sarai* or the inn adapted itself to the ever-changing and constantly growing requirements of the market and has evolved into the modern hotel. From the age of the bullock cart and horses through the age of the rail road into the era of the jumbo jet and supersonic aircraft, the hotel industry developed with the simultaneous development of transportation systems. It also reflects the standard of living and the lifestyle of the society in which it operates.

The development of hotel industry in India is also continuous and satisfactory. The British introduced hotels in India mainly for their own use or for foreign visitors. Some seventy years back, baring the Taj Mahal Hotel in Mumbai, almost all hotels in India were owned and operated by the Britishers and the Swiss. There were Albion Hotels, Victory Hotel and the Hope Hall. The arrangement in these was an excellent one.

Western-style residential hotels are comparatively of recent origin in India. These hotels were first started about 160 years ago mainly for princes and aristocrats and high dignitaries. The credit for opening the first Western-style hotel in India in the name of British Hotel in Mumbai in 1840 goes to Pestonjee who is the pioneer of Western-style hotels in India. The Auckland Hotel was started in 1843 and in 1858 it was renamed as the Great Eastern Hotel.

Today there are a number of western-style hotels in Kolkata—Great Eastern, Oberoi Grand, Kenilworth, Park, Hindustan International, Taj Bengal etc. By the end of the 19th century, there were many western-style hotels in South, like Imperial, Albany, New Woodland, Elphinstone, Napier, Pandyan (Madurai), Bangalore International, West End (Bangalore), Savoy, Ritz (Hyderabad), Palm Beach (Visakhapatnam) etc.

The twentieth century can be called the turning point in the history of the hotel industry in India. It was during this period many big business owners entered into the field.

In 1904, Jamshedji Tata opened the Taj Mahal Hotel in Mumbai. Front facing the Mumbai harbour and overlooking the Gateway of India, it was until recently, the largest hotel in the East. It is rated among the top ten hotels in the world. Jamshedji felt that it was essential for the advancement of the country that it should have an up-to-date hotel to provide facilities and comforts to visitors from all parts of the world.

Today there are many hotels in the chain including the President Hotel, the Fort Auada Beach Resort, the Lake Palace (Udaipur), the Rambagh Palace, Taj Palace (New Delhi), Taj Bengal (Kolkata) and many more.

The Indian Hotels Company Limited, owned by Tatas manages the famous Taj group of Hotels. This chain has fifty-five properties in India and abroad. It has drawn up a plan of Rs. 1,500 crore to add forty more hotels to its present fifty-five. The Taj Hotel in Mumbai, the Taj Palace Intercontinental in New Delhi and the Taj Bengal in Kolkata account for 76 per cent of its profits.

Another entrepreneur who entered the field of hotel industry is Rai Bahadur Mohan Singh Oberoi who opened a chain of Oberoi Hotels in India and abroad. Mr. Oberoi started his career as a clerk but later became a partner in the Clarks Hotels, Shimla.

In 1933, Mr. Oberoi took over the Grand Hotel, Kolkata on lease and gave it a new look and new life. Mr. Oberoi built a hotel on Gopalpur on sea, in Orissa, Mount Everest in Darjeeling, the Mount View in Chandigarh and the Palace in Srinagar to his chain of hotels. In 1973, Oberoi commissioned the 500-room luxury hotels—the Oberoi Sheraton, Mumbai. It is a product of Indo-American partnership. Other hotels of Oberoi chain are Oberoi in Singapore, Abu Dhabi, Sudan, Zambia, Egypt, Saudi Arabia, Fiji, Mauritius, Indonesia, Zanzibar and Colombo.

Oberoi's School of Hotel Management in Delhi recognised by the International Hotel Association, Paris, trains up young people from different countries.

Charle Ritz, son of the Swiss Caesar Ritz started Ritz hotels in India. The Ritzs are located in Mumbai, Kolkata (now defunct) and Hyderabad.

## PALACE HOTELS

India has developed a new concept of holiday making by opening Palace Hotels like the chateau tours in Europe. The magnificent palaces of former Maharajas were turned into Luxury hotels. Kashmir was the first state in India to convert its Maharaja's Palace into a hotel. Maharaja of Jaipur was the next one to convert his Ram Bagh Palace into a hotel. The Maharaja of Udaipur was the third one to do. In Rajasthan the Jodhpur Palace, the Jaisalmer Palace and the Bikaner Palace were also converted into hotels. Palaces by themselves are great attractions to tourists. They can get an opportunity to stay in these palaces and enjoy like Maharajas. Palaces of the former princes in India are now serving as five-star hotels. More than twenty palaces are now five-star hotels.

The Indian Tobacco Company (ITC) entered the hotel industry in 1957 with the opening of the Chola in Chennai. All hotels of ITC are named after the famous period of Indian history. The names Chola, Mughal, Maurya, etc. are chosen from dynasties of different periods of history. The name of its hotel in Chennai is

Chola. The Chola kings were known for their patronage of art and culture; the Mughal in Agra has been named after Emperor Akbar; the Maurya in Delhi has been inspired by the famous Maurya Emperor Ashoka.

ITC has two types of hotels—Welcome Hotels and Indovilles. All hotels functioning at present belong to the first category. It has plans to have Indovilles which will be low cost hotels. It is a combination of Indian town and village. The Welcome group chain of ITC has at present seventeen hotels.

## HOLIDAY INNS

The first holiday inn hotel in India is situated at Juhu Beach, Mumbai, a part of a 1,600-hotel chain that spans the world from USA through Europe, the Mediterranean, Africa, Asia and the Middle East to Australia, opened under the franchise from Holiday Inns. Incorporated USA, the seven-storeyed hotel is the venture of the Eastern International Hotels Ltd.

The Holiday Inn hotels have their own 'Holdiex' system, the world's largest computerized global reservation network that would enable its customers to make reservation in Holiday Inns anywhere in the world, at almost free of cost.

The New Delhi Hilton, an enterprise of Bharat Hotels Ltd., promoted by Delhi Automobiles Private Limited is another deluxe hotel. It is a 540-room Five Star Super Deluxe Hotel and the country's largest shopping-cum-office complex. The Bharat Hotels Ltd. plans to establish hotels at Goa, Mumbai, Diu and another in Delhi.

In 1903, Spencer Hotel, Calcutta was started with a capital of Rs. 3 lakh. There are many good Indian-style hotels in all big cities of India. Many new companies are entering into the hotel field. The Hyatt Regency Delhi, owned by the Asian Hotels Ltd., is a consortium company promoted by a group of non-resident Indian nationals. The hotel is situated at Cama Place, New Delhi.

In the past, construction of hotels has been mainly in the hands of the private sector. The Government paid no attention for the development of hotels in India. There were some rest-houses and tourist bungalows before 1963, which were run by the Department of Tourism and some of them by the state governments.

The tradition of State-owned hotels is quite old in our country. The Ashok Hotel in New Delhi, the Railway Hotels at Ranchi, Puri and Aurangabad, the State-owned hotel at Brindaban Gardens in Mysore, are some of the examples of hotels owned and run by the states.

On the basis of the recommendations of the Jha Committee and with a view to providing facilities needed for the foreign visitors, it was decided to set up three separate corporations:

(*a*) Indian Tourism Hotel Corporation Ltd. (1965), subsequently renamed as HCL Ltd. The main function of the corporation was the construction and management of hotels in public sectors;

(*b*) Indian Tourism Corporation Ltd. (1965). It was established with the object of producing material for tourist publicity; and

(*c*) Indian Tourism Transport Undertaking Ltd., was established in 1964 with a view to providing transport facilities to the tourists.

These three corporations were subsequently amalgamated into one composite corporation—Indian Tourism Development Corporation in 1966. Realizing the importance of tourism in the country, the government of India created a separate Ministry of Tourism and Civil Aviation in 1967.

Indian Tourism Development Corporation (ITDC) promoting tourism backed by the country's largest accommodation chain the Ashoka Group; over three thousand rooms in hotels, forest lodges, travellers' lodges and beach resorts extend from Jammu in the north to Kovalam in the south. The Ashoka in New Delhi has been equated with the best convention facilities available in Asia.

ITDC has a shopping arcade in each of its hotels added to which are five duty-free shops at the international airports of Mumbai, Kolkata, Delhi, Chennai and Tiruchirapalli.

Air India's decision to enter the hotel business is not something unusual. Air India decided not to get into hotel business under its own name. In 1971, it set up a wholly-owned subsidiary called Hotel Corporation of India (HCIL) with the capital of 6.5 million dollars. The HCIL opened the Centaur Hotel at Mumbai airport in 1974. It has also two other hotels.

Yet another entry of public sector in the field of Tourism and Hoteliering was the introduction of 'Palace on Wheels' concept, introduced by Rajasthan Tourism Development Corporation, in collaboration with the Indian Railways.

The hotel industry in India is making a remarkable progress in both sectors-public and private.

## METHODS OF MANAGEMENT

Many lodging establishments especially small motels and inns are managed by their owners. But it is also very common for a hotel to be owned by one party but managed by a different party. The relationship between ownership and management may be one or three basic types:

(*i*) Proprietary ownership,
(*ii*) Franchise, and
(*iii*) Management contract.

### Proprietary Ownership

Proprietary ownership is the direct ownership of one or more properties by a person or company. Small motels are owned and operated by a couple or family are common examples of proprietary ownership.

A chain is a group of hotels that are owned or managed by one company. In general, three or more units constitute a chain but major hotel chains have from 300 to 5,000 properties. A proprietary chain is owned entirely by one company.

In a co-owner chain, ownership of individual properties is shared by the hotel company and by independent investors. Marriott, Sheraton Intercontinental are examples of successful chains.

A chain property has certain competitive advantages over an independently owned hotel. Chain hotels attract experienced employees, it also benefits from national advertising campaigns that independent operators cannot afford. Consumers favour products that are well known to them and hotels are no exception to this principle. A famous chain attracts travellers who recognize and trust the brand name.

### Franchise

Not all hotels that have the same name belong to a proprietary chain. A different type of chain—a franchise chain—comprises properties they have the same name and design but are owned and operated by different parties.

A franchise is a licence given by a company or franchiser, to use the company's ideas, methods or trade marks in a business. By paying a fee, a private investor or franchise can obtain a trademark license, architectural plans, designs, training and operating methods. The franchisee is responsible for financing the construction of the property.

The franchisee may be an individual, a partnership, a small corporation or group of investors. Thus many hotels that have Holiday Inn, Sheraton or Hilton signs are actually owned by local independent investors. A franchisee pays an initial fee upon signing the franchise agreement. Franchisees also pay ongoing royaltise based on the total income of the hotel.

Besides Holiday Inn other wellknown franchise chains include Days Inn, Ramada Inn, Super 8, and the choice chain which includes Quality Inns, Comfort Inns etc.

### Management Contract

Under a management contract, a property owner contracts with a hotel management company to operate the establishment. In some cases a wellknown chain may build a new property and retain ownership, while arranging for a local firm to manage the hotel. In other cases, local investors may fund the construction and development of a property, while contracting with an experienced chain such as Ramada or Marriott, to manage the operations. In either case the management firm receives a share of profits.

## REFERRAL ORGANIZATIONS

Some travellers confuse chains such as Holiday Inn, or Hilton with referral organizations such as Best Western. A Best Western property is neither a chain hotel nor a franchise but rather an independent member's property of a cooperative association that is owned and run by its membership. Best Western is the largest US referral organization. The Golden Tulip network, with headquarters in the Netherlands, provide similar referral services for properties throughout Europe and the Caribbean.

## TYPE OF HOTELS

1. *Motel*—It is a hotel with motorable space.
2. *Rotel*—It is a hotel on wheels.

3. *Flotel*—A houseboat on a flowing river or lake is an example of a flotal *e.g.*, Houseboat on the Dal Lake in Kashmir.
4. *Airtel*—Hotel near airports such as Hotel Centaue, Mumbai.

QUESTIONS FOR ANSWER

1. *Trace briefly the evolution of hospitality industry in India.*
2. *Write notes on (i) Palace Hotels and (ii) Holiday Inns.*
3. *Describe the relationship between ownership and management in the hotel industry.*
4. *Write short notes on the following:*
   (*a*) *Franchise.*
   (*b*) *Management contract.*
   (*c*) *Type of Hotels.*

# 22

# Management of Tourist Hospitality

Accommodation constitute is considered as the most important part of tourism industry because it relates to one of the three basic needs of human being—food, cloth and shelter, hence though a part of tourism industry accommodation is termed as 'Hospitality Industry', therefore, the management of hospitality industry only effects its own growth and development but the tourist industry as a whole, therefore, in this chapter we will discuss various aspects concerning its management, hereunder:

## MEANING

Hospitality is defined as the friendly reception and treatment of stranger with courtesy and warmth as guest. Hospitality is also an industry made up of business that provide lodging, food and other services to travellers. The main components are hotels, motels, inns, resorts and restaurants. In these business the friendly reception and treatment of strangers is paramount to success.

Lodging establishments (hotels) represent the seventh largest industry in the world and generate approximately $36 billion in annual sales.

The hospitality industry is both national and international in nature and in terms of accommodation it ranges from luxury to budget hotel and from city centre business properties to tourism resorts. In the wider sense, time-share, caravanning and camping should be considered a part of the industry.

Hotels are changing and will continue to change. As a result, the techniques of management of modern hotels have to adapt to changing circumstances. Technology in the form of computers and labour saving mechanical equipment, will have a major effect on the way in which hotels are managed and operated.

## HISTORICAL DEVELOPMENT OF HOTEL INDUSTRY

Today's lodging industry is complex and diverse. From the inns of Biblical times to modern resort complexes, the evolution of lodging establishment has been influenced by social, cultural, economic and political changes in society.

The early travellers were mostly traders. Inn keeping was one of the first commercial enterprises and hospitality was one of the first services for which money was exchanged.

The inns offered little more than cot or bench in the corner of a room where sanitation or privacy was non-existent.

It was not until the Industrial Revolution that European traverns began to combine food and beverage service with lodging. In colonial America, inns were modelled after European traverns.

The first American hotel, the City Hotel opened in 1794 in the seaport of New York city. In 1829, Isaiah Rogers built a new hotel in Boston. His creation—Tremont House—was the earliest first class Hotel in America. With the end of World War II, the hotel industry unexpectedly entered a new era of prosperity. With automobile in every house, Americans began to travel with their families.

The early hotels were small owned and operated by couples. California was the site of the first motel revolution.

The historical development of hotel industry is linked up with the development of transportation and in turn the tourism product. With the emergence of railway network there came the need for accommodation and so the building of railway hotels. Increased travel by the upper classes stimulated the building of luxury hotels, since the 60s the hospitality industry grew due to a number of factors—increase in real income, living standards and leisure time.

The increase of car ownership was also a contributory factor. Another influence was the development of air transport since the 60s which played a significant role in the accessibility of resorts and location of hotels. The location of industry and trade and the expansion of motorway network has created a demand for accommodation. In the year 2,000 the largest industry in the world is tourism. Total world arrivals have, over the past two decades, expanded by an average growth rate of 5.1 per cent per year. Receipts from tourism worldwide for the same period have risen by a similar rate.

## GRADING OF HOTELS

The United Nations Conference on International Travel and Tourism held in Rome in 1963 also stressed the need for some regulation of the accommodation for safeguarding the interest of the users. The conference recommend the standardization of methods of classification of hotels into five categories each identified by a conventional sign (stars) in conformity with set standards. Star classification is essentially a guide to the type of hotel, indicating the character of the accommodation and services it sets out to provide, the classification is as follows:

1. *One Star*—Hotels and inns generally of small scale with acceptable facilities and furnishings.
2. *Two Star*—Holes offering a higher standard of accommodation and some private bathrooms and showers. A wider choice of food is provided.
3. *Three Star*—Hotels with more spacious accommodation, large number of bedrooms with private bathrooms and showers. Fuller meal facilities are provided.
4. *Four Star*—Hotels offering a high standard of comfort and service.
5. *Five Star*—Luxury hotels offering the highest international standards.

## PACKAGE OF HOTEL FACILITIES

Each hotel offers its own particular package of facilities. The hotel guests expect to find many auxiliary facilities in addition to the basic ones of accommodation, food and drink. A hotel guest may expect to find a telephone, a radio and TV in the room and be able to telex or fax urgent messages. The guest may wish to purchase newspapers and magazines, have suits dry cleaned, and shirts laundered. Many hotels provide a hair dressing establishment where a guest can get his hair cut, a gift shop where he may buy or presents souvenirs for the family.

The hotel may provide service for reserving tickets for the theatre or making travel arrangements and provide sports facilities such as tennis court or swimming pool. Conference facilities may also be provided. All or some of these auxiliary facilities and the restaurants and bars may also be available to non-residents.

The classic hotel organisation model was built around two major hotel managerial personalities—the chef and the maitre d'hotel. The chef was the chief or 'king' of the kitchen. Like a feudal lord he held sway over everything that had to do with the preparation of food in the hotel. Similarly, the maitre d'hotel was the 'master' of all services in the hotel and it was his responsibility to see that the guests were always served promptly and properly.

In the modern hotel organisation, a complex line and staff structure has emerged. In a hotel those who have a regular contact with the guests are known as line executives. The most important line operations in a hotel are the Rooms Division and Food and Beverage Division.

Staff executive are those who perform 'behind the scenes' activities and have little or no guest contact *e.g.*, engineering is a staff function.

Hotel General Manager occupies a crucial role in the midst of hotel operations as he is in close contact with employees and guests as well as top management. The decision he makes plays a major role in determining the effectiveness of the hotel staff and the satisfaction of the guest.

## MANAGEMENT OF FRONT OFFICE AND RECEPTION

The work of the front office and reception departments in the hotel industry is very important. The front office is referred to as the 'hub', 'the nerve centre' or the 'brain' in the modern hotel. The most important works of the reception staff are as follows:

1. *Welcoming Arriving Guests*—It is the duty of receptionist to put the guests at case at the time of their arrival and welcome them to the hotel which is to be their temporary home for a few days. Guests who are treated in an insensitive way on arrival may prove to be problematic during the rest of their stay.
2. *Completing the Hotel Register*—The legal formality of registration must be fulfilled by the receptionist who sees that all customers supply the details required for record that may be inspected by the police from time to time. Useful marketing information may also be collected at this time.

3. *Recording Reservations*—The selling of rooms is the profit maker in all hotels and consequently vital for effective hotel business.
4. *Compiling Guest's Bills*—The bill that is presented to a guest on departure involves many items of expenditure that may have been incurred by him in different departments of the hotel during his stay. These many small items have to be collected and added on to one bill accurately so that the guest is not overcharged or undercharged. Billing should be carried out swiftly so that a guest's bill is always instantly ready should the guest wish to check out.
5. *Providing Information*—The reception desk is the office of the hotel to the guests and should be able to answer all types of questions not only about the hotel but also about the surrounding areas and activities.
6. *Dealing with Complaints*—The reception desk is the place where many guests come in the event of a complaint. The department must be prepared to handle different types of complaints from customers.
7. *Room Forecasts*—The front office is responsible for maintaining accurate statistics of understays, overstays, early arrivals, cancellations, walk-ins and no-shows. Understays are guests who depart in advance of their check-out date. Overstays are guests who stay on beyond their stated check-out date. Early arrivals are clients who check in before their check-in date. Cancellations are clients who notify the hotel that they will not check in as planned. Walk-ins are guests who check in without a prior reservation. No-shows are clients who place reservations but don't arrive on the stated check-in date and don't cancel the reservations.

The reception desk is one small part of the total front office in a large hotel while it embraces all the work undertaken by a front office in a small hotel.

## DUTIES OF RECEPTIONIST

Many customers arrive at a hotel never having seen the premises before and the first staff they come into contact with is invariably the receptionist. The receptionists are to be found behind their desk which is generally situated near the main entrance to enable them to carry out their main responsibility, *i.e.*, to welcome customers. Guests should be welcomed without delay and the formalities of room allocations and registration dispensed with as soon as possible. Customers are often nervous in a new environment and the receptionist should put them at ease swiftly by removing the psychological worry.

The receptionist should possess a good appearance as well as social skills. The receptionist is the most important public relations man for the hotel.

## Check-in

The purpose of the reception desk is to receive guests and to welcome them to the hotel. The moment of arrival or check-in is the *raison d'etre* of the whole department. It is the duty of the receptionist to make a new guest feel at ease on arrival. The reception staff must be well prepared with all the relevant check-in information to hand so that everything may proceed smoothly.

The receptionist should be able to allocate rooms to customers immediately without their having to wait in the foyer and he must keep a watch that customers do not leave without paying.

The reception desk should be in the front office near the main entrance so that it is easily visible on arrival by guests who do not know their way about the hotel. Another reason for putting the reception desk near the main entrance is to keep an eye on the guests either arriving or leaving the hotel. An entrance which is unsupervised is an open invitation to guests to walk out without paying or to smuggle extra customers into their rooms.

Some customers, who have no previous booking, approach the reception desk. The receptionist should greet this chance arrival and enquire if they have a reservation or not. The receptionist should collect the information regarding the type of room required and if any such room is available. If the answer is in the affirmative the guests should be given registration cards to complete. Next the customers should be asked for a deposit by the receptionist.

The moment a guest arrives at the reception desk it should be ensured that the legal implications of the registration legislature are compiled with. Legally a non-alien has to give only his or her full name along with nationality and address and signature. If the guest is an alien, he has to furnish the following information:

(*i*) The number of his passport or registration certificate.
(*ii*) The place of issue of his passport or registration certificate.
(*iii*) Details of his next destination and if possible his full address there.

The main problem is that the guest, particularly the chance guest, should not leave without paying. The best policy is to ask all guests to pay a deposit on arrivals so that in the event of their departing without payment, a part of the bill may be covered.

Since a hotel is a public place, it is open to many different types of fraud or security problems, which the receptionist has to prevent.

The arrival of a tour or large group puts severe strain on reception and front office staff. When a large group of people, say 40 or 50 arrive at the hotel, all expect to get their rooms as quickly as possible. Registration of a tour group through the checks-in process may be a problem. If the tour company send the guests' details in advance, there is no necessity for each customer to register individually.

It should be remembered that legally a hotel is obliged to accept every traveller who arrives and the only grounds for refusing a person a room are if the hotel is already full or if it is felt that the customer is unfit to be received. By unfit, the law could mean a person who is drunk or who is a known prostitute. In either case it is better to simply say that the hotel is full.

## The Guest In-house

It is the responsibility of the front office staff of any hotel to deal with any information the guests might request and to answer any enquiries. The staff of the front office should be able to provide guests with information. If any front office staff feels that it is not his responsibility to answer to queries from the guests it might be disastrous to guest relations.

Having completed their stay in the hotel the final morning arrives when customers have to pay for all those services that they have made use of during their stay.

The Cashier in hotels are generally responsible for accepting payment for guests' bills as well as dealing with the exchange of foreign currency. It is also an important task to undertake the safe custody of guests' valuable if so required.

It is an offence to leave a hotel without paying and the hotel may prosecute in order to obtain payment.

**House Keeping**

House Keeping is perhaps the most important front office support department. The house keeping department inspects rooms for sale, cleans the occupied and vacated rooms and co-ordinates a room's status with the front office.

Within the rooms division there is the uniformed service—packing attendants, door attendants, porters, drivers and bell persons. Uniformed service personnel have a great degree of contact with guests. They greet and help guests to the front desk and to their rooms. At the end of the stay, they take guests to the cashier and to their means of transportation.

## THE GUEST CYCLE

Guest transactions during a stay at a hotel determine the flow of business which can be divided into a four stage guest cycle.

During the pre-arrival stage the guest chooses a hotel to patronise. The choice can be affected by a variety of factors including previous experiences with the hotel, advertisements, recommendations, etc. The attitude, efficiency and knowledge of the front office staff may influence a caller's decision to stay at a particular hotel.

The arrival stage of the guest cycle includes registration and rooming functions. When the guests arrive at the hotel they establish a business relationship with the hotel through the front office staff. It is the staff's task to clarify the nature of the guest-hotel relationship and the expectations from the hotel of the guest.

Throughout the occupancy stage front office represents hotel to the guests. The objective of the front office is to satisfy needs of the guests in a way that will encourage a return visit.

The last stage of the guest cycle is departure. Both the guest services and guest accounting aspects of the guest cycle are completed during this phase. Once the guest has checked out, the room's status is updated and the house keeping department is advised.

**Refusal of Accommodation**

A hotel may legally refuse accommodation to person due to any of the reasons.

(*i*) When no accommodation is available in the hotel.
(*ii*) If the prospective guest is a known criminal or a prostitute.
(*iii*) When the hotel believes that the prospective guest might create disturbance.

But a hotel cannot refuse accommodation to a prospective guest on the basis of age, race, colour or creed.

**Meals**

The restaurant meals are produced for immediate consumption on the premises and are not bought and consumed in another context as in the case with many other consumer goods, for example, food from super markets. The result is that customers are more closely tied into the organisation structure than they would be in other organisation contexts such as retailers.

In a car factory, contact between the producer of the product and the actual customers does not exist. But in a hotel there is a direct contact between the producer of the products and the actual customers.

**Food**

The food and drink service is the second major activity of most hotels next to accommodation.

*Food Cycle*: The food operation of a hotel may be viewed as a cycle, which consists of several stage—purchasing, receiving, storing, issuing, preparing and selling.

Purchasing is the beginning of the hotel food cycle. Normally, one person has a responsibility for food purchases—a purchasing officer in a large hotel and the food and beverage manager in a medium sized hotel and in the smaller hotel purchasing may be undertaken by the owner or managers.

The purchasing function extends from identifying the best sources of supply, making arrangements with suppliers and placing orders to close liaison with the kitchen and other user departments.

Receiving involves the hotel is being supplied with food of the ordered quantity and quality at the agreed price and its transfer to stores or directly to the user departments. Receiving takes place by a comparison of delivery notes against orders and by a physical inspection of the deliveries.

Preparing or food production presents the conversion of the purchased foods by chef and cooks into dishes and deals.

Storing and issuing consists of maintaining an adequate stock of food for the day-to-day requirements of the hotel, without loss through spoilage and pilferage and without capital being tied up unnecessarily through overstocking and of issues of food to user departments. Issues to the kitchen and other user department are normally made at set times in the day against authorized requisitions.

Selling is the final stage of the hotel food cycle and consists of the service of particular foods, dishes and meals by various categories of foods service staff to the customer in a restaurant. The main aspects of the selling stage are the menu, the form of service and the physical environment in which the sale takes place.

The menu is the focus of the food operation and there are two main types:

(*a*) *A table d'hote* menu is a limited choice menu with single price for any combination of items chosen or with a price determined by the choice of the main dish.

(*b*) *An a la carte* menu provides a choice of items, each of which is priced separately.

Three basic levels of service may be identified;

(*a*) *Self-service,* where the customer orders and collects the food from a counter and takes it to a table where he consumes it.

(*b*) *Counter service,* where the customer is presented with the food he had ordered and consumes it at the counter;

(*c*) *Table service,* where the customer is served by a waiter who takes the order and serves the meal at the table.

QUESTIONS FOR ANSWER

1. *"The development of hotel industry, is linked up with the transportation and tourism." Justify.*
2. *Describe the facilities provided by a modern hotel.*
3. *Write a note on Hotel grading schemes.*
4. *Explain the functions of the front office and reception departments in the hotel industry.*
5. *Describe the functions of the receptionist in a modern hotel.*

# 23

# Functioning of Hospitality Industry in India

## INTRODUCTION

Culturally India is very rich in hospitality. Our concept of hospitality is based on the dectum of '*Atith Devo Bhav*' which means that the guest equals the God and it is His blessing on us if we receive a guest. Therefore, even today accord a friendly reception and generous treatment to our guests.

## FORMS OF ACCOMMODATION

Many different forms of accommodation are available to the modern tourist. Holiday accommodation is available to the modern tourist. Holiday accommodation may be classified into four main categories.

1. Service accommodation including hotels, pensions, guest and boarding hoses.
2. Self-catering accommodation including camping, caravans, rented flats and houses.
3. Homes of friends and relatives where no payment is made for the use of accommodation.
4. Other accommodation including boats, youth hostels, etc.

The UN Conference of International Travel and Tourism held in Rome in 1963 considered, *inter alia*, the problems of accommodation. In recognised the importance of means of accommodation, both traditional (hotel, motels) and supplementary (camps, youth hostels) as incentives to international tourism. The conference recommended that governments should establish special corporations for tourism.

Hotels and motels constitute the largest sector of accommodation. Hotels and motels are similar except that motels are roadside hotels with parking space to accommodate travelling tourists.

Supplementary accommodation includes accommodations for tourists but not necessarily hotel services. It includes government rest houses, tourist bungalows, dak bungalows, youth hostels, *dharamshalas*, etc.

Accommodation may also be classified into two sectors: the commercial sector which includes hotels, motels, guest houses and supplementary sector to cover all others forms of accommodation. The supplementary sector includes private permanent residences used for hosting friends and relatives and second homes *i.e.*, a permanent building which is the occasional residence of a household that usually lives elsewhere and which is mainly used for recreational purposes. Camps and caravans may constitute an intermediate category where in private tents or caravans are sited in commercial camping grounds.

Apart from the traditional accommodation provided by hotels, flexible and functional forms such as rented apartments are available. Flexibility in ownership is also apparent. Resort apartments or condominiums in many places may be purchased out right or may be arranged on a time-sharing basis where by a series of owners acquire rights to a property for specified periods of the year.

## CONCEPT OF HOTELS

We have discussed this concept in the earlier chapters. Hotel is a place which supplies boarding and lodging or a place for the entertainment the travellers. From users point of view hotel is an institution of commercial hospitality which offers its facilities and services for sale.

Its location places the hotel geographically in or near a particular city or village; within a given area location denotes accessibility and the convenience and attractiveness of surroundings and the appeal it presents, freedom from noise and other nuisances.

Its facilities which include bedrooms, restaurants, bars, function rooms, conference halls, and recreation facilities such as swimming pools, represent facilities for the use of its customers.

Its service comprises the availability and extent of particular hotel services provided through its facilities and the quality of these in such terms as degree of personal attention, speed and efficiency.

Its image may be defined as the way in which the hotel portrays itself to people and the way in which it is perceived as portraying itself by them. It is a by-product of its location, facilities and service but it is enhanced by such factors as its name, appearance, atmosphere and what other people say about it.

Its price expresses the value given by the hotel through its location, facilities, service and image and the satisfaction derived by its users from these elements of the hotel concept.

First hoteliers in India were the *Pandas* or priests who accommodated their clients in *Dharamshalas* or in their houses at places of pilgrimage like Banaras, Haridwar, Mathura, Puri, etc., for in those days most travels were for pilgrimage.

The modern tourist is increasingly mobile and enjoys greater freedom and independence than his predecessor. The aircraft and the motor car enable him to be more adventurous, more flexible and less formal. As a result, there are changes in the demand for accommodation in three main directions—in location, requirements and in its volume and distribution in time.

The availability of new forms of transport exercises a growing influence on the choice of holiday area. More remote regions are increasingly accessible and new holiday areas are growing up with a new demand for accommodation facilities as popular tourist destinations cease to attract new hotels and holiday villages meet the accommodation demand in new locations.

An hotel is defined as an establishment of a permanent nature of four or more bedrooms, offering bed and breakfast on a short-term contract and conforming to certain minimum standards.

The greater self-sufficiency of the tourist finds an expression in caravan and camping holidays and in self-catering accommodation ranging from chalets to flatlets which are also conducive to weekends and shorts holidays away from home, at all times of the year.

Accommodation facilities provide an outstanding example of location in relation to the market. They are located where the demand is exercised.

Inn-keeping and hotel keeping are two parts of an evolutionary process which followed the developments of the means of passenger transportation. Inns were situated along the roads and at destinations serving terminal traffic. The railways gave an impetus to terminal hotels at destinations. Motor transport created a new demand for transit accommodation. The influence of passenger shipping can also be seen on the provision of accommodation in ports for incoming and outgoing traffic. Air transport has exercised a distinct influence on the location of accommodation facilities near airports.

As the railways of the nineteenth century found it necessary to build hotels to safeguard their main business, the transportation of passenger, so do the airlines of the twentieth century. Some major hotels chains are subsidiaries of airlines.

## TYPES OF HOTELS

From the viewpoint of size and amenities provided, there are different types of hotels:

(*a*) *International Hotel*—These are modern western type hotels in the metropolis and principal tourist centres. These hotels are ranked in different star categories, *i.e.*, from five star to one star depending upon the facilities provided. There are some international chains which own a large number of such hotels.

(*b*) *Resort Hotel*—Resort Hotels are mainly near the sea or in mountains and cater to the needs of the tourists. The motive of a person to visit a resort hotel is rest and recreation. Resort hotels provide recreational facilities to the tourists in an informal atmosphere. Resort hotels may be Summer Resorts, Winter Resorts, All Season Resorts, Hill Resorts and Health Resorts.

(*c*) *Commercial Hotel*—Commercial hotels cater mainly to travellers who visit a place for commercial or business purposes. These are mainly located in important towns and cities. Commercial hotels may be licenced or unlincened.

(*d*) *Pensions*—These are found in Europe and USA. These are accommodation facilities operated by a family usually living in building. Pensions also known as residential hotels were developed in the USA where people discovered that permanent living in hotels has many advantages. These pensions are located mostly in big cities and provide accommodation to the tourists.

## CLASSIFICATION OF HOTELS BY PHYSICAL CHARACTERISTICS

Physical characteristics determine whether a lodging establishment is a hotel, motel, resort, conference centre, condominium hotel or bed and breakfast inn.

The world *hotel* means *mansion* in French, implying a high level of comfort luxury and personal service. A hotel provides private accommodations, usually with food and beverage service on the same premises and maintain a fulltime service staff.

As automobiles and road travel become popular, motor hotel or motel became a prominent component of the travel and lodging industries. A motel provides ample parking space for automobiles.

To meet the needs of business travellers, hotels adopted a wide variety of amenities such as swimming pools, tennis courts, golf grounds, health clubs creating the resorts.

As there are more conventions and meetings now than at any previous time, there are also more convention hotels. A convention hotel is a lodging house that has special facilities and service for large groups that hold conferences, meeting and large exhibition hall and several meeting and banquet rooms. Conference centers are designed for smaller meetings.

A condominium hotel or 'condotel' offers apartment style accommodation with a full kitchen for guests who wish to prepare their meals. *Bed and breakfast* inns are private residences that provide temporary lodging to guests with breakfast included.

## CLASSIFICATION OF HOTELS BY PRICE LEVEL

Hotels are also classified by price level. The average room rates offered by hotel determine whether it is a luxury, superior, mid-market or economy hotel.

The term luxury indicates the highest standard of excellence in the lodging industry. Luxury hotels are also called Deluxe hotels.

A superior hotel also called a first class or executive hotel in near-luxurious and has on-premises food and beverage service.

A mid-market hotel, also called a tourist-class hotel, is a traditional hotel with above average luxury and comfort.

An economy hotel also called a standard or budget hotel, provides private, sanitary rooms at affordable rates. Most economy hotels do not have their own food and beverage operations. Instead they are located near a fastfood restaurant for the convenience of guests.

### Hotel Chain

A chain consists of three or more properties owned or managed by the same company under the same brand name, *e.g.*, Marriot, Sheraton.

### Paying Guest Accommodation

To augment the room requirements at the major tourist centres, paying guest accommodation scheme has been introduced. In all, 1,476 units have been registered. This scheme is open to the house owners having lettable rooms of requisite standard.

In India, we also have floating hotels as in Hong Kong and elsewhere. In Kashmir, Floating hotels in the form of houseboats are very popular and Hirilling with tourists.

### Major Hotel Chains in India

At present there are four major hotel chains in India.

(*a*) *Ashok Hotel Chain* run by the Tourism Development Corporation of India has 37 hotels with 3,800 rooms.
(*b*) *Taj Group* owned by the Tatas has 28 hotels in India and 15 overseas. The Taj Group has also started a second chain of budget hotels for middle class people called Gateway hotels.
(*c*) *Oberoi Hotel Chain,* has 26 hotels—14 in India and 12 abroad.
(*d*) *Welcome Group* has 21 hotel in India.

Air India's Hotel Corporation has four major hotels—two in Mumbai, one in Delhi and one in Srinagar, these are called Hotel Centaur.

Major international hotel chains operating in India are Sheraton. Holiday, Intercontinental, Ramada, Inn, Quality Inns, Hyatt and Meridian.

## Heritage Hotels

A new classification standard of heritage hotels has been introduced to cover functioning hotels in palaces, *havelies*, castles, forts and residences built prior to 1950. As the traditional structure reflects the ambience and lifestyle of the bygone era, it is immensely popular with the tourists. The scheme is aimed to ensure that such properties, landmarks of our heritage are not lost due to decay and disuse; at the same time, by bringing such properties into the approved sector, they become financially viable besides providing additional room capacity for the tourist.

QUESTIONS FOR ANSWER

1. *Describe the various types of tourist accommodation available in India.*
2. *Trace the emergence of hotels. What are the different types of hotels?*
3. *Give a classification of hotels by physical characteristics.*
4. *Write notes on:*
   (*i*) *Classification of hotels by price level.*
   (*ii*) *Major hotel chains in India.*
   (*iii*) *Heritage Hotels.*

# 24

# Tourism: The Existing Pattern and Future Trends

The reports of World Tourism Organisation (WTO), which covers 185, destination countries divided in 10 regions, for its data clearly presents the existing pattern of global tourism and visualizes the future trends as discussed hereunder:

## THE EXISTING PATTERN

People in general now view tourism as a way of life rather than a luxury items reserved for the affluent and the elite. Tourism has emerged as the largest service industry globally, in terms of gross revenue, as well as foreign exchange earnings.

According to the World Tourism Organisation (WTO), the number of international travellers has risen to more than 700 million per annum. With rapid developments in the field of transport and communications, the global tourism industry is likely to double in the next decade.

Tourism is the industry of industries and has a great multiplier effect on other industries. Tourism serves as an effective medium for transfer or distribution of wealth because here income earned in places of "residence" is spent in places "visited".

WTO forecasts that international arrivals in the year 2010 will top on billion and that by 2020 it will reach 1.6 billion—nearly three times the number of international trips made in 1996 which was 592 million.

The 21st century will see a higher percentage of the total population travelling, specially in developing countries, and people will be going on holiday more often. Travellers of the 21st century will also be going farther. The "Tourism 2020 Vision" forecasts predict that by 2020, one out of every three trips will be long haul journeys to another region of the world.

Tourism is the highest generator of employment. A total of 250 million people are now being employed globally through direct and indirect opportunities generated by this industry. This means that one out of every eight persons now earns a living from tourism. Tourism is also highly employment intensive. For every million rupees of investment, 13 jobs are created in the manufacturing industries, 45 jobs in agriculture, and 89 jobs in hotels and restaurants. Tourism, is therefore considered to be an important area for intensive development for all governments. As the fastest growing foreign exchange earner in developed and developing countries, it is being given priority attention.

## LIST OF WORLD'S TOP 30 COUNTRIES IN TERMS OF TOTAL EXPENDITURE ABROAD

There 30 countries account for 92 per cent of all tourist spending worldwide.

1. USA
2. Germany
3. Japan
4. UK
5. France
6. Canada
7. Italy
8. Netherlands
9. Austria
10. Sweden
11. Switzerland
12. Taiwan
13. Saudi Arabia
14. Belgium/Luxembourg
15. Mexico
16. Hong Kong
17. Australia
18. Spain
19. Denmark
20. Norway
21. South Korea
22. Kuwait
23. Finland
24. Brazil
25. Malaysia
26. New Zealand
27. Israel
28. Argentina
29. Republic of Ireland
30. South Africa

## LIST OF 15 COUNTRIES HAVING MAXIMUM INTERNATIONAL TOURISM EXPENDITURE (Excluding International Transport)

| *Rank* | *Country* | *Rank* | *Country* |
|---|---|---|---|
| 1. | USA | 9. | Austria |
| 2. | Germany | 10. | Sweden |
| 3. | Japan | 11. | Switzerland |
| 4. | UK | 12. | Taiwan |
| 5. | Italy | 13. | Belgium |
| 6. | France | 14. | Spain |
| 7. | Canada | 15. | Australia |
| 8. | Netherlands | | |

## LIST OF TOP 15 TOURISM EARNER COUNTRIES (Excluding International Transport)

| *Rank* | *Country* | *Rank* | *Country* |
|---|---|---|---|
| 1. | United States | 9. | Canada |
| 2. | France | 10. | Hong Kong |
| 3. | Italy | 11. | Singapore |
| 4. | Spain | 12. | Mexico |
| 5. | Austria | 13. | Australia |
| 6. | United Kingdom | 14. | Netherlands |
| 7. | Germany | 15. | Thailand |
| 8. | Switzerland | | |

India does not find place in any of the above three lists though we have very good potentials for the development of tourism at par with any country in the world, therefore, in future we must go all out to develop tourism infrastructures to ensure maximum national income from tourism, a foundation of which have been laid in last five years in particular by the NDA Government.

## FUTURE TREND IN TOURISM

Making long term projection is a very uncertain business. Tomorrow is unknown to us, and the more tomorrow we put together, the more likely it is that events will take an unexpected turn. But in order to plan properly forth future growth of tourism, it is necessary to make certain forecasts. Planning based on future forecasts must take place now in order to supply the goods and services for quality tourism in the future.

## SPACE ODYSSEY—TRAVEL OF THE FUTURE

In the not-too-distant future, space travel to distant cities will become commonplace. People willing to pay the price may travel by space shuttle say from New York to Tokyo, a trip which will take only 45 minutes.

Of trips to places off the earth's surface, a journey to the moon will be the most popular vacation tour, a space station located between the earth and the moon will be used as a stopover. NASA will operate the tours, since private airlines cannot afford the cost, and NASA will build a beautiful hotel on the moon at the base of spectacular mountain range. Moon visitors will have an opportunity to view space manufacturing of many products made advantageously in zero gravity and will learn about scientific experiments taking place on the moon.

During their visit to the moon, tourists will be provided space suits or walks on the surface, so that everyone can enjoy the exhilaration of low-gravity moon walking as well as the spectacular visits of moon mountains and craters and the eerie view of the earth in the sky.

By operating these exotic and very expensive tours, NASA can recover some of the money spent on developing the space programmes. A tremendous demand for lunar tours has developed, although the tours would be high price, the prestige of being able to tell friends about a walk on the moon will be well worth the cost to the adventurous affluent.

Trips to other planets will be the ultimate in travel—the epitome of one's lifetime of travel experiences. Mars will be the most popular destination. As on trips to the moon, passengers will wear ordinary street clothes and will be accommodated in a passenger module, seating 40 to 50 people. The space vehicle's first stop will be at a luxury space hotel orbiting the earth about 100 miles up. Here the passengers are refreshed and rested for a few days while receiving instructions and preparing for their 280-day flight to Mars. Passengers would be divided into two groups. Those of normal range of weight to height remain alert during the entire trip, and they would be required to participate in rigorous physical exercise each day to keep up their physical well-being. Those who are quite overweight will spend most of the trip in a comatose state, reached by being wrapped in a refrigerated blanket. This device slowly lowers body temperature to –76 degrees Fahrenheit, inducing hibernation until they reach the Red Planet.

At an appropriate time prior to arrival, the refrigeration blankets would be removed by the flight crew and each passenger would gradually warm up to normal body temperature. A series of exceptionally nourishing meals is served prior to arrival to renew body strength and vigour.

Upon arrival, passengers are transferred to a beautiful NASA hotel where complete recovery from the long trip is accomplished under the guidance of experienced space physicians. Donning streamlined space suits, the Mars visitors can explore the most interesting features of the Red planet by battery-operated automobiles and, if they desire ski cross-country on the north polar ice cap.

After a two week visit, it would be time to prepare for the long homeward trip. Again hearty meals would be served in the hotels to help to rebuild those needing fat reserves. When this would be accomplished, passengers embark for the trip back to the space orbiting hotel and then back to the starting point. Upon return to earth, they would be awestruck by the lush greenery and beautiful blue water of their earthly home, and they would be amazed by the changes that would have taken place since their departure into space.

## QUESTIONS FOR ANSWER

1. *Write a note on the existing pattern of world tourism.*
2. *Discuss the concept of space-odyssey as the travel of the future.*

# 25

# Theory of Statistical Measurement in Tourism

The need to develop the theory of statistical measurement in tourism rose as the volume of tourist traffic began to reach significant proportions after World War I, which we will discuss hereunder:

World tourism statistics are compiled by the World Tourism Organisation (WTO) in Madrid from the information received from the various National Tourist Organisations. Statistics relating to foreign tourist arrivals are compiled by the National Tourist Organisation of each country.

The reasons for statistical measurement in tourism are as follows:

1. Statistics are required to evaluate the magnitude and significance of tourism to a tourist destination. Statistics quantify the role and contribution of tourism to the economy and to society and for a country also the part played by tourism in the balance of payments.
2. Statistics are essential in the planning and development of physical facilities. To assess the requirements of hotels, airports, roads and other facilities, the volume and the characteristics of the tourist movement have to be determined quantitatively.
3. Statistics are required in marketing and promotion which can be effective only if they are based on the assessment of the actual and potential markets.
4. Statistics of tourism are useful to the government tourist organisations and the providers of tourist services.

Government are mainly interested in travel as an item in the balance of payments and in tourism as a source of employment and as a user of resources.

5. They provide a means of marketing forecasts.

## INTERNATIONAL SOURCE

The most comprehensive source of international tourism statistics readily available is that published annually by the World Tourism Organisation (WTO). Other international organisations such as the Pacific Asia Travel Association (PATA) and the Organisation for Economic Cooperation and Development (OECD) also collect and publish statistics concerning tourism in their member countries.

The WTO, an intergovernmental organisation, compiles and distributes travel statistics furnished by member and some non-member states. These statistics is an attempt to provide internationally uniform and accurate figures, it remains dependent on the respective national tourist organisations, immigration or statistics departments for the nature and quality of the data received.

Travel statistics worldwide are most frequently expressed in terms of "frontier arrivals," that is, the number of visitors entering a country as determined by some form of frontier check. Where the majority of arrivals are by air through limited points of entry, there the degree of control is usually very high and most related statistics can normally be considered reliable. Where there is a large volume of traffic arriving overland through a number of entry points, as is the case in much of Europe, the degree of control is much less.

A second source of international travel statistics is that based on accommodation returns. Many countries require international visitors to complete registration cards in hotels and other forms of accommodation which are then collected and analysed.

The principal statistics of tourism may be divided into three main categories:

1. *Volume*: Such arrivals and stays.
2. *Expenditure*: Spending at the destination and on the journey.

3. *Characteristics*: Information on the behaviour of tourists.

## Volume Statistics

The basic statistic of volume is the number of tourists to a destination over a given period say, a year.

The total number of international tourist arrivals to a country and the total number of international tourist departures from that country are key figures.

The weakness in using international tourist arrivals is that the length of stay is not taken into account. The length of stay is important for accommodation establishment, beach managers, retail outlets and so on. A better measure of volume for many purposes is total tourist nights.

## Statistics of Expenditure

The value of tourism to an economy is reflected in tourist expenditure at the destination. For International tourism this covers all tourist expenditure in a country including expenditure on transportation purchases.

The total visitor expenditure at the destination is divided by the number of arrivals, the result is the average expenditure per visit. While global estimates of tourist expenditure provide a general indication of the value of tourism to an economy, visit and daily averages provide respectively general indications of the type and quality of the traffic to a destination.

Total visitor expenditure is a simple measure of the economic value of foreign visitors to a country. It normally includes spending within the host country and excludes fare payments made to international passenger carriers for travel into and out of that country.

## Tourist Characteristics

The behaviour patterns of tourists will provide meaningful information for marketing and developmental purposes. In case of international tourism, the place of origin is the country of residence which supplies the major flow of tourists to a country. In domestic tourism the major source of tourist traffic to a region are other regions of the same country.

The information collected contains the following details:

| *The Visitor* | *The Visit* |
|---|---|
| Age | Origin and destination |
| Sex | Mode of transport |
| Nationality | Purpose of visit |
| Occupation | Time of visit |
| Income | Group type (alone, family) |
| | Length of stay |
| | Accommodation |
| | Places visited |
| | Activities engaged in |

The principal characteristics of tourists are age, sex, nationality, occupation and income. The behaviour characteristics include time of visit, whether travelling alone or in a group, type of accommodation used, means of transport used and the activities at the destination.

For promotional purposes the behaviour characteristics include such information as the readership of newspapers and magazines, the impressions of the tourists of their visit and information on how and when holiday plans are made.

## DOMESTIC TOURISM

Use of domestic tourism statistics is made in a variety of ways.

1. To measure the contribution of tourism to the overall economy. Although it is impossible to assess accurately, estimates can be made which measure the effect of tourism on a country's gross domestic product (GDP).
2. For promotion and marketing policies.
3. To assist area development policies. This can involve attempting to ensure a high quality of environment in the main tourism areas, as well as developing other areas to relieve congestion.
4. To aid social policies. A statistical knowledge of the holiday taking habits of nationals is required for providing aid to the underprivileged, in the form of subsidies to socially oriented sites.

## LIMITATIONS OF STATISTICS

The interpretation of tourism data is fraught with danger. Following points should be kept in mind.

1. Tourism statistics are normally estimates, often derived from sample surveys. As such, they are subject to various forms of error.
2. For measurements which result from sample surveys, in general the smaller the sample size, the greater is the likely error.
3. Even a large sample size for data relating to a region may give rise to acceptable levels of error. Analysis of a subset of the data pertaining to a smaller region may not be feasible due to the much reduced sample size.
4. Where the methodology in collecting data changes, it is dangerous to compare results.
5. There are serious problems involved in attempting to compare figures collected by different countries.

In the tourism phenomenon the unit of measurement is the tourist. Naturally the question arises who is a tourist. In the common language, a tourist is one who makes a journey for the sake of curiosity or for pleasure. But this definition does not serve the purpose of measurement. It was the League of Nations which gave a definition of a tourist for the purpose of statistical measurement.

The League of Nations defines a 'foreign tourist' as 'any person visiting a country, other than that in which he usually resides, for a period of at least twenty four hours.'

## DEFINITION OF TOURIST

The following persons are considered tourists according to this definition.

1. Persons travelling for pleasure, for domestic reasons, for health etc.
2. Persons travelling for meetings or in a representative capacity of any kind.
3. Persons travelling for business purposes.
4. Persons arriving in the course of a sea cruise, even when they stay for less than twenty-four hours.

The following categories are not to be regarded as tourists:

1. Persons arriving with or without a contract of work, to take up an occupation or engage in any business activity in the country.
2. Persons coming to establish residence in the country.
3. Students and young persons in boarding establishments or schools.
4. Residents in a frontier zone and persons domiciled in one country and working in an adjoining country.
5. Travellers passing through a country without stopping, even if the journey takes more than 24 hours.

The above definition of tourist was accepted by the United Nations in 1945. It stated that a tourist is one who stays in a foreign country for more than twenty-four hours and less than six months for any non-immigrant purpose.

The definition of foreign tourist adopted by the Government of India is based on the recommendation of the United Nations' Conference on Travel and Tourism held in Rome in 1963. It is as follows:

A foreign tourist is a person visiting India on a foreign passport, staying for at least twenty-four hours in India and the purpose of whose journey can be classified under one of the following headings:

1. Leisure (recreation, holiday, health, study, religion and sport),
2. Business, family mission, meeting.

The following persons are not regarded as 'foreign tourists.'

1. Persons arriving with or without a contract, to take up an occupation or engage in activities remunerated from within the country.
2. Persons coming to establish residence in the country.
3. Excursionists, *i.e.*, temporary visitors staying for less than twenty-four hours in the country.

All international tourists have three actions in common:

1. They cross international frontiers,
2. They exchange their own currency for foreign currency, and

3. They spend time outside own country and this implies using some form of accommodation.

A domestic tourist is one who travels more than fifty miles from home and spends at least one night in a hotel or some place where he has to pay. If a man goes to another city and stays with his relatives or friends, he is not considered a tourists. However, there is no standard definition of domestic tourist which is accepted by all countries.

There is a basic difference between international tourist and a domestic tourist. In case of domestic tourist, as the travel place within the limits of the boundaries of country, various travel formalities which are necessary for international tourist are not required. The barriers of foreign exchange, passport, visa, health documents, etc., are not to be faced by a domestic tourist.

## QUESTIONS FOR ANSWER

1. *Who compile world tourism statistics? What are the reasons for statistical measurement in tourism?*
2. *What are the uses and limitations of statistics?*
3. *Discuss the sources of international tourism statistics.*

# 26

# Status of Tourism and Tourism Education in India

Though history of tourism in India is as old as human civilization, yet in modern concept of tourism and its allied field of hospitality establishments India's entry in world market of tourism is a new concept, as we have discussed in earlier chapters. Before 1950 the arrival of foreign tourist in India could be accounted on finger tips and we have no publication on tourism and no institution to impart tourism education, therefore, our earning of foreign exchange from tourism was almost nil, but now tourism in India is a big industry and we have enough institutions which impart instructions in tourism as well as many periodical publications on tourism.

Hereunder, we will discuss our success story in the field of tourism and tourism education.

## GOVERNMENT OF INDIA TOURIST OFFICES

Particularly after World War II the question of tourism promotion was under active consideration of Government of India, therefore, when India became republic in 1950 it opted to establish four tourist offices—two in India and two abroad, one each in U.K. and U.S.A. Since then our efforts in this regard are continuing. At present we have tourist offices as per following list which contain 21 inland and 17 abroad offices.

| INDIA | |
|---|---|
| 1. Agra<br>191 The Mall, Agra 282001<br>Uttar Pradesh<br>Tel: 363377, 363959 | 2. Aurangabad<br>Krishna Vilas, Station Road<br>Aurangabad 431005<br>Maharasthra Tel: 31217 |

*(Contd.)*

(*Contd.*)

3. **Bangalore**
KFC Building
48 Church Street
Bangalore 560001
Karnataka
Tel: 5585417
4. **Bhubaneshwar**
B-21, BJB Nagar
Bhubaneshwar 751014
Orissa
Tel: (0674) 432203
5. **Mumbai**
123 M Karve Road
Opp. Churchgate
Mumabi 400 020
Maharasthra
Tel: 2032932, 2033144
Telex: 011-82922
Fax: 91-22-2014496
6. **Kolkata**
'Embassy', 4 Shakespeare
Sarani, Kolkata 700071
West Bengal
Tel: 2421402, 2421475, 2425813
Telex: 021-8176
(Gram: "INDTOUR")
Fax: (033) 242-3521
7. **Guwahati**
B.K. Kakati Road, Ulubari
Guwahati 781 007 Assam
Tel: 547407
8. **Hyderabad**
3-6-369-A-30, Sandozi
Building, 2nd Floor,
26 Himayat Nagar,
Hyderabad-500 029
Tel: 660037
9. **Imphal**
Old Lambulance, Jail Road
Imphal 795 001, Manipur
Tel: 21131
10. **Jaipur**
State Hotel, Khasa Kothi,
Jaipur 302 001, Rajasthan
Tel: 372200, Fax: 0141-373496
11. **Khajuraho**
Near Western Group of
Temples, Khajuraho 471606
Madhya Pradesh
Tel: 2047, 2048
12. **Kochi (Cochin)**
Willingdon Island,
Kochi 682009, Kerala
Tel: 668352 (R) 666218
Telex: 0885-6847-INDT-IN
13. **Chennai**
154, Anna Salai,
Madras 600 002
Tamil Nadu,
Tel: 8524785, 8524295
Telex: 041-7359
Fax: 044-8522193
14. **Naharlagun**
Sector 'C', Naharlagun 791110,
Arunachal Pradesh
Tel: 328
15. **New Delhi**
88, Janpath,
New Delhi 110001
Tel: 3320005, 3320008, 3320109,
3320266, 3320342
16. **Panaji (Goa)**
Communidade Building Church
Square, Panaji 403 001 Goa
Tel: 0832-43412.
17. **Patna**
Sudama Palace,
Kakarbagh Road,
Patna 800 020, Bihar
Tel: 226721, 345776

(*Contd.*)

(*Contd.*)

18. **Port Blair**
VIP Road, Junglighat P.O.
Port Blair 744 103,
Andaman & Nicobar Islands
Tel: 21006
19. **Shillong**
Tirot Singh Syiem Road,
Police Bazar,
Shillong 793001
Meghalaya, Tel: 225632
20. **Thiruvanthapuram**
Airport, Thiruvanthapuram
Kerala Tel: 451498
21. **Varanasi**
15B, The Mall,
Varanasi-221002
Uttar Pradesh, Tel: 43744

Most State Governments have their own Tourist Information Offices in their State Capitals.

OVERSEAS

1. **Australia**
Lebel, C/o H.C.I. 17, Castlereagh Street, Sydney, NSW 2000
Tel: 0661-2-232-1600/17961
0061-2-233-7579
Fax: (02) 2233003
2. **Bahrain**
P.O. Box 11294, Villa No. 5
Gudaibiya Manama,
Tel: Off/Res. 00973-715713
Fax: 00973-715-708
3. **Canada**
60 Bloor Street (West), Suite 100,
Toronto, Ontario M4 W3 B8
Tel: 01-416-962-3787/3788
Fax: 01-416-962-6279
4. **France**
8, Boulevard de la'Madeleine,
75009 Paris
Tel: 00331-42-65-83-86,
00331-42-65-77-06
Fax: 00331-42-65-0116
5. **Germany**
Govt. of India Tourist Office,
(INDISCHES FRENDENVERKEHSAMT)
Baseler St. 48, 60329, Frankfurt
Tel: 0049-069-235423/24
Fax: 0049-069-234724
6. **Italy**
9 Via Albricci, Milan 20122
Tel: 00392-804952, 8053506
Fax: 00392-72021681
7. **Japan**
Pearl Building, 9-18 Ginza,
7, Chome, Chuo-ku-Tokyo 104,
Tel: (33) 571-5062/3
(33) 571-5197
Fax: (33) 571-5235
8. **Malayasia**
Wisma HLA, Lot 203
2nd Floor, Jalan
Raja Chulan,
50200 Kuala Lumpur
Tel: 00603-2425285
Fax: 00603-2425301
9. **Netherlands**
Rokin 9-15, 1012 KK,
Amsterdam, Tel. 020-6208991
Fax: 003-120-6383059
10. **Singapore**
20 Kramai Lane, #01-01A
United House
Singapore-0922
Tel: 235-3800,
Fax: 235-8677

(*Contd.*)

(*Contd.*)

11. **Spain**
    C/o Embassy of India
    (C/o Embajada-de-la-India)
    Avenida PIO XII30-32
    Madrid-28016,
    Tel: 00341-3457339, 3457340
    Fax: 00341-4577996/3453430
    Telex: 22605 EOIME
12. **Sweden**
    Sveavagen 9-11, 1st Floor,
    S-III 57,
    Stockholm 11157
    Tel: 00468-215081/101187
    Fax: 00468-210186
13. **Switzerland**
    1-3, Rau de Chantepoulet, 1201
    Geneva Tel: 0041-22-7321813/
    1677, Fax: 0041-22-7315660.
    Telex: 412727
14. **Thailand**
    3rd Floor, 62/5, Thaniya Road,
    (Silom) Kentucky Fried Chicken
    Building Bangkok 10500.
    Tel: 00662-2352585, 2356670
    Fax: 00-662-2352585/2368411
15. UAE
    Post Box: 12856, NASA Building,
    A1 Maktoum Road,
    Deira, Dubai
    Tel: 00971-4-236870, 274848
    Fax: 00971-4-274013
16. UK
    7 Cork Street, London WIX 2AB
    Tel: 71-437-3677/8 (Gen),
    71-734-6613 (Direct line)
    Fax: 004471-494 1048
17. USA
    3550 (Wilshire Boulevard)
    Room 204, Los Angeles,
    California 90010,
    Tel: 001-213-477-3824 380-8855
    Fax: 001-(213) 380-6111
    30, Rockerfeller Plaza, Suite 15,
    North Mezzanine, New York,
    NY 10112
    Tel: 001/212/586/4901/4902/
    4903/4904
    Fax: 001-212-582-3274
    Telex: 9102508316

In addition to government of India tourist offices abroad our ambassadors in each and every country provide tourist information in their own offices. As a result of this effort tourism in India has developed in a big way and same is the case of our foreign exchange earnings which is highest and thus tourism in India seems to have much scope to develop more, for which our policy planners are trying their best.

Here, it needs to be mentioned that alike Government of India, each state government is devotedly working to develop adequate infrastructure to promote tourism in their states and this dual coordinated effort of the Central and State Governments in five to ten years time will double the inflow of foreign tourists in India and very soon India would find a place in first ten countries as most attractive tourist destination in the world.

## TOURISM AWARENESS

The publicity programmes of the Centre and State Governments about the tourism destinations and infrastructural facilities are creating tourism awareness among foreign as well as domestic tourists. There was a time when India did not publish any periodical on tourism, but now we have many periodicals published on tourism in India. These publications create environment for the foreign as well as domestic tourist to feel interested to visit our tourist destinations. Hereunder, we mention some of the travel guides in India and periodicals published in India on tourism:

## TRAVEL GUIDES IN INDIA

Biswas, Sukumar, *Traveller's Guide to India;* Rupak Publishers Kolkata.

British Airways BA, Explorer 2-A London/Threshold Guide: *Guide to the Orient and Pacific,* Threshold Books Ltd.

Chellani, Ramesh A, *Look India—Tourist Guide,* R.A. Chellani.

Chatterjee, D., *Handbook of India* (Vol. I and II); Kolkata, Print and Publication Sales.

Fodor E and Curtis, W. (Eds.), *Fodor's Guide to India;* New York, Fodor's Modern Guides, Inc.

George, A. Simon, *India—Simon's Handbook on*; Ernakulam, International Advisers and Publishers.

Gupta, S.P. and Krishna Lal, *Tourism Museums and Monuments in India;* Delhi, Oriental Publishers.

Publications Division, *Handbook of India;* New Delhi, Publications Division, Ministry of Information and Broadcasting.

Roy, P.B., *India—Handbook of Travel,* Kolkata.

Rushbrook Williams, L.F. (Eds.), *Handbook of Travellers in India, Pakistan, Burma and Sri Lanka,* London, John Murray.

Waldo, Myra, *Travel Guide to the Orient and the Pacific,* London, Macmillan and Co.

Insight Guides, *India,* APA Productions (HK) Ltd., P.O. Box 219 Orchard Point Singapore 9123.

Pran Seth, *India: A Travellers' Companion,* Sterling Publishers Pvt. Ltd., New Delhi-110020.

PATA, *Asia Pacific Business Travel Guide,* Priory Publications Ltd., Brackley, Northants NN 13, 5HH, UK.

## TOURISM PERIODICALS PUBLISHED IN INDIA

*Air Observer*, Air Observer Publications, Warsha House, 6, Zakharia Bunder Road, Sewri, Mumbai 400 015, India.

*Destination India*, Cross Section Publications, 7 Dwarka Sadan, C/42 Connaught Place, New Delhi 110001, India.

*Indian Hotelkeepr and Traveller*, Oberoi Intercontinental, 90-91, Maidens Hotel, Delhi 110006, India.

*Indrama*, Sita World Travel (India) Pvt. Ltd., F-12, Connaught Place, New Delhi 110001, India.

*Indian Magazine*, Wadia Building, 17/19 Dalal Street, Mumbai 400 023, India.

*India: Best of the Best*, Durga Das Publications Pvt. Ltd. 72 Todarmal Road, New Delhi 110001, India.

*Explore India*, Durga Das Publications Pvt. Ltd., 72 Todar Mal Road, New Delhi 110001, India.

*Travel and Tourism*, Indian Express Newspapers (Bombay) Ltd. Ist Floor, Express Towers, Nariman Point, Mumbai 400021. E-mail: ehc@vsnl.com.

*Hotelier and Caterer*, Indian Express Newspapers (Bombay) Ltd., 1st Floor, Express Towers, Nariman Point, Mumbai 400021.

*Indian Travel Guide*, Post Box No. 423, 72 Big Street, Triplicane, Chennai 600 005, India.

*Magic Carpet*, Air India, Air India Building, 218, Nariman Point, Mumbai 400021, India.

*Namaskaar*, Air India (Inflight Magazine), Media Transasia, 3rd Floor Sarasin, Building, 14 Surasak Road, Bangkok, Thailand.

*Namaste*, Welcomegroup Publication, The Hotels Division of ITC Ltd., 28, Community Centre, Basant Lok, Vasant Vihar, New Delhi 110057, India.

*Safari India*, Young Asia Publications, 7, Ansari Road, New Delhi 110002, India.

*Soma*, East India Hotels Ltd., 7, Alipur Road, Delhi 110054, India.

*The Taj*, The Indian Hotels Company Ltd., Apollo Bunder Road, Mumbai 400039, India.

*Travel News*, Travel Agents Association of India, 35, Anjali, 1st Floor, Arthur Bunder Road, Colaba, Mumbai 400005, India.

*TCI News*, Travel Corporation (India) Private Limited, Chander Mukhi, Nariman Point, Mumbai 400021, India.

*Travel World*, 160, Chittaranjan Avenue, Kolkata 700 007, India.

*Signature,* Diners Club of India Pvt. Ltd., Raheja Chambers 213 Nariman Point, Mumbai 400021, India.

*Tourism and Wildlife,* 24, Gole Market, Netaji Subhash Marg, New Delhi 110002, India.

*Tourism and Travel,* National Press Agency, 182, Jor Bagh, New Delhi 110003, India.

*Youth Hosteller,* Youth Hostel Association of India, 5 Nyaya Marg, Chanakyapuri, New Delhi 110021, India.

*Trav Talk,* Durga Das Publications Pvt. Limited, 72 Todar Mal Road, New Delhi 110001, India.

*Travel Trends Today,* Cross Section Publications Pvt. Ltd., F-74, Bhagat Singh Market, New Delhi 110001, India.

Outlook Traveller, AB-10, S.J. Enclave, New Delhi 110029, India.

In addition to the above mentioned travel guides and tourism periodicals we may find many more such periodicals and travel guides in domestic and foreign market on tourism in India. Apart from these we also find, off and on, travel accounts of travel destinations in India in various other periodicals and newspapers, which create tourism awareness amongst the domestic and foreign tourist. Thus, we feel confident that future of tourism development in India is very bright.

## TOURISM EDUCATION

Prior to 1950 tourism education was a distant dream but now it has developed as an inter disciplinary as well as an independent academic discipline. Now we find that tourism education in India has developed in a big way and provision for such education exist in every part of India. Hereunder, we mention some very important institution of tourism education in India:

### Tourism Courses in India

University of Delhi, College of Vocational Studies, Sheikh Sarai, New Delhi-110007.

(*a*) Degree Course
Duration: 3 years (Full time)

(*b*) Post-graduate Diploma Course
Duration: 2 years (Part time)

University of Garhwal, Faculty of Tourism, Srinagar, Garhwal, Uttaranchal.

Post-graduate Diploma Course
Duration: 2 Years (Full time)

Marathwada University, Marathwada, Maharashtra

Post-graduate Diploma
Duration: 2 years (Full time)

University of Madras, Department of Audit and Continuing Education, Chennai.

Post-graduate Diploma
Duration: 1 year

University of Rajasthan, Institute of Correspondence Studies and Continuing Education, Jaipur, Rajasthan

Post-graduate Certificate
Duration: 1 year (Correspondence Course)

Kurukshetra University, Kurukshetra, Haryana
Department of Ancient Indian History, Culture and Archaeology

(*a*) Paper in Tourism in Graduate Course
Duration: 3 years
(*b*) Postgraduate course in Tourism Administration (MTA)
Duration: 2 Years

Annamalai University, Faculty of Professional Management Courses, Annamalai Nagar, 608101 Tamil Nadu.

(*a*) B.A. (Tourism)
Duration: 3 years
(*b*) Post-graduate Diploma
Duration: 1 year (Part time)

Academy of Management Science and Studies, 5 Padmanabha Nagar, Adyar, Tri Junction, Chennai, 600 020, Tamil Nadu.

Diploma Course in Travel and Tourism Management
Duration: 6 months

University of Lucknow, Isabella Thoburn College, Lucknow, Uttar Pardesh.

Diploma in Travel Counselling and Tourism
Duration: 6 months

University of Agra, Agra, Uttar Pradesh

Postgraduate course in Tourism
Duration: 1 year

Lady Amritbal Daga College for Women, Nagpur, Maharashtra, Mumbai.

Post-graduate Diploma
Duration: 1 year

K.C. College of Management Studies, Mumbai

Diploma Course
Duration: 1 year

Sophia College, Shri Sasant Kumar Somani Memorial Polytechnic, Mumbai.

Post-graduate Diploma
Duration: 1 year

Godavarish College of Vocational Studies, Department of Travel, Tourism and Hotel Management, Nageswar Tangi, Bhubaneswar 751 014 Orissa.

Degree Course (Specialising in Tourism)
Duration: 3 years

Madurai-Kamraj University, University Building, Palkalai Nagar, Madurai 625021.

Master's Degree in Tourism Management
Duration: 2 years

Alagappa University, Directorate of Distance Education, Alagappa Nagar, Karaikudi 623003.

Post-graduate Diploma in Tourism Management
Duration: 1 year

Devara College, St. Patricks Complex, Opposite Opera Theatre, Residency Road, Bangalore 560 001, Karnataka.

Diploma Course
Duration: 1 year (Full time)

Similar Courses available in Mumbai and Chennai.

YMCA School of Commerce and Management, 12-N Parekh Marg, Mumbai 400 039, Maharashtra.

Diploma Course in Travel and Tourism
Duration: 6 months

YWCA Women's Technical Training Institute, Bangla Sahib Lane, Jai Singh Road, New Delhi 110 001.

P.G. Diploma Course in Travel and Tourism Management
Duration: 1 year

South Delhi Polytechnic for Women, N-9, South Extension, Part I, New Delhi 110 049

Diploma in Tourism
Duration: 1 year

India International Trade Centre (IITC), 105 Nirmal Towers, New Delhi 110 001.

Diploma in International Travel and Tourism Management
Duration: 6 months
(Similar Courses available in Mumbai, Chennai, Bangalore and Secundrabad)

Bhartiya Vidya Bhavan, Rajendra Prasad Institute of Communication Studies, New Delhi and Mumbai.

Sita Academy, M-135, Connaught Place, New Delhi-110001

Travel and Tourism Management Course
Duration: 1 year
Postgraduate Diploma
Duration : 1 year

Institute of Management Studies, H.P. University, Shimla-171005.

Master of Tourism Administration
Duration: 2 years

Indian Institute of Travel and Travel Management, Govindpuri, Gwalior 474002, M.P.

Basic and Advanced Management Courses leading to award of Postgraduate Diploma in Tourism Management

Duration: 14 months

Indira Gandhi National Open University IGNOU, New Delhi

Correspondence courses leading to
Master's Level (MTA) in Tourism Administration
Bachelor's Level (BBA) in Tourism Administration
Diploma in Travel and Tourism
Duration: 1-3 years

In addition to the above institutions more than 100 others institutions under various universities in India are imparting tourism education.

The above detailed account clearly bear it out that the future of tourism industry as well as tourism education in India is very bright as our present is satisfactory.

## QUESTIONS FOR ANSWER

1. *Name ten overseas cities which house Government of India Tourist Offices.*
2. *Name ten Indian cities which house Government of India Tourist Offices.*
3. *Give details of Four Travel Guides on India.*
4. *Name ten tourism periodicals published in India.*
5. *Name ten institutions which impart Tourism education in India.*

# 27

# Areas of Career Opportunities in Tourism Industry

Tourism is a complex, yet fastest developing service industry, therefore, it provides many areas of career opportunities to our present and future youths as per their capabilities, which we will discuss hereunder:

Tourism today is one of the world's largest industries, made up of various segments, the main ones being transport, accommodation, food service, shopping, travel arrangement, and activities for tourists, such as history, culture, adventure, sports, recreation, entertainment, and other similar activities. The businesses that provide these services require knowledgeable business managers.

Familiarity with tourism, recreation, business, and leisure, equips one to pursue a career in a number of tourism related fields. Even during times of economic recession, tourism has performed well. Tourism skills are critically required and there are many opportunities available in a multitude of fields.

Because tourism is so fragmented and each sector has innumerable job opportunities, it is virtually impossible to list and describe all the jobs available in this fields. However, we have tried to give a broad outline of the avenues available for a person seeking a career in tourism.

**Airlines:** The airlines are a major travel industry employer, offering a host of jobs at many levels ranging from entry lever to top management.

**Bus Companies:** They require management personnel, ticket agents, sales and tour representatives, hostesses, information executives, personnel people and training employees.

**Cruise Companies:** The cruise industry is the fastest growing segment of the tourism industry today. Job opportunities include those for sales representatives, market researchers and recreation directors. Because of its similarity with the lodging industries there are many similar jobs in both.

**Railroads:** Passenger rail service hire service and sales representatives, reservation and station agents.

**Rental Car Companies:** With increased air travel and the growth of fly/drive programmes, rental car companies are becoming an even more important segment in the travel and tourism industry. This sector employs reservation and sales agents and District and Regional managers.

**Hotels, Motels and Resorts:** The range of jobs in hotels and motels is extremely large. To mention a few are, general manager, resident manager, management trainees, directors of various departments like sales, research, personnel, convention sales, etc., front office manager, housekeepers, lobby managers, etc. The American Hotel and Motel Association estimates that the lodging industry employs approximately 1.4 million people and creates 100,000 new jobs every year.

**Travel Agencies:** They range from small to very large businesses. In large offices, opportunities are more varied which include domestic and international travel and tours counsellors, research directors, sales personnel, tour planners, tour guides, group coordinators, operations, administration and advertising specialists.

**Tour Companies:** They offer employment opportunities in posts as tour manager or escort, tour coordinator, tour planner, publicist, group tour specialist, incentive tour coordinator, costing specialist, hotel co-ordinator, office supervisor, and other managerial positions.

**Tourism Education:** As tourism continues to grow, the need for training and education also grows. Vocational schools have expanded their present programmes and there are job opportunities for administrators, teachers, professors, researchers, counsellors and support staff.

**Tourism Research:** Tourism research consists of the collection and analysis of data from both primary and secondary sources. The tourism researcher plans market studies, consumer surveys, and the implementation of research projects. Research jobs are available in tourism with airlines, cruise lines, management consulting firms, state tourist offices, etc.

**Travel Journalism:** There are a number of opportunities available in travel writing as editors, staff writers, and free lance writers. Most travel firms have a need for public relations people who write and edit, disseminate information, develop communication vehicles, obtain publicity, arrange special events, do public speaking, plan public relations campaigns, etc. A travel photographer can find employment in either public relations or travel writing.

**Recreation:** Jobs in recreation include coaches for sports, drama and dance directors, etc. Many recreation workers teach handicrafts. Resorts, parks, and recreation departments often employ recreation directors who hire specialists to work with senior citizens or youth groups, to serve as camp counsellors, or to teach such skills such as boating and sailing. Management, supervisory and administrative positions are also available.

**Attractions:** Attraction such as amusement parks and theme parks are a major source of tourism employment. Large organizations such as Disney World, Disneyland and Sea World provide job opportunities in various departments, from top management to maintenance jobs.

**Tourist Offices and Information Centres:** Numerous jobs are available as director, deputy director, economic development specialist, public relations, public information manager, media liaisoning, marketing coordinator, package tour co-ordinator and many more.

**Convention and Visitors Bureaus:** As more and more cities enter the convention industry, employment opportunities in this segment grow. They require managers, assistant managers, directors, marketing and public relations staff and sales personnel, etc.

**Meeting Planners:** A growing profession is meeting planning. Many associations and corporations are hiring people whose job responsibilities are to arrange, plan and conduct meetings.

**Other Opportunities:** Though we have tried to give a comprehensive list of career opportunities, there are many that do not fit in the general categories, such as club management, corporate travel departments, hotel representative companies, in-flight and trade magazines and trade and professional associations, to list a few.

The information provided is an important starting point for you. However, it is up to you to explore further and gain additional information regarding prospects in this industry.

## QUESTIONS FOR ANSWER

1. *Discuss in brief nature of various career opportunities in tourism industry.*
2. *Discuss the concept of career in the fields of :*
   (*a*) *Tourism Education.*
   (*b*) *Tourism Research.*
   (*c*) *Travel Journalism.*
   (*d*) *Convention and visitors bureaus.*

# 28

# Problems Faced by Tourists and Tourism Industry

Tourists move out of their home for pleasure and tourism industry aims at providing satisfaction to the tourists, while ensuring good fortune for itself and for the nation, but this goal gets lost on account of some problems faced by both the tourists and tourism industry together, which are being discussed, very briefly, hereunder:

The problems that the tourism industry faces today are complex and multifold. Broadly, these problems may be divided into two parts:

(*i*) Problems in the private sector
(*ii*) Problems in the public sector

## PRIVATE SECTOR

Private sector plays an important role in providing facilities to the tourists. It has hotels/guest-houses in all major tourist centres and it is natural that all these wish to earn maximum profit. Obviously, in such a service-based sector only profit-orientation cannot work and thus leads to numerous problems quite similar in nature as faced by the public sector units. Hereunder an effort is made to highlight on some of the problems that the private sector faces:

### Quality of Accommodation

1. It is commonly observed that barring in the five-star hotels, the regularity of air-conditioning and air-cooling facility in the hotels is by and large not up-to-mark. It was

observed that even in a two-star hotel air-conditioning facility is irregular. This is, in fact, a common complaint against a majority of hotels.

The question that arises here is that if this is the situation with the star class hotels in the state what better can be expected of the other class of hotels.

2. Most of these hotels do not provide for hot and cold water beyond a certain time. This always gives a bad taste to tourists and keeps them away from such hotels.
3. It is also commonly observed that the moment a tourist reaches at the Bus Station, Railway Station or Air Port, middlemen for Hotels etc. mob tourists like a honey bee and try to influence his decision. These people sometimes tell a lie to the tourist that the hotel where he wants to stay has no vacancy or is taking higher charges whereas the hotel that he proposes is cheap and the best. These trends make a tourist scared of the place itself and he does not dare visit the spot again. These trends are observed everywhere but they are particularly serious at pilgrim centres.
4. Sometimes even travel agents do not give full and correct information to tourists. They fail to satisfy tourists about reservation of tickets, train and plane timings and other travel facilities.
5. Hawkers are another source of embarrassment for foreign tourists. These hawkers mob tourists and try to sell junk to them. As the tourist realises this fraud he is permanently unhappy with the place and the people.

## Guides and Guiding

1. It is commonly observed that none of the hotels, barring a few five-star ones, provide any facility of guides. Even if they do provide in some cases, these guides suffer from language problem. This leads to cropping up of unauthorized guides who work as hawkers. These then mislead the tourists with little knowledge or wrong facts regarding the monuments.
2. Another aspect emerges from this problem is of inadequate facility of guides. It is the absence of proper maps and guiding material. The Department of Tourism,

which is responsible for bringing in authoritative maps does not do so regularly. Most of such material is old and outdated. This compounds the problems of the tourist.

**Transport and Package Tour**

1. The private operators provide for daily tours and package tours at various places. Most of these tours are conducted primarily for pilgrims. The pilgrims and tourists, however, complain of many problems that they face during such package tours like inadequacy of lodging, impolite behaviour of the tour managers, lack of time-discipline, insufficient time for sight-seeing, heavy charges, non-availability of good guides, etc. These are enough to cause serious problems to any tourist.
2. Transport is the backbone of successful tourism. In fact, tourism development is based on the development of transport facility. Therefore, more buses and package tours are needed to boost tourism; however private tour operators are not able to do so due to lack of funds, licence or registration problem etc. This casts its shadows on effective development and management of tourism.

Besides, there are certain problems which the people managing the infrastructure encounter affecting the discharge of their duties. Some such problems are illustrated below:

1. Most of the hotel employees suffer from lack of motivation, they feel that they are not adequately paid. This affects the quality of their services.
2. The problem is further compounded when some managements obtain their signatures on more amount than actually paid to them. Demotivation is the only logical result and ultimate victim, of course, is tourist.
3. Most of the employees of majority of hotels are inexperienced and raw hands. Managements prefer them because they ask for less salary. But, ultimately these people neither benefit the organisation nor do they serve tourists in a professional manner. Here too, both management and tourists remain unsatisfied.
4. It has been observed that in some of the non-starred hotels anti-social elements occupy a lot of time and space. Their

presence and behaviour together with hotel employees' helplessness creates a lot of problems to tourists who either do not wish to go to such hotels or leave them immediately.

5. Even the cooks and waiters in these hotels are ill-trained. They are neither able to prepare choice food nor serve it properly.

Tourism is now an industry, yet, it has not been given its due nor has it been properly classified as to what facilitation will be given to this industry. Most of the aforementioned problems are faced by middle-class hotels who are neither able to charge exuberantly nor are able to sacrifice quality.

The five-star hotels on the other hand, do not face any such problems and they are working satisfactorily. However, a deeper probe reveals that some facilities are not available even in these hotels. For example some such hotels does not have package tour facility nor do they provide for sight-seeing. At some places air and rail reservation facilities are not up-to-the mark.

Thus, it is clear from the above account that although private sector has enough potential to develop tourism to newer heights, it has certainly not received matching support from government. The schemes that exist are not applied or only partially applied. The entire system is under the grip of red tapism and suffers from severe bureaucratisation and hypocrisy. So long as middle level structures are not developed, mass-tourism cannot take place and all attempts to boost tourism will become superficial. The role of tourism in economic development, in removal of unemployment will remain a distant dream if private sector does not get enough promotion.

## PUBLIC SECTOR

The basic responsibility of providing accommodation to tourists in public sector but at most of the places the facilities provided do not match with the facilities required. Moreover, they suffer from a number of problems and handicaps, some of them are listed below:

1. Most of the tourist bungalows do not reflect their regional specialty and their upkeep is far from satisfactory. This makes the stay of tourists uncomfortable.

2. The public sector has failed to recognise the importance of dual-rate policy, *i.e.*, one for peak season and the other for off-season. Already charging higher rates, the tourist bungalows become highly unpopular during off-season.
3. At all tourist stations, as against one Government Tourist bungalow, there are a good number of private hotels offering equally good facilities at lower rates.
4. The Government accommodations do not have any extra facility to attract tourists nor are they given any encouragement in this regard. This is why they are at an unequal position vis-à-vis private hotels which try their best to attract tourists.
5. At most of the places, as the tourist comes out of the airports, railway station or bus station, there is no one to tell him as to where the government facility exists. The counters opened for the purpose on some tourists stations do not function satisfactorily.

To conclude, one feels that accommodation units in the public sector are not functioning properly. There is also a problem of too much job security which has made their personnel defiant and unprofessional. In most of the cases it was observed that their personnel do not bother about tourist needs and do not behave in courteous manner. Since the higher officials are also non-professionals, the removal of their problems also faces bureaucratic solution. These units are not mentally prepared to take on the market.

### Food and Breakfast

Tourism is a dynamic phenomenon. Therefore, it attracts tourists from all places. These tourists when out of their homes aspire for only two things: comfortable stay and good food at reasonable prices. This is unfortunately not happening Government owned hotels and tourist bungalows. An observation of some hotels revealed that firstly, the rates of food items are higher in Government owned hotels; secondly, the quality of food is not good and thirdly, the regional specialities are not given in many cases.

## TRANSPORT SYSTEM AND SIGHT-SEEING

Although package tours, conducted tours, sight-seeing and daily tours are important part of tourists services, public sector units are seemingly not aware of it. In most of the units such facilities either do not exist or exist in an unorganised manner. However in most cases they too suffer from lack of time-schedule, discourteous behaviour of our operators, and non-availability of deluxe buses. The other problems are as follows:

(*i*) In most of the cases, rail and air reservation facilities are non-existent giving a lot of problems to the tourists.

(*ii*) The facilities of entertainment are also inadequate at most of the places. It was found that in some cases where people tried to present local tradition-based cultural programmes, the officers did not support such ideas.

(*iii*) Most of the tourist hotels/bungalows are situated at inconvenient places which face tremendous problems including that of security.

(*iv*) It is commonly observed that the room tariffs that these hotels/bungalows charge are too high for a middle class tourist. Keeping in mind that domestic tourists outnumber foreign tourists, these hotels/bungalows fail to attract them.

(*v*) Like room tariffs, the rates of eatables in Government hotels/tourists bungalows are comparatively higher. It goes even higher because public sector imposes sales tax/service charges/surcharge also. Naturally, tourists do not want to make use of these facilities and prefer to eat elsewhere.

## TOURISM INDUSTRY AND POLLUTION

Tourism brings pleasure and leisure. However, an uncontrolled tourism may lead to pollution and in extreme cases to sheer disaster. This pollution may take many shapes—that of destruction of natural resources, that of socially unlawful activities and that of cultural exploitation. Either of these may change the entire scenario of tourism in any area.

### Natural Pollution

Tourism has been, barring in recent years, an activity of the opulent classes. This class due to sheer money power, believes that money can bring anything anywhere. These tourists do not actually contribute to the earnings but take a heavy price by destroying wonderful natural resources. Garhwal hills the regular organisation of Himalayan Car Rallies has put a grave danger to an already fragile eco-system. In fact in 1989, people of Garhwal stood up against the onslaught of automobiles and blocked the Rally. Such instances are many that are not recorded properly nor any scientific study had been taken up to evaluate such dangers.

It is commonly observed that tourists visiting popular places particularly in hills, take along with them a lot of cans and plastic sealed materials. These matters are not dissolved easily and have started creating a permanent damage to the environment. In fact serious view has been taken by government. Regarding adventure tourists as things left out by them are degrading the eco-system. However, much needs to be done in this regard. If this is not done the day will not be far when like Ganga, entire Himalayan region will be without greenery.

### Social Pollution

Instances of tourists being cheated by locals are now in numerous. However, the local population is also cheated by itself. For example, in the hill areas local people provide all the facilities to visiting tourists with a smile on their faces. During summers people of Nainital, Almora, Ranikhet, Mussoorie etc. even rent out their houses for the tourists. Such actions of locals make such spots popular. However, due to this popularity, the city gets costlier and the ultimate victim of this situation is the local person. This is why whereas the popularity of the hill areas is on the up, the poverty of the local area has showed no signs of coming down.

### Cultural Pollution

Cultural integration is said to be one of the objectives of tourism development. Because of this monuments are saved, festivals are popularised, new outlets are provided to traditional craft and performing arts and align industries are benefited.

However, given a deep-insight, it will be apparent that all is not well with tourism. Although it does save monuments, however, it does so only for a few popular ones. In fact when monuments are preserved through tourism, market forces concentrate all work on the most prominent and accessible buildings, leaving others to rot untouched. This is so, because like other industries its actions too are dictated by the market forces and usually by short-term profit rather than by long-term investment. Tourism's most obvious disadvantage for conservation is the physical destruction of buildings and streets under pressure of tourism-based development.

Furthermore, it is true that tourism provides new outlets for traditional crafts and for the performing arts, work done for tourists is rarely of the quality produced for a more experienced market. Therefore, quantity is achieved at the cost of quality.

Similarly, although tourists may be interested in traditional culture, they bring with them alien values whose superficial attraction leads the local people away from tradition. Tourists can be seen as wealthy and successful role models. Tourism, thus, creates dissatisfaction with the local culture and is unable to supply anything of value of its place.

Therefore, too great a dependence on tourism may result in a chain of unpredictable economic, social and cultural changes which may cause irreparable damage to the society.

## QUESTIONS FOR ANSWER

1. *Write a note on the problems faced by tourists on account of the apathy of private and public sectors of tourism industry.*
2. *Enumerate the difficulties faced by private and public sectors of tourism industry.*
3. *Write a note on tourism industry as creator of natural, socio-economic and cultural pollution.*

# Bibliography


Aerni, M.J., *"The Social Effects of Tourism"*, Current Anthropology, 13 (1972).

Alastair, M. Morrison, *Hospitality and Travel Marketing* (New York: Delemar 1989).

Aldous, T., *Battle for the Environment* (London: Fontana/Collins, 1972).

Anand, M.M., *Tourism and Hotel Industry in India* (New Delhi: Prentice-Hall of India, 1976).

Anderson, N., *Work and Leisure* (London: Routledge and Kegan Paul, 1961).

Archer, B.H., *"Tourist Research in the United Kingdom"*, Journal of Travel Research, 10; 4 (March 1972).

Archer, B.H., *Demand Forecasting in Tourism* (Cardiff: University of Wales Press, 1974).

Archer, B.H., *The Impact of Domestic Tourism* (Cardiff: University of Wales Press, 1973).

Ashworth, G.J., *Marketing in the Tourism Industry* (London: Routledge, 1990).

Ashworth, G., *Recreation and Tourism* (London: Bell and Hyman 1984).

Avvill, R., *Man and Environment* (London: Penguin, 1967).

Balsdon, J.P.V.D., *Life and Leisure in Ancient Rome* (London: Bodley Head, 1966).

Beazely, E., *Designed for Recreation* (London: Faber, 1970).

Bernecker, Paul., *Methods and Media of Tourist Publicity* (Vienna: Austrian National Tourist Office, 1961).

Bhatia, A.K., *International Tourism: Fundamental and Practices* (New Delhi: Sterling, 1991).

Bhatia, A.K., *Tourism Development, Principles & Practices* (New Delhi: Sterling, 2001).

Bhatia, A.K., *Tourism Management and Marketing* (New Delhi: Sterling, 1997).

Bhatia, A.K., *Tourism in India—History and Development* (New Delhi: Sterling, 1978).

Boniface, B. and Cooper, C., *The Geography of Travel and Tourism* (London: Heinemann, 1987).

Brunner, E., *Holiday Making and the Holiday Trades* (London: Oxford University Press, 1945).

Bryden, John M., *Tourism and Development* (Cambridge: Cambridge University Press, 1973).

Buhalis, D. and Flicher J., *Environmental Impact on Tourist Destinations: An Economic Analysis*, University of Aegean, Mytilinine, 1992.

Bull, A., *The Economics of Travel and Tourism* (London: Pitman, 1991).

Burkart, A.J. and Medlik, S. *Tourism: Past, Present and Future* (London: Heinemann, 1976).

Burkart, A.J., *The Management of Tourism* (London: Heinemann, 1975).

Burton, R., *Travel Geography* (London: Pitman, 1995).

Burton, T.L. (Ed.), *Recreation Research and Planning* (London: Allen and Unwin, 1970).

Butler, R.W., *"The Social Implication of Tourism Development"*, Tourism Research 2, 2 (1974).

Galder, N., *The Environment Game* (London: Panther, 1969).

Checchi and Co., *The Future of Tourism in the Far East* (1961).

Cherry, G.E., *Town Planning and its Social Context* (London: Hill, 1970).

Chuck, Y. Gee., *The Travel Industry* (New York: Van Nostrand Reinhold 1989).

Clare, A. Gunn., *Tourism Planning* (Washington, DC: Taylor and Francis, 1993).

Clare, A. Gunn., *Tourism Planning* (New York: Taylor and Francis, 1988).

Clayne, R. Jensen., *Leisure and Recretation: Introduction and Overview* (Philadelphia: Lea and Febiger, 1977).

Cleverdon, Robert, *The Economic and Social Impact of International Tourism on Developing Countries* (London: The Economic Intelligence Unit Ltd., 1979).

Cohen, Eric., *"Towards a Sociology of International Tourism"*, Social Research 39, 1 (1972).

Colley, G., *International Tourism Today* (London: Lloyds Bank Review, 1967).

Cooper, C., *Tourism Principles and Practices* (London: Pitman, 1993).

Cosgrove, Isabel and Jackson, R., *The Geography of Recreation and Leisure* (London: Hutchinson, 1972).

Crampon, L.T., *An Analysis of Tourist Markets* (Colorado: University of Colorado Press, 1963).

Crampon, L.T., *The Development of Tourism* (Colorado: University of Colorado Press: 1963).

Dale, E., *Management Theory and Practice* (New York: McGraw-Hill, 1973).

Davidson, R., *Business Travel* (London: Pitman, 1994).

Davidson, R., *Tourism in Europe* (London: Pitman, 1992).

Davis, H.D., *Potentials for Tourism of Developing Countries* (London: Finance and Development, 1968).

Donald, E. Hawking (Eds.), *Tourism Planning and Development Issues* (Washington: George Washington University, 1980).

Donald, E., *Tourism Marketing and Management Issues* (Washington: George Washington University, 1980).

Douglas Pearce., *Tourist Development* (Longman, 1989).

Douglas, Pearce., *Tourism Today: A Geographical Analysis* (New York: Longman, 1987).

Dower, M., *The Challenge of Leisure* (London: Civic Trust, 1965).

Dumazedier, J., *Towards a Society of Leisure* (New York: Free Press, 1967).

Ed Gell, D.L., *International Tourism Policy* (New York: Van Nostrand Reinhold, 1990).

Edmunds, *Environmental Administration* (New York: McGraw-Hill, 1973).

Edward, J. Mayo., *The Psychology of Leisure Travel* (Boston: CBI Publishing Company, 1981).

Edwards, Francis, G., *How to Focus Your Marketing Efforts* (London: Louis A. Allen Associates, 1976).

Engel, James F. (Eds), *Market Segmentation: Concepts and Applications* (New York: Holt, Rinehart and Winston 1962).

Feiffer, M., *Giving Places* (London: Macmillan, 1985).

Forster, John, *"The Sociological Consequences of Tourism"*, International Journal of Comparative Sociology (1964).

Foster, D., *Travel and Tourism Management* (London: Macmillan, 1985).

Frank, R.E., *Market Segmentation* (New Jersey: Prentice-Hall, Inc; 1972).

Gearing Charles, E., *Planning for Tourism Development* (New York: Praeger Publishers, 1976).

Glasser, R., *Leisure: Penalty or Prize?* (London: Macmillan, 1970).

Gray, H. Peter, *International Travel—International Trade* (Lexington: Health Lexington Books, 1970).

Gunn, C., *Tourism Planning* (New York: Taylor and Francis, 1988).

Hammarskjold, K., "*Economics of Air Transport and Tourism*" (Montreal: I.C.A.O., 1972).

Heath, E. *Marketing Tourism Destinations* (New York: Wiley, 1992).

Hibbert, Christopher, *The Grand Tour* (London: Weidenfel and Nicolson, 1969).

Hiller, Herbet L., "*The Development of Tourism in the Caribbean Region*", Air Travel and Tourism (August 1972).

Hodyson, A., *The Travel and Tourism Industry* (Oxford: Pergamon, 1987).

Hollander, S., *Passenger Transportation* (Michigan: Michigan State University, 1968).

Holloway, J.C., *Marketing for Tourism* (Harlow: Longman, 1995).

Holloway, J.C., *Marketing for Tourism* (London: Pitman, 1988).

Howard, *Marketing Made Simple* (London: W.H. Allen, 1972).

Hudson, E., "*Vertical Integration in Travel and Leisure Industry*", Institute of Air Transport (Paris, 1972).

Hunziker, W., *Social Tourism: Its Nature and Problems* (Geneva: Aliance International de Turisme, 1951).

Hurdman, L.E., *Tourism: A Shrinking World* (New York: Wiley, 1980).

Ian M. Matley, *The Geography of International Tourism* (Washington: Association of American Geographers, 1976).

Inskeep, E., *Tourism Planning* (New York: Van Nostrand Reinhold, 1991).

Jefferson, A., *Marketing Tourism* (Harlow: Longman, 1988).

Jefferson, A., *Marketing Tourism: A Practical Guide* (Harlow: Longman 1991).

Jenkins, J.R. and Zif, J.J., *Planning the Advertising Campaign* (New York: Macmillan, 1973).

John M. Bryden, *Tourism and Development* (London: Cambridge University Press, 1973).

John, Lea, *Tourism Development in the Third World* (New York: Routledge, 1988).

Joseph, D. Firdgen, *Dimensions of Tourism* (East Lansing, Michigan: American Hotel and Motel Association, 1991).

Kaiser, Charles Jr. and Larry E. Helber, *Tourism Planning and Development* (Boston: CBI Publishing Company, Inc., 1978).

Kotler, P., *Introduction to Marketing Management, Analysis, Planning and Control* (London: Prentice-Hall, 1975).

Kernan, J.B., *Promotion* (New York: McGraw-Hill, 1970).

Kerry Godrey and Jackie Clarke, *The Tourism Development Handbook* (London: Cassell, 2000).

Kotler P., *Principles of Marketing* (New York: Prentice-Hall, 1999).

Krippendorf, S.J., *The Holiday Makers, Understanding the Impact of Leisure and Travel* (Oxford: Heinemann, 1987).

Lansing, J.B. and Blood, D.M., *The Changing Travel Market* (Michigan: University of Michigan, 1964).

Law, C., *Urban Tourism: Attracting Visitors to Large Cities* (London: Mansell, 1993).

Laws, E.C., *Tourist Destination Management: Issues, Analysis and Policies.* (London: Routledge, 1995).

Lawson, Maclom, *Teaching Tourism Education and Training in Western Europe: A Comparative Study* (London: Tourism International Press, 1975).

Leadley, P., *Leisure Marketing* (Harlow: Longman, 1992).

Lickorish, L.J., *Tourism and International Balance of Payments* (Geneva: International Institute of Scientific Travel Research, 1953).

Lickorish, L.J., *Tourist Promotion and Publicity Media* (Geneva: National Institute of Scientific Travel Research, 1955).

Lickorish, L.J. and Kershaw, A.G., *The Travel Trade* (London Practical Press, 1974).

Loughlin, Carleen, "*Tourism in the Tropics: Lessons from the West Indies*", Insight and Opinion (1970).

Lundberg, D.E., *The Tourist Business* (New York: Van Nostrand Reinhold, 1990).

Lundberg, Donald, *The Tourist Business* (Boston: Cahners Books, 1974).

Lundberg, *International Travel and Tourism* (New York: Institute of Certified Travel Agents, 1970).

Mathieson, A., *Tourism: Economic, Physical and Social Impacts* (London: Longman, 1982).

McIntosh, R.W., *Tourism Principles, Practices and Philosophies* (Ohio: Grid, 1977).

Medlik, S. and Middleton V.T.C., *"The Tourist Product and its Marketing Implications"*, International Tourism Quarterly (1973).

Medlik, S., *Economic Importance of Tourism* (Surrey: University of Surrey, 1972).

Medlik, S., *Higher Education and Research in Tourism in Western Europe* (London: University of Surrey 1966).

Medlik, S., *Profile of the Hotel and Catering Industry* (London: Heinemann, 1972).

Middleton, V.T.C., *Marketing in Travel and Tourism* (London: Heinemann, 1988).

Middleton, V.T.C., *Marketing in Travel and Tourism* (Oxford: Heinemann, 1988).

Mill, R.C., *The Tourism Business: An Introductory Text* (London: Prentice-Hall, 1985).

Mill, R.C., *The Tourism System* (London: Prentice-Hall International, 1985).

Mill, R.C., *Tourism—The International Business* (New Jersey: Prentice-Hall, 1990).

Mitchell, Frank, *"The Value of Tourism in East Africa"*, East African Economic Review, 2, (June 1970).

Morisson, A.M., *Hospitality and Travel Marketing* (New York: Delmar, 1989).

Murphy, Peter E., *Tourism: A Community Approach* (New York: Methuen, 1985).

Neulinger, John, *The Psychology of Leisure* (Springfield: Charles C. Thomas, 1974).

Nicholson, M., *The Environmental Revolution* (London: Penguin, 1972).

Norval, A.J., *The Tourist Industry* (London: Issac Pitman and Sons Ltd., 1936).

Ogilvie, F.W., *The Tourist Movement: An Economic Study* (London: Staples Press, 1933).

Page, S., *Urban Tourism* (London: Routledge, 1995).

Parker, S., *The Future of Work and Leisure* (London: Mac Gibbon and Kee, 1971).

Patmore, J.A., *Land and Leisure* (London: David and Charles, 1970).

Peaker, A., *"Holiday Spending by the British at Home and Abroad"*, National Westminster Bank Quarterly Review (August, 1973).

Pearce, D., *Tourism Organisations* (Harlow: Longman, 1992).

Pearce, D., *Tourism Today* (Harlow: Longman, 1987).

Pearce, D., *Tourist Development* (Harlow: Longman, 1989).

Pearce, Sales, J., *Travel and Tourism Encyclopedia* (London: Blandford, 1959).

Pearee, M., *International Tourism*, Hutchison, 1969.

Peters, Michael, *International Tourism*, "The Economics and Development of the International Tourist Trade" (London: Hutchinson, 1969).

Pigram, J., *Outdoor Recreation and Resource Management* (London: Croom Helm, 1993).

Pimlott, J.A.R., *The Englishman's Holiday* (London: Faber, 1947).

Pudney, John, *The Thomas Cook Story* (London: Michael Joseph, 1953).

Rae, W.F., *The Business of Travel* (London: Thomas Cook and Són, 1891).

Ram Acharya, *Civil Aviation and Tourism Administration in India* (New Delhi: National Publishing House, 1978).

Raymond, F., *Ecological Principles for Economic Development* (London: John Wiley, 1978).

Reilly, R.T., *Travel and Tourism Marketing Techniques* (New York: Delmar 1988).

Richards, G., *Tourism and the Economy* (Surrey: University of Surrey, 1972).

Roberts, K., *Leisure* (London: Longman, 1970).

Robinson, G.W.S., *"The Recreation Geography of South Asia"*, Geographical Review (October, 1972).

Robinson. H.A., *Geography of Tourism* (London: MacDonald and Evans, 1976).

Ross, G.F., *The Psychology of Tourism* (Melbourne: Hospitality Press, 1994).

Rothfield, Crampon, Wahab, *Tourism Marketing* (London: Tourism International Press, 1975).

Ryan, C., *Recreational Tourism: A Social Science Perspective* (London: Routledge, 1991).

Schmoll, G.A., *Tourism Promotion* (London: Tourism International Press, 1977).

Sessa, Alberto, *Tourism in Developing Countries* (Paris: Reprint from Manual on the Conservation, UNESCO, 1970).

Seth, P.N., *Successful Tourism Planning and Management* (New Delhi: Cross Section Publications, 1978).

Sethi, Praveen, *Tourism Today and Tomorrow*, Anmol Publication Pvt. Ltd., Delhi, 1999.

Sigaux, G., *History of Tourism* (London: Leisure Arts, 1966).

Smith, S.L.J., *Recreation Geography* (Harlow: Longman, 1983).
Smith, S.L.J. *Tourism Analysis* (Harlow: Longman, 1995).
Susan Horner, *Marketing Tourism Hospitality and Leisure in Europe* (London: International Thomson Business Press, 1996).
Sutton, Geoffrey, *How to Sell Travel* (London: Travel Topics, 1959).
Tata, J.R.D., *"The Story of Indian Air Transport"*, Journal of Royal Aeronautical Society (London: 1961).
Tiwari, S.P., *Tourism Dimensions*, Atma Ram and Sons, Delhi.
Trease, Geoffrey, *The Grand Tour* (London: Heinemann, 1967).
Tull, D.S., *Marketing Research: Measurements and Methods* (London: Prentice-Hall, 1993).
Turner, Louis and Ash John, *The Golden Hordes—International Tourism and the Pleasure Periphery* (London: Constable and Company, 1975).
Wahab, Crampon Rothfield, *Tourism Marketing* (London: Tourism International Press, 1976).
Wahab, Salah, *Tourism Management* (London: Tourism International Press, 1975).
Walter, Pasini, *Tourist Health: A New Branch of Public Health* (Rimini: WHO, 1988).
Waters, Somerset R., *"The American Tourist"*, Annals of the American Academy of Political and Social Sciences (1966).
White, J., *History of Tourism* (London: Leisure Art, 1967).
Witt, S.F., *Tourism Marketing and Management*, Handbook, Prentice Hall, New York.
Woodruff, H., *Services Marketing*, Macmillan India Ltd., Delhi, 1997.
Young, George, *Tourism: Blessing or Blight* (London: Penguin, 1973).
Yukic, T.S., *Fundamentals of Recreation* (London: Harper Row, 1963).
Zeithaml, V.A., *Services Marketing* (London: McGraw-Hill, 1996).

# Index